A Matter of Conduct

The True Story of a Man
Who Battled a Bank and Won

by Dalton Yap
with Alex Lee

Library and Archives Canada Cataloguing in Publication

Yap, Dalton
    A matter of conduct : The true story of a man who battled a bank and won / Dalton Yap, Alex Lee.

Also issued in electronic format.
ISBN 978-0-9869413-4-4

    1. Yap, Dalton. 2. Bank fraud--Jamaica. 3. Judicial error--Jamaica. 4. Computer engineers--Jamaica--Biography.
I. Lee, Alex, 1966- II. Title.

HG2824.Y36 2011   364.16'8092   C2011-907545-8

Sassy Sunflower Books.com
Published by Sassy Sunflower Books, Ottawa ON, Canada

To Dad—let's go and take some breeze.

*To Kimmy, Jeremy and Jason—I hope you
have rediscovered your father; the man in
this book.*

To Pauline—you are everything to me.

I love you all.

To Dudley,
Enjoy the read!

Walt
2/2/10/08.

FROM THE AUTHOR:

This is the true story of my legal battle with my former employer that lasted almost a decade. It would be impossible to remember every detail exactly as it happened, but the important ones remain clear in my mind to this day. I have also relied on the help of friends and family who were close to me and to the case, as well as on the documents used in the actual court proceedings. The real names of those involved have been used, with the exception of one, for whom a fictitious name was chosen.

Dalton Yap

ACKNOWLEDGMENTS

This account could not have been written were it not for those who entertained my numerous requests for their time and patience.

Christopher Dunkley and Hilary Phillips sat with Alex Lee and me on several occasions to help reconstruct the case in agonizing detail, when they had more important things to do and people to see. It was, and always is, great fun to walk down memory lane with them. David Wong Ken, attorney-at-law and friend, has my deepest gratitude for his comments and expertise. I will not forget his generosity of time, encouragement and support. To my team of editors: Dr. Victor Chang and Aileen Cho who looked at the first drafts, and Dawn Hugh and Camille Lee Chin who combed through the final drafts, I offer my heartfelt appreciation. To my co-author, Alex Lee, I thank you for the energy and dedication you maintained throughout this project.

It goes without saying that my family stood by me patiently as I threw myself into this very personal journey. I thank them for reading the drafts, for their honest contribution, and for making their own comments and suggestions. This is as much their story as it is mine.

PROLOGUE

T he tall man in the black suit appeared with stealth and paused at the doorway between the respondent's room and the main chamber. For a split second, all you could focus on was the pristine white bow tie. It was in perfect balance with the silvery hair that sat atop his poised head. He was, without question, unlike any other court clerk we had ever seen before.

He broke the silence with a near whisper, the kind that had a crispness that made you automatically pull your shoulders back and give your full attention.

You may enter now.

We emerged from our respective entrances into the huge chamber—the appellants and the respondents. The morning light crept in through the stained glass windows that spanned the high walls. Above us, the stalactite chandeliers shimmered.

We all stood before their Lordships who were already seated in the centre. The addition of the five law lords did little to fill the cavernous room in which we were now assembled. I immediately recognized three from our reconnaissance visit. I wondered if they would recognize us as the odd group of spectators from the day before—and if they did, would it help or hinder?

On the respondent's team we were two men, two women. All Jamaicans. Tourists in casual garb one day, court officers and players in robes and suits the next. Not your normal occurrence. *Normal.* That was a word I hadn't been able to define in almost a decade.

We were at Downing Street, home of the Privy Council. For my esteemed lawyers, Christopher Dunkley and Hilary Phillips, Queen's Counsel, this was the Holy Grail—the highest court of appeal for member nations of the British Commonwealth. I tried for a fleeting moment to feel pleased for them. After watching the duo work together, I knew that if there were two lawyers worthy of a chance to deliver a memorable performance, it was this pair. That I was the reason they were here was almost an honour. Almost.

I felt a slight pressure on my back as if to say *this is it.* I was glad she hadn't grabbed my hand. It was already cold and clammy with sweat. I stole a glance at my sister standing next to me, raw determination fixed on her face. Pat had put her family and medical practice on hold to see me through the final steps of my legal ordeal. For my spirited sibling, dressed in her signature warrior black, this was to be the knockout punch that would end the war waged against her brother and good family name. I had never been quite the natural fighter that she was.

As for me, the accused, this was the final destination in a trip through hell that had scorched some ten years of my life. The faces of my loved ones flashed in my mind, one by one, and finally paused on the image of my father.

On cue we all bowed to their Lordships. They each returned a nod. Again the clerk spoke.

Counsel, please state your representations.

A wave of nausea stirred in my stomach. The hearing had officially begun.

It's like standing before a firing squad and not knowing if or when the bullets will hit. Your life—someone else's decision. Your name—one final chance to clear it.

I stood there, paralysed, as the voices began to swirl around me, filling the huge chamber. My nightmare was coming true. How would this new set of law lords sieve through the evidence and view the case that had stalked me for so long? What if they missed something? What if my attorneys simply ran out of steam? They were only human. What if I was just meant to be another sad example of a good guy who finished last? What if that was, in fact, my sorry fate?

I squeezed my eyes shut and let my world go black for a few seconds. It was nothing short of ludicrous the way one's life could sink into a horrible abyss with just a few ill-fated twists and turns. And then I put the question out to the universe. How did it come to be that I, Dalton Yap, just another hard-working husband and father, would be here today on official business in a building next to the residence of the British Prime Minister?

ONE

I was never one to entertain omens or superstitions. Not when my official start date at the bank was thwarted by that historic menace, Hurricane Gilbert, and not even when my normally jovial father offered an unwittingly prophetic: "What's this? A stormy start? Not good, eh, son?" At the time I dismissed his candid observation with the naiveté of the twenty-eight year-old young aspiring professional that I was—a YAP as I called myself—and gave him my signature laugh. Head thrown back, cheeks bulging, teeth exposed, and the stomach, depending on how diligent I'd been at exercising, moving in tandem with my raw howl.

It was a genuine reaction. My appointment to Jamaica's first and oldest indigenous bank was no ordinary feather in my cap. The fact that my former boss thought highly enough of my work to pull me along in his wake was a double honour I didn't take lightly. No hurricane was going to rain on this guy's parade.

And it didn't. I'd give Jamaica Citizens Bank—JCB—nothing short of excellent work for the next five years. No one had to take my word for it. The bank's performance evaluations said it for me.

So when my eyes suspiciously popped open that fateful Friday morning at five o'clock instead of the usual five thirty or so, I thought nothing of it. I had no reason to. Life was good.

More than good. October had always been a friendly time of year for a corporate man like me. No more debilitating summer heat, no new projects to hammer out, and Christmas's relaxed upbeat vibe was just two flips of the wall calendar away.

The first Sunday in October also meant another garden party at the Chinese Cultural Association, this time to celebrate China National Day. I was a proud founding member of that association and a willing fixture at their functions. A handful of us had started out just by teaching English to new Chinese immigrants during the week after working hours in a small room in New Kingston. Born and raised in Hong Kong until the age of twelve, I was fluent in Cantonese and Hakka. As time went by, the Chinese Cultural Association grew in membership. Now it had a modest brick-and-mortar home on Barbican Road, with enough lawn space for a bunch of kids to play a game of basketball, or for a few hundred to gather for a grand Chinese New Year's dinner. That was the sweetest thing about perseverance. It usually got you to your destination.

I eased out of bed a bit more carefully that morning—toes gingerly first on the cold tile followed by heels. It was too early for Pauline to wake up.

I had married a hard-working woman who spent her days and evenings running her own haberdashery business and caring for our two young children. She needed her rest. Pauline was what those in the Chinese Jamaican community called a *good Hakka woman*—devoted to her family, dedicated to her work, devoid of complaint. If she did in fact harbour complaints, she rarely voiced them. I can only admit that some of my indulgences required her forbearance.

She could have, for instance, protested about how little time I spent with the family. I was an enthusiastic young father who loved to read to the kids, play board games, or splash around with them at some beach in Negril, but the time left at the end of my workday and week was usually not enough. It was a matter of simple math. I was usually gone before they awoke, and back home after eight or nine at night with barely enough time to check their homework and tuck them under the covers. Then I'd spend most evenings doing paper work for the family business until about midnight. Whenever the bank's work kept me too late, I'd overnight in Kingston with my sister Pat, and brother-in-law Chris.

Weekends weren't necessarily a break either. On Saturdays I'd often pop my head into the office for a few hours in the morning, and devote the rest of the day to the family business. As for Sundays? Some Sundays you could find me chopping balls on the tennis court at the ALCAN sports club over by Ingleside with my Mandeville "choir boys" posse, or "church" as we shamelessly called it. Admittedly, the closest I'd ever gotten to church was sitting on the Boy Scout Committee with Father Boyle, my hometown's affable Roman Catholic priest.

There was no question about it—I wasn't afraid of hard work, and there was no question that Pauline allowed my self-imposed punishing schedule. It was the only way I knew how to live as an ambitious young man with a growing family. You work hard to give the ones you love everything they need. You prove yourself while you still have the energy to burn, mouths to feed and dreams to fuel your journey. I wish I had known more then about a balanced life, but I would learn that significant lesson soon enough. I'd also pick up a few other unwanted ones along the way.

I pulled the blanket over Pauline's exposed shoulder before standing to take my first stretch. She barely stirred.

Pauline and I had met in 1984 while she was vacationing from Hong Kong and staying with an aunt in the nearby town of Spaldings. Theresa, one of my three sisters, introduced us. I don't know which was harder for the shy visitor to do—control her urge to giggle, or conceal the smile in her eyes, which she kept trying to place anywhere but on my own broad grin. I admit I had not dated a hell of a lot before. My old-fashioned father had raised his sons to treat girls like we wanted our sisters to be treated. He was unwavering about that. When I met this girl, I decided then and there that she was the most amazing creature I'd ever laid eyes on.

First came the instant attraction, then the amateur love poems. That was followed by endless teasing from my sisters. After a short courtship I persuaded her to stay in Jamaica and move in with me. I was a young pup renting a small apartment in Kingston. I had absolutely nothing to my name. Nothing. So it occurred to me one morning over coffee that if this woman could love me just as I was then, she could love me no matter what.

On the morning of February 28, 1985, we started our life as husband and wife at the Marriage Registrar on Widcombe Road, a stone's throw from our apartment. I wore one of my work suits. My young bride looked beautiful in the simple knee-length white summer dress she had found in her holiday suitcase. We took pictures with the same joy and enthusiasm of a couple getting married in an elaborate church ceremony with hundreds of well-wishers. Exactly two months later, we hosted a more formal reception in Mandeville for our family and friends. And wish us well they did. The following year on September 9, we became the young and hope-filled parents of a smiling baby daughter we named Joanne Kimberly. Kimmy, as we called her, would be followed by a son, Jeremy, a few years later. We couldn't have been happier.

Choosing Pauline Lee as my life partner was one of the best things I ever did. It is a fact of life few appreciate or even consider, but it matters who sits in the trenches with you.

It is a privilege to wake up in Mandeville. Deliciously chilly, the morning air is so fresh and crisp you can almost taste the sweetness of the dew as you breathe in. Considering its agreeable climate, the Brits had done well to settle here.

Snuggled high in the lush hills of Manchester parish, this small community had long remained a well-known secret, conveniently made so by the tedious two-hour plus drive that kept "town" and its big-city residents at bay.

It was colder than usual that October morning. My body must have felt it. Without pausing for my usual wardrobe assessment, my hands landed on a wool suit I hadn't worn in ages. It had been an old favourite, and I greeted it with an instinctive "hey, long time no see" grin.

It is perplexing when you realize which details are subconsciously committed to memory, and which are purged. I know exactly what I wore that day. I had on a grey suit with black pin stripes made of lightweight wool. The pants were baggy and cuffed. Wing-tipped burgundy shoes had socks to match. A cotton shirt sported magenta and white stripes. The tie was silk with flecks of burgundy, black and blue. A cursory check in the bathroom mirror confirmed that it sat just above my belt buckle.

As was common with Chinese families, there were three generations living in our home. My old man was my usual pre-dawn companion in the kitchen. That's where we shared a fifteen-minute serving of coffee and conversation. The first was always piping hot and fresh. The second was usually meaningful in its sketchiness, the kind that comes only with familiarity. That morning we'd indulge in a few minutes more together.

In many ways we were each other's opposite. He was of slight build at five feet five inches, compared to my six feet. Socially, he'd chat up a storm for hours while I'd crack a couple of jokes and then settle down. Semi-retired from his demanding life as a shop and restaurant owner, these days he was bronzed from his daily work in his vegetable garden. He grew choice Chinese greens for us and anyone else who praised his green thumb. Just pulling into second gear as a bank's chief "techie," I was pale from my daily work inside an air-conditioned building.

My father and I did share one common trait, however—a nasty temper. That temper was coupled with a healthy repertoire of colourful Jamaican adjectives. Our redeeming characteristic was that we always knew when an apology was in order.

My father had been born as Llewellyn Yap in a small town called Ballards Valley, in the parish of St. Elizabeth. As was customary in those days, he had been sent back to China as a child to learn the ways of his father's heritage. Upon his arrival, the village elders named him "Yap Get-Gui".

Years later as a young man, he would decide that it was time for a different life, and set his sights on Hong Kong. His journey sent him over mountains and across a lonely harbour. Moving only at night, my father's sole companion and comfort was the sea of stars that faithfully lit his path. When he finally climbed out of the water and pulled himself onto Hong Kong soil, he decided to change his name to Yap Sing-Hoi. It meant "Sea of Stars."

Llewelyn Yap was a man of habit. Always an early riser before daybreak, he indulged in short but daily afternoon naps, and enjoyed nothing more than a post-dinner glass of Napoleon brandy with a slice of political discussion—the more animated the tastier. We knew how to push his buttons. It was politics that drove him from his home. It was politics once again in the 1970s that made him take notice when Jamaica's young Prime Minister, Michael Manley, began flirting with the same idealisms from which my father had already fled. Always one to walk his talk, he'd eventually offer some of his time and support to Southern Manchester's Labour candidate, Arthur "Teacher" Williams.

That morning he must have heard me stir early, because the welcoming aroma of that necessary brew had already found its way to my nose by the time I walked into the dark kitchen, where he sat waiting. It was the kind of long, deep kitchen that automatically drew you in, enticing you to open its cupboards, take a peek here, take a whiff over there. As was customary, I, the younger of the two, was the first to greet him. We spoke as we usually did, in his native Hakka dialect.

"Jao sin, ba-ba." (*Good morning, father.*)

"Jao sin, jao sin." He pointed to the lone mug waiting for me on the table. A plain blue one was already nestled in his right hand, poised just inches from his mouth. The steam temporarily clouded the reading glasses perched on his nose.

I carefully lifted and pulled a chair out with both hands to avoid the rude scraping sound. It was way too early for that kind of noise. "Doa cha. Thanks."

"You up early this morning, son."

Barely seated, I pulled the mug to my lips. "Mm."

"Busy day?"

I shrugged. "No more than usual. Just woke up early. Figured I may as well get up and go."

"Ah," he said with an approving nod.

Hard work was a way of life in the Yap household. My father had always made two things clear. One, he would ultimately prefer to see me flourish in a business of my own. Two, in the meantime he couldn't be more proud to see me blaze a trail in my chosen career. He bragged behind my back to just about anyone who would listen. *You hear Dalton got another excellent performance evaluation? Or, do you know he just got another big promotion?*

It had never been my intention to work at the bank until retirement. Sure, that worked out very well for some, but in my mind, if you think you're going to be in one place forever, then you might run the risk of pacing yourself and just dragging things out until you can no longer button up your suit. I wasn't interested in punching in the clock until I got my gold watch. I mean—damn!

Just entering my thirties, I had recently sown the seeds for my eventual transition into business. It would still be several more years before I could or would make the move—but while I was still a salaried man, I was determined to turn in a stellar performance. In the meantime, my father was like a football dad attending his son's every game, cheering wildly. He couldn't get enough.

"How are things at work? Your boss still away? Everything good with him?" He sipped loudly from his mug as he glanced up, his eyebrows following.

Nothing pleased me more than to know that I made my father beam inside. When I was happy, he was too. So I deliberately ignored his last question. "Work good, man. And yes, Mr. Wiggan is still at that conference in Singapore."

The truth was I felt that my boss's vibe had somewhat cooled towards me ever since August, when I returned from my holiday in Toronto. It could have been my imagination, of course, but gone were the jokes about our snazzy threads. Vanished was the easiness in his speech. Eye contact seemed to be scarce too. It was as if he'd gone all business overnight. For a while I assumed he was still cheesed off about one of the bank's new projects that had just disintegrated on us—a telemarketing credit card processing service that the bank quickly shut down just months after it began due to some complications.

Initially my boss seemed to be annoyed with me about it, even interrupting my vacation to vent a little. In my mind it was an uncharacteristic panic, coming from him. Then the bank opted to end it and let the project fizzle out. So when his odd mood continued, I figured the culprit was personal. *Must be some big heap problem*, I kidded myself at the time.

Now almost two months later, little had changed. The tension between my boss and me lingered. I decided to change the subject on my unsuspecting father to avoid his speculation. "How's your old vegetable patch coming along these days, Daddy?"

"Oh! Forgot to tell you! Gave away some nice fat *choi sim* and *lopet* to Mrs. Wong and Mrs. Chen yesterday. They were so happy to get them."

I grinned. "Daddy, man. Who you fooling? You were happy to *give* them away."

DAY WAS STILL tentatively breaking as I shifted gears out of Mandeville that morning. Alone in the Nissan Cefiro with no one else's comfort to consider, I rolled down the windows and let the wind blast my face. The volume on the radio was already turned up, and I could hear radio hosts Dorraine Samuels and Alan Magnus signing on over the *whrrr whrrr* of the wind. They were my faithful commuter companions.

I glanced at my small collection of motivational tapes wondering which to choose today. Whenever the mood hit me, and it often did, I'd alternate between the radio and the tapes while tackling the long drive. I had some great ones: Zig Ziglar's *How to Get What You Want*, and a favourite by the dynamic Les Brown would often help ease the journey. That morning I selected a tape I had just started listening to a few days earlier. It was a series by Tom Peters called *Thriving on Chaos*.

Within five minutes I had reached the very steep Winston Jones Highway. That particular morning, I could barely make out the western spur of another hill that sat beyond like a mist-covered fortress. Not yet visible to the left lurked the Windalco bauxite residue lake in the gorge below.

I was the only one on that hill. As I sailed down the crest, I could feel the slick Cefiro inhaling the sheer slope. The silver sedan was a company perk and my vehicle of choice. I was the only manager to have chosen this particular make and model. It had been my morning send-off for the past five years. Just the Cefiro, the road and me. Most thought I was certifiably insane to commute from Mandeville to Kingston daily and sure, sometimes I took issue with the evening commute, but most of the time I felt lucky.

MY WATCH SAID it was just about seven when I pulled into downtown Kingston. A popular dancehall tune was stirring it up on the airwaves as the capital city stretched to face the last day of the workweek. Admittedly I was more of a Motown-oldies kind of fellow, but I could still manage to appreciate some of the more contemporary hits.

A quick five-second time-management decision later and I was buying a *Gleaner* from one of eager newspaper boys. *Gleanah! Gleanah! Gleanah, Missa Chin?* It would help to fast forward the few minutes I'd have to wait in the parking lot before the Burger King on Harbour Street opened for my breakfast.

At half past seven, my office greeted me with what felt like a quiet cheer. I knew that room like I knew my own face. I could even tell blindfolded where I was just by the feel of the carpet under my feet. Some parts had been worn thin. Other parts were still thick and soft. It was my own private sanctuary.

On my desk, my diary sat open to October 1. As it was Friday, the first item on the list was my division's weekly meeting at eight. The regular pow-wow was a practice I had started when I took over the problem-riddled operations side of the bank's Credit Card Centre in June of 1992. My promotion to General Manager of Operations and Technology would come a few months later.

I never denied the general consensus that I had become Lloyd Wiggan's protégé. I was proud of it, actually. He had only been JCB's General Manager of Operations for a few months when he recruited me from Citibank as his second in command. I had enjoyed working with him before, so I didn't hesitate to work with him again. The man had long been a well-respected executive, even before his appointment as the first Jamaican Vice-President at Citibank. He had been a true mentor to me, starting right after he interviewed and then hired me as a wet-behind-the-ears college graduate, eager to start his own career.

The competition had boiled down to two candidates. Me, just out of the Radio College of Canada and making few demands, and another Chinese-Jamaican fellow with similar qualifications but much more experience and a higher price tag.

I was the lucky candidate. I showed my appreciation by doing a smashing job for the multinational bank, eventually becoming one of the few to win the service excellence award twice. It was an achievement that secured me a much-prized personal letter of commendation from a high ranking official—the Chairman of Citicorp himself. I kept that letter on my bedside table for weeks.

I did what every boss wanted. I took the problems he presented, found solutions, and made our team look good in the process. I was glad to. He had taken the time to smooth whatever rough edges I had arrived with and shaped me into being as close to the textbook executive as I could get. He had helped me finesse my English, taught me how to survive office politics, present myself to other managers and executives, and even how to wear a suit properly.

He himself sported a more militaristic appearance—shoes usually shined to a glare, stiff posture, always in control, always the polished executive. Before long, I too was sporting monogrammed shirts and Armani suits. No question about it, I was enjoying the education.

Joining an environment like Citibank right out of college had been a good move. I developed an immediate appreciation for established procedures that were not only meticulously documented, but carefully followed. Like a kid mesmerized by comic books, I read Citibank's internal procedures manuals cover to cover. I found a certain comfort in the structure. You didn't have to rely on someone to show you the ropes or for time to unveil the procedures layer by layer. It was all there in plain black and white. That's why it was a bit of a shock the day I stepped through the doors of Jamaica Citizens Bank. Incredibly, I would not even be given a written job description.

My boss's strength was his ability to know when and how to shore up one's weaknesses. I considered him a true manager and respected the fact that he wasn't afraid to stop and ask for the damn directions. *Forget playing hero. If we don't have the expertise, we get it*, is what he taught us. And at that time JCB needed the help. From a bottom line point of view they were riding high, but technologically they were short-circuiting. After years of disappointing systems managers, they were choked with vendor-supplied hardware that no one seemed able to implement. Staffers were fatigued from constantly putting out fires. It was no wonder then that I was received by the other managers with what I thought to be a discernible skepticism.

The questions seemed to flare from their eyes. Who was this young grasshopper from Citibank who would leap up the stairs several steps at a time, and burn the candle at both ends without fading? How good was he anyway? All natural questions, I thought.

That's the challenge when you make an entrance wearing big shoes. You have to prove yourself right away. The team of Wiggan and Yap had done much for Citibank, including implementing Jamaica's first online banking system. So the pressure was on at JCB from the first handshake.

Our team got to work right away. Instead of filling order forms for new equipment, we literally pulled the old machines from the storage shelves, dusted them off and made them compute. And we didn't play hero. We hired consultants from India just to make sure we got it perfect. I'd venture to say that over time we erased the doubt some of the other managers might have had concerning my ability.

I had proven myself to be good. Perhaps too good. Seasoned technologists understand two basic tenets. If you're doing your job well, your days should be boring with no fires, no remarkable adventures. It was a lot like the Eastern approach of preventive care. In the earlier days of China, affluent families often had their own resident physicians. The physician was considered to be working effectively as long as everyone remained healthy. The moment someone in the family took ill, the physician stopped being paid.

The second tenet is that if you're doing your job well, you should be able to see everything with the eyes of an x-ray technician. Before long, I had discovered a scheme involving some middle managers with access to unsecured and interest-free credit cards and lines of credit. I shared my discovery at a management meeting with some of the aforementioned present. Admittedly, that little disclosure didn't help to bolster my popularity, but I didn't lose my breakfast over it. I was doing what was right, and taking your employer for a ride was not.

I continued working hard, making no attempts to veil my enthusiasm for my work or for the bank. I quickly got to the task of establishing procedures for the Operations and Technology Division, and literally wrote the manual myself, a first for the bank. Wiggan followed by doing the same for several of the bank's other departments. He also championed the use of annual performance evaluations—a practice that soon became the norm for the entire bank. Now JCB had official records of each employee's performance to which its executives could refer. I'd soon catch the attention of the Group Chairman, who made me an offer to become CEO of the group's technology company specializing in systems development. As flattering as the offer was, I graciously declined and stayed right where I was.

By the time 1993 rolled around, the financial industry had just taken a roller coaster ride through a dizzying boom.

The Jamaica Stock Market was growing like an athlete on steroids. Boutique merchant banks were popping up all over like jerk pork stands, competing frenziedly for customers who were looking for somewhere fertile to plant their cash. Advertisements and commercials tempted customers with offers of 40 percent plus interest rates, enticing even once-bitten Jamaican expatriates to take a second look home. Many decided to risk a quick conversion and short-term position in Jamaican funds for a taste of the red carpet rates. Several boarded airplanes to roll those dice.

By now JCB was in full-growth mode, opening more branches island-wide, all streamlined and generating real time reports, thanks to my staff's 'round the clock hard work. The bank had also begun offering customers the option of U.S. accounts with online access to view them, a move for which my boss won and deserved full credit. JCB was ahead of the game.

Up to the time my boss and I received our promotions, the dam had not yet burst; banks and bankers in Jamaica were generally still very much sacrosanct. We were both deserving of our thumbs up. He became Managing Director, now in charge of the general managers, and I took his former slot as General Manager of Technology and Operations. I was now responsible for the technical and operations staff of about one hundred. The honeymoon was still going strong and I was leaping up those stairs faster than ever.

To make General Manager at thirty-two back then was no common feat. We were all quite young in the division, actually, and by now were the undisputed heavyweights of the bank. We had toiled non-stop, and our boss made sure to reward us appropriately. We got whatever tools we needed to get the job done, even if we felt sheepish about it—like having cellular phones at a time when they were still very new and way too conspicuous. Edward Gabbidon, one of my star technicians, confessed to literally slipping around corners to dodge the rude stares as soon as the submarine-sized device began to ring. Sometimes smaller really is better.

The office was part of my promotion, an inheritance from my boss who had moved into the bigger one across the hall. Before the promotion my office had sat by a window on the second floor surrounded by glass walls, the curtains and door pulled open so that I could communicate quickly with my staff. No appointment necessary, all visitors welcome. Of course, it also meant that I couldn't even scratch an itch without them seeing me. I enjoyed being that close to my staff, but had since become quite comfortable in my new space. I even moved in a small refrigerator to help with my long hours and Saturday morning stints.

The meeting that morning began at eight o'clock sharp, as always. My division managers knew what my commute was like, so no one cared to suffer the embarrassment of a late arrival with "traffic" as the excuse.

Eight of us gathered together that day by my round table. I'd say I ran a fairly efficient meeting. We took minutes at each one without fail. The purpose of the regular knocking of heads was simple. Beyond trying to encourage a clean flow of information throughout the newly-merged division, I had the dubious honour of being asked to scrub out some old calluses that had come with the added responsibility—like blurred task assignments, work load difficulties, report distribution, overloaded equipment and documentation issues. An independent study done the year before by an American-based consultant offered us its bottom-line assessment. Clean out the mess before it became quicksand.

The only strict part about our meetings was our respect for time. Other than that, it was an easy-going hour of exchanged ideas, reports and good humour. I enjoyed mentoring where I could and used our meetings to share my own career lessons. We were all technology people at heart first and foremost, and any conversation that led to solutions was a welcome one. In the world of the techie, every genuine problem has a logical solution. That was the basic premise of life as we saw it. I was openly boastful about the efficiency of my lean team while we took care of the bank's seventeen branches with a team smaller than most in the industry. And we delivered.

THE CALL FROM Helen Byles came not long after the meeting ended.

By then I was alone in my office working at my computer. I greeted her with a tone that reflected the easy-going rapport I shared with the bank's head of human resources. "And a very good morning to you, Helen!" Meanwhile, my secretary Debbie walked in with a handful of pink notepaper bearing messages she had taken while I was still in my meeting. I nodded a *thank-you* to her while listening to Helen on the other end of the line.

"There's a what?" I exclaimed. "A meeting at four o'clock *today*?" Her words were few, but her voice was discernibly even. I remember noting it was a strange tone coming from her. She had always been relaxed and pleasant with me.

"I see," I laughed politely. "Squeezing in a last-minute meeting before the weekend, huh?" When no quip was returned I continued, but this time I sounded a bit off-centre myself. "Well ah, well yes, sure thing—. Ewart's office. Right, okay then, Helen."

Before I could ask what the meeting was about, she hung up.

Two

4:00 P.M.

I threw my secretary Debbie a smile and a *have a good weekend* as I sailed past her on the way out, leather briefcase in hand.

It had been a full day and so I figured on a beeline move to my car right after the meeting. Debbie returned a respectfully familiar *you too, boss.* She was the only one who used the term "boss," or who called me Mr. Yap, for that matter. Everyone else called me by my first name, at my insistence, but Debbie was a pleasant "young miss" who was happier with old-world traditions and pleasantries. Yet she also happened to be an incredibly modern-day working woman. There was never a time she didn't want to learn new skills on her computer. By the time I was finished teaching her, she knew more than any other secretary at the bank did, hands down.

At the time, the bank's address was 4 King Street, at the corner of King Street and Port Royal Street in the historic section of downtown Kingston. Rapid expansion and limited space had forced JCB to rent more space across the road. This second building used to house the once famous and now defunct Bank of Commerce and Credit International, or "BCCI" as it was commonly called. Now it housed JCB's large Retail Banking Division headed by Ewart Scott. There were three other divisions—Corporate Finance, Treasury, and Technology and Operations led by Karl Thompson, Neville

Parkinson and me respectively. I was the junior in the senior management team.

I stepped out of my building with a purposeful stride. It was a picture-perfect sunny Friday afternoon, and the road to home wasn't long from now. The sun, still bright but gentler at that hour, was accompanied by a slightly anxious breeze, compliments of the funky-smelling Kingston Harbour that sat within walking distance to the south.

The guard out front caught my eye, and with a quick smile flashed a good set of teeth. "Afternoon, Mr. Yap. Yuh gone already, sir?" Although they technically worked for a security firm, these guards had become a part of the JCB family. I knew each one, and they knew me.

I dropped a hand on his shoulder when I got closer. "Hey, chief, what's going on?"

"Everything alright, sir?"

"I'm going to a little meeting before heading home."

The smile flashed again. "Yes, sir. Okay."

"But if I don't see you afterwards, enjoy the weekend."

"Yes, sir, Mr. Yap. Safe drive to Mandeville."

"Thanks, man."

I turned right towards the pedestrian crossing. The noise of stubborn car alarms punctuated the afternoon air, already thick with the familiar scent of fried chicken coming from the busy KFC across the intersection. I mentally smacked my lips while wondering what meal Mom or Dad had whipped up for us today. My thoughts turned to the only thing left standing between me and a home-cooked meal. *What the hell could Ewart want so late on a Friday, man?*

I heard the resetting of several alarms—tu! tu!—but one disagreeable one kept sending out the annoying wail. *The poor idiot probably forgot where he put his keys.* The hustlers-turned-car-washers were noticeably busy getting all manner of vehicles in tiptop shape. It was a clear sign that the weekend had arrived in Kingston.

I stopped at the pedestrian crossing. To my right, the one-way traffic streamed down from Port Royal Street, a main thoroughfare sandwiched by concrete buildings on both sides for several blocks. The engine songs echoed and bounced off the walls, mixing with the gas and diesel fumes from the vehicles. The roaring stream blasted everyone on the sidewalk. My tie fluttered furiously, hitting both sides of my face until I finally held it down to my stomach.

I ran through a gap in the oncoming traffic and reached the other side without getting maimed. I'd won the first round, but would have to face the second when the meeting was over. That would be a more pleasant task, though, as I'd be hopping into my car and heading for Mandeville. For sure, I'd be driving into a sweet sunset this evening. A nice weekend was in store for the Yap family. No tennis on Sunday for me, but a family garden party instead at the Chinese Cultural Association. *The kids will enjoy that*, I thought. I'd have to squeeze in some exercise time, though. *Need to get this tummy flatter*, I complained to myself as I patted it.

As I stepped into the building I quickly scanned my hair and tie with my hands, my body already turning towards the staircase and Ewart Scott's second-floor office. Elon Beckford had appointed him General Manager of the Retail Banking Division before Elon left JCB to establish his own merchant bank, Horizon Merchant Bank. Today, however, Ewart was sitting in as Acting Managing Director for a still absent Lloyd Wiggan.

I won't deny it. I was not a big Ewart Scott fan. To his credit he was pleasant enough, certainly highly qualified and all— but I personally preferred a more decisive approach when doing business. He had, on at least a couple of occasions, led me down a path of hair-raising frustration. There was the time he asked Wiggan, still my General Manager back then, to have us develop a dial-in system allowing corporate customers to check their balances at leisure. Citibank and Bank of Nova Scotia already had their systems, so, logically we needed one of our own. It was a great idea. Of course, we also needed it, like, yesterday.

Ewart didn't have to ask twice. We got to work immediately with the due diligence, worked out the particulars, designed it, put it through several tests, ran it, re-ran it, and only surfaced for air once the auditors had signed off on the security aspect of it. We proudly presented Ewart with his dial-in system within two months. Then, just days before the launch, he backed off because of some nervous talk about hackers. No amount of proof that the system was secure would make him stay the course. I admit that perhaps the problem was mine. For Dalton Yap, as long as it still made sense, you finished what you started. Perhaps my faith in technology was simply stronger than most.

I sprinted up the stairs while tossing out quick "good-byes" to those coming down. *Lucky bastards getting an early start to the weekend.* Ewart's office was just within eyesight when I noticed Helen sitting in the distance talking to someone. *Bad time for her to get stuck in a conversation,* I thought. I waved an arm to get her attention, and possibly help her out.

"Helen! You coming in?" I smiled as I pointed ahead with some amount of exaggeration toward Ewart's office. She continued talking to the person in front of her and barely took a few seconds to give me what seemed a somewhat awkward "be with you soon" kind of gesture. Her cemented posture suggested it would be later than sooner. Of course, she never would join us.

Body language is a true whistleblower. The trick is learning to trust it. I noticed Ewart's eyes the moment I stepped into his office. They went everywhere but to mine as I offered him a friendly "hello, hello." He wasn't someone I ran into daily, so as I took my seat we struggled through the necessary pleasantries. His body was noticeably shifting forward and then back in his chair. There was some swiveling, some shuffling of paper on his desk and a lot of general uneasiness, but I dismissed it, figuring he didn't want to be here either.

The small talk went on for just another couple minutes. Finally, he cleared his throat. I went quiet to give the man centre stage. Ewart began choosing his words carefully, and yet I couldn't quite grasp their meaning. Whatever he was trying to say was sticking in his throat. I gave him a polite smile-frown combination, and leaned forward to perhaps hear a bit better. Never before had I had seen my colleague quite like this.

Please just spit it out! As if reading my mind, Ewart suddenly stopped trying to speak, placed his fingertips on two documents on the desk immediately in front of him, and pushed them towards me, one hand per document. He indicated that the first, a report from the Group Auditor, was for me to read only, while the second was for me to keep.

I pulled the chair closer to the desk and stretched my back forward for a closer look. Slowly, my brows inched up as I began to read. The tone of the auditor's report came at me like an FBI document. The subject: my personal bank account activity and business travel over the last couple years. Somehow this document was trying to imply that the two were linked in some way. The curious frown I had been sporting seconds before now switched to one of confusion. I raised my head to look at Ewart.

"What the—? Ewart, what the hell is this? Some kind of practical joke?" I forced a small laugh but it wasn't enough to hide my bewilderment. By now I was holding the documents in my hands, my back straight and stiffening.

He began offering me words that seemed to bounce somewhere between regret and discomfort over the task at hand.

I dropped my eyes back to the letter. As the words loomed larger and larger, his voice began fading to a murmur in the background. I was struggling now to read. Something about transferring large sums of money into my Miami accounts, then something about the bank missing funds—. My eyes started jumping ahead, searching for the panacea sentence that would explain this mess. Inside, a stream of nausea began to flow. *What kind of sick joke was this?*

Ewart's voice was coming back now. I wanted to shout at him to stop so that I could process what I was reading.

Gross negligence and conspiring to do what???

And then my eyes jumped to the second letter. That's when it all became clear. *Dear Mr. Yap. Recent investigations concluded by our Group Audit Department—*. I sat frozen, staring at the words as they unfolded one by one on the poisonous paper. They stared back, refusing to budge. A cold dampness gripped my body as I turned the page. My hands started to shake. Scott and the room fell silent. That's when I finally raised my head. "Ewart—Ewart, you're *firing* me?"

He nodded, but barely.

I fought the warm tide now surging in my stomach so I could engage my vocal cords again. "What are you doing to me? This is pure rubbish! Come on, Ewart! Tell me this is a mistake! A bad joke of some kind!"

He offered some more dialogue without eye contact about wishing he didn't have to do this.

This time I lurched forward to the edge of my seat. "Ewart, please! This is insane! It's all rubbish! I haven't done *any* of this, man! None of it! You have to know that!"

Still looking away, Ewart slowly turned a helpless hand up in the air and started referring to the auditor's report, still in mine.

"My God! This can't be happening. What's happening?? They're wrong, Ewart! This whole thing is wrong! I can prove it! Let me respond to this. Please let me respond to this!" I pushed further when I got no reply. "A copy of the report! Can I get a *copy* of the report?"

This time he shook his head.

I shook the paper at him. "You mean to say I can't even get a *copy* of a report that has my name all over it?"

He met my plea with a shrug.

"Look here, Ewart," I raged. I could hardly hold air in my lungs as I struggled to make sense of the rabbit hellhole wonderland I had just fallen into. "Is there someone I can talk to about this? I can prove that this is a mistake of some kind. I can address everything in this report. Please, Ewart! Can I see Lloyd when he gets back? What about Mr. Williams?" I was shouting now and didn't care who could hear beyond the closed door. "Can I at least talk to Mr. Williams? Ewart, I am begging you. Please at least let me talk to the Chairman!"

Finally he looked up. It was not uncommon knowledge that I had a pretty good rapport with the bank's much-respected Chairman. I pushed carefully, not wanting Ewart to drop his eye contact with me. "Ewart?"

Finally he relented. He agreed to let me try to see the Chairman on Monday, but said that they'd tell me when he was available to talk.

Grateful, I forced my voice down to a calm level and tried to take in a deep breath. I thanked him a few times. Still shaking, I staggered to my feet, this time in silence. I had found a lifeline and I wasn't about to risk having it yanked away by saying the wrong thing—or saying anything for that matter.

By now I felt numb and was having trouble focusing. After busting my ass for five sterling years, after commuting in the darkness, racking up the hours, eating and breathing the bank, I'd been unceremoniously dismissed—like fast food served on a plastic tray in an easy and convenient five minutes. I was corporate chump tossed out with one easy letter. The day I was fired marked the very last time my colleague and I would ever speak.

With one careful step at a time, I made my way toward the stairs. Everything in my path now blurred as if I'd just opened my eyes after a deep sleep. I gripped the railing. That's when I saw Helen again. This time she was just sitting there alone. I thought about her call that morning and the nightmare I had just walked into. Her call, the way she had just waved me off. Had she known all along while I bubbled through the day like a damn fool? She glanced from the side and briefly met my confused gaze. We exchanged no words. I turned away and walked through the door.

Outside, the sun that just minutes before had been warm, suddenly felt cold. I shivered.

I HEADED BACK to my office, this time hardly aware of the sea of traffic I had to cross. Thankfully, Debbie had already left. An explanation for my sudden return was not something I could handle right now.

I shut the door, dropped the letter on my desk, and sank into my chair. For a moment I let the office wrap itself around me. It was a great room, the kind that made you want to sit back and let your eyes take in the details. Four wood-paneled walls, warm recessed lighting to make up for the lack of a single window, and a beautiful round wood desk where I worked. Round tables held a special meaning for me. They represented equality. Teamwork. Oneness. I let my eyes roam on the little things that had made this place like home. Family photos on my desk, intriguing artwork, elegant crystal, a shelf rich with books and manuals. My computer. This had been my sanctuary. I had done lots of work here. Good work. Was this the same office I had stepped into this morning? Was this the same bank I had made my life? And who were these people I had just spoken to? Had we not spent the last few years working side by side?

I picked up the offending letter again. This time I let my eyes lock onto every word as they came at me off the paper:

Dear Mr. Yap,

Recent investigations concluded by our Group Audit Department on September 29, 1993 have revealed that you have been involved in and facilitated major breaches of the Bank's policy and have exposed the Bank to serious legal and financial risks.

These Audit investigations have identified and revealed:

1. Gross negligence in the establishment by you of Visa/MasterCard transaction processing relationships without any credit card checks as well as at least "willful blindness" in respect of the relationships;
2. By non-compliance with Visa International and MasterCard By-laws for establishment of Merchant relationships;
3. Non-compliance and/or delays in compliance with instructions from Visa/MasterCard;
4. Circumvention of Executive Management's instructions to terminate processing arrangements by facilitating "A Ghost" office in Kingston for Travel Connection;
5. The withholding of information from Executive Management;

6. Unauthorized release by you of agreed reserves;

8. Attendance by you at an Audio Text convention on June 9 and 10 in California which could cause Visa International to sever its relationship with the Bank;

9. Your involvement in transactions which could give rise to grounds for Visa International to terminate our licensing arrangement.

You have exposed the bank to:

a) Possible legal action by Telemarketers.
b) Possible fines from VISA/MASTERCARD.
c) Potential suits against our Miami agency.
d) Potential irrecoverable chargebacks which could lead to financial losses of up to US$695,710.89.

In light of the above you are hereby dismissed with immediate effect. You will be held accountable for all losses sustained by us as a result of your negligence and / or unauthorized actions.

Until the Bank has satisfied itself that no loss has been suffered, any sum which may be due to you will be withheld.

All indebtedness to the Bank must be settled immediately. Kindly immediately return to me your Staff Identification and Health Cards, your JCB Credit Cards and Cheque Books and any other property of the Bank which may be in your possession.

Yours faithfully,

Ewart Scott

Actg. Managing Director

C: Emanuel Obasare

Chief Internal Auditor

I have absolutely no recollection of what happened over the next couple of hours. According to my family and friends, the first call went to my brother just before five o' clock. Afen was still at the family's business in Kingston.

Afen, I said weakly. *Afen, the bank just fired me—Fired —Yes—What? I can't explain now. There's a letter full of—I don't understand either. My office—just happened—No. It was Scott—What? No. I'll go to Chris and Pat's—Yes—Yes, I'll call him—Okay—See you there.*

The next few calls would be similar. Brief, sketchy, potholed with moments of silence and disbelief. A lot of *"what?"* in my ears. With my wife I was as vague as possible, telling her that I'd be staying in Kingston for the night and ending with some empty promise that I'd sort it out soon. I didn't want to worry her. I couldn't prop her up right now. I needed to catch my own breath, steady myself first. My brother-in-law, Christopher Berry, gave the longest pause before reacting to the news. "Meet me at my house. We'll talk there," is what he finally said.

I CAN'T RECALL when exactly I pulled into Chris and Pat's driveway, but I do remember wondering how I'd gotten there at all. I had no notion of driving, no memory of traffic lights, of turning at jammed intersections, of braking, accelerating. Nothing. Only the occasional blaring of horns reminded me that it was evening and that people were impatiently heading for their homes. I don't even remember how I handled Chris's erratic rottweilers.

Once inside the house, I switched on the lights, removed my jacket, loosened my tie and eased onto the sofa. For a while I just sat there floating in the silence, the familiar hum of the old refrigerator keeping me company.

Blue Castle Drive was my Kingston refuge. The couple's modest home was tucked away in the cool foothill community of Mona, not far from the University of the West Indies. This was where Chris and I used to kick back and eat bachelor food without apology until Pat's return from completing her studies in dermatology in London. My choice meal was any kind of Campbell's soup with Grace elbow macaroni. His was whatever was within arm's reach and he had a belly to show for it. We were family and good friends. He was the tough banker and I was the hardcore techie. We chatted about our latest projects at work, new dilemmas and well-earned victories. We were two sounding boards giving our careers our all. The only difference was that he was sweating it out in his family's stockbroker business, and openly wondering why I didn't put my energy into my family's business ventures.

One quality I had always appreciated about my brother-in-law was his frankness. Beating around the bush was not his style. Even his speech was clear and steady. I remember when I first told him about what was to be the last promotion I'd get at the bank. It was late one night, and I was relaxing on my bed pointed at the television, hands under my head, my lungs in full-blown howl at David Letterman's monologue, my nightly comedy fix. I must have been particularly loud that night, being in a good mood over the promotion and all, because the first thing Chris did when he got in was stick his head in the door and take a jab at me about the neighbours complaining. That's when I announced my good news.

"Whah," he had said approvingly. "Excellent, chief, excellent. About time. And how's the raise? Nice and fat?"

"It's just okay, I guess," I replied truthfully.

Chris pulled his head back. "Look here, now. You already have the bank coming out of your ears as it is. Now you're taking on even more responsibility. Just you make sure you're not playing martyr."

That was late 1992. A few months later the credit card processing business began to develop a small rash.

The credit card processing business was a new venture that had started back in 1991, about a year and a half before my promotion. Elon Beckford was still with the bank. He introduced me to the project after one of the monthly executive meetings and asked me to meet with a fellow by the name of Mel Reaume, a Floridian with a merchant bank in Antigua. Apparently this Reaume fellow had approached JCB about doing some transactional processing for his merchant bank. Elon asked me to do some research and find out what needed to be put in place.

I jumped on it and called the gentleman. In a nutshell, Reaume needed us to process credit card paper acquired from his telemarketing merchants, a business his bank had just moved into.

As Jamaica Citizens Bank was in the Caribbean, both banks were in compliance with VISA International's rules that allowed for processing to occur within the same region. After our initial meeting and my report to Elon, Reaume put us in touch with other individuals to help us get the business link going. By early 1993 all systems were a go. Ewart Scott had taken over the project once Elon left the bank. By then I had already pulled Lesley-Ann Hew from Citibank to help with the new business; it was going to have JCB swimming in gravy. It needed top-notch performers like Lesley. Like me with Wiggan, she didn't hesitate to follow.

What the hell was I going to say to Lesley? What about my staff? No. No way could this be happening. Mr. Williams would sort it out with me on Monday. Or Lloyd when he gets back from Singapore. It was all just a nasty mistake. They have it wrong. They have it all wrong.

My brother-in-law was the first one to arrive at the house. His key grated the front door, bailing me out of my trance. His stride thundered as he stepped in.

"Dalton," he said, his face already searching mine for some glimmer of a logical explanation. "What the hell, man?"

ATTORNEY-AT-LAW Christopher Dunkley stared at the phone he had just hung up seconds before. The caller, now gone, had been Leo Campbell with our SOS for help. Leo was my other brother-in-law, my youngest sister's husband. He and Dunkley knew each other through the Jamaica Defense Force. Captain Dunkley was a reserve army officer, while Leo was a Major, and therefore Dunkley's superior officer. Leo also happened to be Chris Berry's cousin. To complete the circle, my brother Afen had also been a schoolmate with Dunkley at deCarteret College. The close relationship of this small group reduced the matter of my rescue to a matter of minutes.

As I sat paralysed in Pat's home, watching Chris Berry reach into his briefcase for a pen and sheet of paper, attorney Dunkley sat alone in his downtown office, and scribbled my name at the top of his own fresh notepad. Next to it he drew a huge question mark and circled it.

THREE

F OR THE next few moments, I gulped down mouthfuls of cold water while trying to ignore the fact that my brother-in-law was ignoring my insistence that the horrible mistake would be sorted out. I just needed to speak with my chairman or boss, I kept repeating. It would be okay then. But his face did not respond to my wishful rambling as he read my dismissal letter for the second time.

Finally, he put it down on the table between us and looked at me. "Dalton, this is not going to disappear just like that. They're talking fraud here."

For a few seconds we sat there in silence. Nearby, the fridge continued to hum. Chris squeezed the space between his eyes and then looked up.

"Look, Dalton," he said. "Something's obviously gone wrong. Forget the details right now, those don't matter. The basic fact is they've gone rabid over some major money gone missing over there. And you know that when it comes to money, fingers go-a-pointing."

"My God, Chris. What are you saying? That they picked me just like that?"

Chris barely blinked and slowly placed his hand on the letter. "No. Not just like that. They obviously *feel* they have reason to look your way."

I clenched my fist. "No. *No.* I refuse to believe they could even think of me as an incompetent, much less a thief. That bank was my second home. They were like family to me."

Chris gave a small nod but his face bore no expression. "To *you*, yes. Time to get real, Dalton. Friends and family can and do sometimes turn on one another."

I couldn't move. My brother-in-law's words were rumbling in my ears like a roller coaster slowly crawling to the top of a very steep ramp. "Chris—you're talking about people who think *highly* of me. All those performance evaluations, the promotions and raises. You're talking about five years of—"

But this time he cut me off. "Afen's gotten in touch with your lawyer. He's going to meet with us tomorrow. Until then, let's do some work right now. Right now, Dalton."

Dunkley? You called my lawyer? The roller coaster was cresting now, preparing for a spiral fall. I wanted off. Before I could begin to question or object to the need for legal help, my brother-in-law began firing detailed questions about the transactional processing business. I watched as his notes grew on the pad.

He had known about it to some extent through our intermittent exchanges, but this time Chris went narrow and deep. *Exactly how were the accounts opened? Who were the signatories? At what point were the monies transferred? Who actually moved the funds around? Who approved the merchants? Who introduced them to the bank? Who this? How that? When? Why?*

They came at me like practice tennis balls from one of those automatic machines. I returned them with relative ease. I felt I knew the project like I knew the road to Mandeville. After scribbling for what seemed like an eternity, he paused, pen still in hand and looked up. "But, Dalton, based on what you're telling me—between how the bank operated, how decisions were made and what your responsibilities were—no reasonable person could come to the conclusion that you could have stolen the money, even if you wanted to."

"I know! That's why this is so ridiculous!" His assessment offered me some immediate reassurance. I waited for more.

Chris stared back at me, carefully thinking his next step through. "Let's back up a bit. What really brought the telemarketing down? In *your* opinion. I'm just trying to understand what happened."

I fell silent for a moment. What I really wanted to say was *foolish panic*. Nothing more than that. Instead, I tried to focus and think objectively. It had happened all so quickly. Quite frankly, I wasn't so sure I understood it all myself. So I told him what I thought.

"If I had to sum it up, I'd say a combination of pressure and confusion. We'd gotten these telemarketers on board, and the next thing we know, we're getting pressure from VISA about their integrity, okay? VISA is asking our marketing department questions like '*Who are these people engaged in selling to their cardholders? What are they selling?*' That kind of thing. They were worrying about chargebacks. Because if the telemarketers are con artists, the cardholders have recourse through VISA, as you probably know."

"At the acquiring bank's expense."

"*If* the telemarketers are crooked. Yes. And then there's the whole bad publicity concern on VISA's part. So naturally VISA has to be worried about their integrity and JCB's homework on them—which is why they were on our backs. But yes, it's potentially at JCB's expense because we're basically the first ones to be out of pocket before we can confirm whether the chargeback is valid or not. Anyway, so now JCB is getting nervous and is talking to the merchants about closing their accounts." I took a deep breath. "You follow?"

Chris gave a slow and single nod while continuing to write. I moved on.

"But we investigated all of VISA's concerns. Even the merchants were trying to help us out by saying, look, if you're worried about possible chargebacks and costs to the bank, we can offer you Letters of Credit as protection. *We can sort it out so we're all happy,* kind of thing. But VISA keeps applying the pressure, and begins to send us written correspondence—some of it directly from the Vice-President of the Latin American Region officially warning us that these merchants could be, you know, 'bad people' so to speak. And then there seemed to be some confusion about the local paper rule."

Chris stopped his pen and looked up. "The what?"

"VISA had something called a 'local paper rule.'"

"Explain that one."

"The rule stipulates that the transactions must originate within the same country in which you process them. But apparently an exception was made for those islands that did not have a principal member, okay? They could go through a principal member elsewhere but within the same *region*. It was based on that exception that we came to start processing for some Antiguan merchants, since they had no principal member. The thing is, I'm not sure how clear the Marketing Department was on it at the time. I don't remember if *I* was aware that such a rule existed at that time. Anyway, long story short, soon after Mel Reaume's Antiguan merchant bank came on board, JCB started processing for other merchants. Eventually it was discovered that some of them were outside the region." I paused for a breath. "You still with me?"

Again Chris gave a deep nod. "Go on."

"So for a short while there's a lot of panicky correspondence between us and VISA. Correction—more like from VISA to us. Just doing their job, I suppose. Right? Then all of a sudden the bank is instructing me to shut down certain accounts. This is July now, literally just four months after operations began. So my division does as it's asked, and shuts down the named accounts so that no further business can be done. However, we leave it in such a way that we can accommodate credit situations, you understand. And at this point now my vacation is just days away."

"And of course, up until now you have no reason to think there's trouble brewing for you."

I shook my head and scoffed at the image of me happily boarding a plane for Toronto, family in tow, confident that all was in good hands. Suddenly I didn't feel so smart. I paused for breath and squeezed my eyes shut. I began to see the script that was unfolding, and didn't want to believe it. In my head, one of my father's favourite Chinese sayings now taunted me. *Only trust 70 percent of those around you, son.* Seventy percent? I'd been way off. It was all snapping into place now—all the bits and pieces that didn't seem to fit at the time. The puzzle was finally coming together—and it was a picture of me in a court jester's costume.

Chris broke my thoughts. "Dalton?" I returned his stare and let out a deep breath. "Sorry, Yap, but we need to do this."

I held up a hand. "I'm fine. At this point now—I'm guessing that while I was away, the shit hit the fan. Because right in the middle of my vacation, I get a call from Wiggan. And he's—he's angry like I've never seen before. I mean really pissed off, Chris."

Chris jerked his head back. "Hold on. Lloyd Wiggan pissed with *you*?" He was no stranger to the good history I had with my boss.

I nodded.

"What about?"

"He's upset and saying something along the lines of *how could I bring in these people, and how could I do something like this to the bank.*"

Chris frowned but kept his tone even. "That makes no sense, chief. Soliciting merchants and doing background checks simply don't fall under your umbrella. Your thing is technology. Machines, software, gadgets. You're the man who makes the big engine work so that all everyone else needs to do is hit the power switch."

"I know," I said with flick of a hand in the air. "*He* knows. I swear, Chris. If I didn't know better, I'd say the man was talking as if he had just met me. I mean, it was cold."

Chris studied me for a bit. "Odd. Very odd."

"Boy, Chris," I said, "It was the weirdest thing hearing him talk like that. It seemed so—irrational. Almost, surreal. Like absolutely *nothing* in that conversation made sense—know what I mean?"

Chris threw more questions out. "Did he not attend the meetings, man? I mean, this is a respectable bank, not a family-run shoe shop. No one person makes a decision on anything. Meetings are held, minutes are taken, distributed, confirmed and so forth. It's a group effort. Was he not a part of all that? Weren't all the executives, for that matter?"

I nodded emphatically. "Yes, of course."

"So what was the outcome of this telephone conversation?" I could barely manage a shrug for an answer. Chris shook his head. "Amazing. Okay then, so what did you say to your boss?"

"What I assumed he already knew—that I had nothing to do with bringing these people in. That the project had been started by others and I was just following orders. But it was weird, man. I mean, I wasn't telling my boss something that was new to him, okay?"

"Agreed. What next?"

"Well—none of that seemed to help. At the end of the call I was still confused—I mean, Chris, this had to be the strangest conversation Lloyd and I had ever had in all the years we've worked together. But I was on holiday and figured he was just reacting very badly to a very big problem. Maybe the man needed to vent, you know? He's still human—right?"

"Mm—" Chris said, carefully opting for a neutral response.

He offered nothing else so I continued. "The next thing I know, my vacation is over, I'm back in the office, and within a couple hours Ewart Scott's right-hand man, George Lumsden comes in to update me on the project. And that's when I find out it's now flat-lining. That's when I learn that while I was gone, the bank pretty much shut down the whole damn thing. It completely shut down all the telemarketing accounts so that no new business could be processed, but the real problem was that chargebacks could no longer be facilitated either. It was a mess."

This time Chris spoke. "So now you're—"

"Stunned! I honest to God thought they'd figure something out. Work on some letters of credit like the telemarketers were offering. Have a face-to-face meeting with the VISA people. Something. Anything!"

Chris raised an eye. "They never met with VISA?"

I didn't even pause. "Not face-to-face. Not to my knowledge, that is."

"Are you sure?"

"If it happened, then I sure as hell didn't know about it."

Chris folded his arms for a few seconds. "Unbelievable."

I threw my hands open in agreement. "Exactly. But you know—it wasn't the content of the conversation with Lumsden that bothered me the most. It was his delivery." I shook my head slowly, my eyes staring ahead of me. "Lumsden was acting—you know how you stiffen up when you're in the company of someone you don't want to be seen with?"

"Like—?"

"Your voice goes a little flat while your eyes search for the nearest exit."

"He was like that with you?"

"Not just him. Suddenly I'm greeting people in the corridor who can't stop to chat, or they're barely returning my smiles or good mornings. At the most I'm getting a hasty nod. My usual jokes don't seem to work now—even the really corny ones. It's like my fly's undone and they'd rather dodge me than tell me."

"And your boss?"

"He seemed cold. Unusually preoccupied. Can't catch his eye for long. Manufactured smiles, if any. At least that's how it felt."

"So how were you interpreting all of this?"

I gave a helpless shrug. "I just figured that they were all still upset about the project in general. Disappointed, you know. I mean, I could understand why. The whole telemarketing business could have made the bank a tidy sum. It had that kind of potential. So I figured they were just pissed off. And then—and then later that same day when I walked into his office—"

Chris glanced up from his note pad. "Wiggan's?"

"Yes."

"Go on."

"It was bizarre again. This time I caught him reading a memo I had sent to VISA earlier in response to their panic. From the shine on the paper I could tell that it was a fax copy of the original. I even saw my signature. But when I walked in he started to cover it up just as I said something like *Oh hey, Lloyd, how come you're reading that memo?*"

"What about that scene made you uneasy?"

"The fact that he was trying to hide my own memo from me. And the fact that he never really answered. He just changed the subject and started making conversation. You tell me.

How does that make any sense? This is my boss we're talking about. Up until then the man was thrilled with my work. But still, Chris, even with that sticky moment, I didn't suspect a thing. At least, nothing as sick as this."

"What about your staff? How were they acting?"

"Lesley Hew, Debbie and some others did come and ask me what was going on. They were on edge—friendly as usual, of course, but visibly anxious. Wearing frowns and unable to stand still. Not even wasting time to ask me about my vacation. I mean this was a project we'd rallied around for a year and change—and with the snap of their fingers management just shuts it down. My division viewed that move the same way I did—illogical. Well, apparently they hadn't been told very much in my absence while everything was being mashed in the blender. So I told them what I knew. That management had already made its decision. And I just left it at that. What the hell else could I tell them? Believe it or not, Chris, up to that point I still thought they could have worked out a solution."

"And up until the time you left for holidays, had any chargebacks occurred?"

"No more than the usual, as far as I could tell. Chargebacks are a normal part of the credit card business, and even then each case is checked for validity. The problem really only starts when the bank shuts down the merchants' accounts without warning or explanation. Because all of a sudden there are no accounts through which to process the valid chargebacks. So as soon as I'm back from vacation I begin to get the calls directly from the telemarketers."

"Why you?"

"I guess because in the setting up of the accounts, I got to know most of them. So even Mel Reaume is calling, this time from Antigua, asking me what the hell is going on. Man, he was livid."

"Okay, Dalton," he said. "In the auditor's report—the one they did not give you a copy of—you say they highlighted your personal accounts, and seem to have tracked movements of funds. You have personal accounts with the bank, yes?"

"Here in Jamaica and with the Miami branch."

"Go on."

"Remember that I started that plastics manufacturing company with some other people."

"Yes. About a year now, right?"

"Right. Well, my partners and I used my accounts to transfer funds as we needed it. You know, to pay for raw material, purchase equipment and so on."

Chris raised an unhappy eye. "Through your personal accounts, Dalton? You can't be serious."

I nodded and swallowed hard. I knew a reprimand was coming. "I know, Chris, I know. It was stupid of us. I just figured that it would be okay for a short while until we set up our own company account. Especially since we have it all clearly documented. I mean, trust me, we can account for every penny. No question about that."

"So this money was used to run the company then. How much would you say you had in terms of movement of funds?"

"During the course of the first year? Maybe close to US$400,000?"

Chris couldn't hide a grimace. "I can't believe you ran your business through your personal account."

I swallowed nervously. "It was just so convenient at the time." I shook my head. What I really wanted to do was take a bat to it. "No need to say it, Chris. It wasn't the smartest thing to do, I know. But I swear to you that everything has been carefully documented and accounted for. I have a paper trail. The bank doesn't have to take my word. My partners can confirm where the money came from."

Chris chewed on that for a few seconds. "Okay. At least we have that. But you're telling me that Scott never gave you a chance to answer the allegations? He never asked you where that money came from?"

"No."

"Same with the auditor? Did he ask to interview you while preparing this report they wouldn't let you have?"

"No. No interview. No questions. Not one."

"Are you telling me you were never given a chance to defend yourself before being fired?"

I looked at him numbly. "I, I guess that's what I'm saying."

Chris bit down on his lips and shook his head slowly. I could tell he was furious. "So much for the principle of natural justice."

"Principle of what?"

"Natural justice. Give a man a chance to defend himself before taking action. You weren't given that opportunity."

"No. I wasn't." I could feel defeat creeping over my shoulders as I slumped in my chair.

Chris raised his eyes with a sarcastic nod. "So in a nutshell, there's money missing, they see lots of movement in your personal accounts, and suddenly a seemingly credible argument against you develops and the executives take swift action."

I looked at him helplessly, the sick horror of his summary now fresh in my head. "Looks so."

"I don't believe it," Chris shook. "All they had to do was ask you some of the same questions I just did and they'd realize you could *not* have done this." I nodded, grateful for the logic and support my brother-in-law was offering. "That's the trouble with some of these big companies. Too often the ones at the top get a more filtered vision of reality."

A rush of air escaped my nostrils. "Meaning?"

"Look. The head of a big bank is not going to conduct an investigation himself. Let's be fair. He's going to rely on others to do that—his internal auditors, his managers, his lawyers and so on—because that's their job. Big companies pay these professionals big money for their opinion and expertise. But it's also only natural that these professionals are going to want to advise the company on the basis of their being right. Yes? The CEO or whatever he or she is—but a paid professional nevertheless—is going to listen to these advisors because that's what they're supposed to do and also because money's at stake. Believe me; that CEO is going to hold firm to their advisors' opinions and counsel. The human factor is not going to be as strong. They don't necessarily think like a smaller business owner who might be more inclined to consider someone's reputation or track record—who might sit with you in private, talk to you personally. Get to the bottom of it, man to man."

"I see what you mean."

Chris glanced at what he'd scribbled. After a minute or so he tapped the pen on the table. "Well. Clearly they have a lot of faith in this internal auditor. He certainly has them pointing in a certain direction." And then he looked straight at me. "A potentially expensive one too."

I cleared my throat. His last statement sounded loaded. "What are you thinking?"

"It's not what I think. It's what I know."

"Which is?"

"That no one likes to lose—especially when you're a corporate big-wig. Dalton, did Scott complete the dismissal, though? I see you still have the car. Did he take your company particulars—like your building pass? Did he have you escorted out with security and all that?"

I answered by shaking my head. At least Ewart had been kind enough to spare me the sick embarrassment of being treated publicly like a common thief. "I asked him to let me speak to Mr. Danny Williams first. He agreed to let me try on Monday. I figure he's waiting on that to happen."

Chris didn't move, but looked at me hard. "Dalton. You need to get yourself together, and you need to do it now." I pulled back with a frown. His voice had taken on a controlled sense of urgency that I didn't like. "You need to make sure you understand everything there is to know about this telemarketing project."

I returned a blank stare. "I don't—I don't get you."

"Dalton." Chris looked like he wanted to shake me but his voice remained steady. "A business deal has gone sour and people are upset. *You* are the object of their anger. Just look at what's happened so far. Up until recently these people thought so highly of you they'd seek your help with problems *outside* your division. They sang your praises review after review, handed you promotions like candy. Suddenly they're so convinced you're an incompetent and a thief, that they don't even extend you the basic courtesy of the chance to defend yourself? Doesn't that just ring wrong to you?"

"But, Chris what can I do?"

"Do you really want to be left standing there with just your word, brother-in-law? Because clearly not even your spotless track record matters to them any longer." He leaned forward. "Dalton, this time they're handing you candy *and* pink slips, except they're all out of candy. You get me now?" Furious, confused and more embarrassed than anything else, I could only nod silently at the tongue-lashing. "Look, Dalton, I'm sorry, man. But this is no time to be a boy scout."

This time Chris paused as I recoiled. His words triggered in my head a scene from one of my favourite Harrison Ford movies. My face twitched—first in confusion, and then in recognition. I heard Chris's voice again. "You've stumbled into a deep hole, Dalton. Make sure you have the tools to dig yourself the hell out."

It was then that I understood what I needed to do.

SATURDAY, OCTOBER 2. Sleep would not come that night. As the world rested, the creaks and whispers of the night taunted me. My worst thoughts raced and collided until I was beyond numb.

That first day in October had left me a withered man by the evening's end. I had to face my wife who had come in from Mandeville, and my siblings who came rushing to their big brother's side. They all tried to say the right things, pour the right teas, squeeze my hand as hard as they could. On the phone, my bewildered mother begged for an explanation I could not give.

I knew there was more to come. Much more. I had yet to face my staff, my friends. The huge Chinese community, my mother—my father. My proud father. What would I do for money? What about my bills? My children? Was I really about to go bankrupt? Could I actually end up in jail? Was that a possibility? There are moments when a man cannot be comforted. For the first time in my life, I was there. But there was no time to pause for even dark imaginings. My lifeline was still intact, floating quietly in the dark water. I needed it to remain undetected. At least for the next few hours.

That Saturday morning I got dressed inconspicuously, but I still felt like I had a huge arrow pointing at me that said *look here*. Suddenly the blue jeans seemed too well ironed. The polo tennis shirt, too white. Pauline kept reassuring me. *You look okay, D. Yap. We'll be okay. Please try to eat something.* By nine o'clock we were in my car on our way to King Street. I had timed it so that I'd get there at my usual Saturday arrival slot—in my usual Saturday attire. At least a hundred scenarios ran through my mind as we drove in silence. *What if the guard stopped me? What if my door was bolted? What if the other managers were there?*

At about a quarter after nine the Cefiro turned on King Street and pulled up alongside the grimy sidewalk, almost directly in front of the bank. Thankfully, the downtown area was always more accommodating on a Saturday, when some of the uptown executives stayed home. A stray dog scurried out of our way as the car came to a complete stop. Now parked and still in our seats, I put my hand across my stomach and stretched my torso to get air in my lungs. Pauline touched my arm and squeezed.

I looked for the guard. I knew that once I established eye contact with him, I could tell how the next hour was going to unfold. And then I spotted his uniform. It was the same fellow from the evening before. I froze. *Did Ewart give him his orders right after my dismissal? My God. Did he?* And then the guard turned my way. Immediately his face broke into his usual broad grin at the sight of a familiar face. As if to calm me further, he held up a friendly hand. It was exactly what I needed to see.

Pauline trembled as she smiled but kept pace as I played the part of Dalton Yap, hardworking executive in for his usual Saturday morning stint. The building was largely quiet. Few had come in yet. My nose picked up traces of the cleaning detergents the office maintenance crew had used the night before.

I held my breath until we were standing at my office door. No one was around. I slipped my key in, and turned. It was the most beautiful sound I'd ever heard. With a push of the door we were in. Everything was as I had left it. I pulled open my filing cabinet and immediately fixed my eyes on what I needed. They were all still there—my files on the telemarketing project. I grabbed an empty computer monitor box, threw it on my desk, and got down to work.

Within an hour we were heading out the door, the same plastic but pleasant smile on our faces, my heart beating wildly against my chest. I barely made it to the waiting Cefiro before my legs began to shake under me and the now not-so-empty box.

THE YOUNG LAWYER SAID he thought he'd encountered some strange situations before, but the previous evening's call from his friends, Leo Campbell and then Afen Yap, kept him awake for most of the night.

Christopher Dunkley and I had all but lost touch after my graduation and departure for studies in Toronto. We would only step back into each other's lives years later, thanks to an irate dog that had taken a chunk out of one of the workers at my new plastics factory in Savanna-La-Mar. Prior to that, I had never needed a lawyer for anything serious. With a shared alma mater and love for food, we became like old friends as I became his new client. That had only been six months ago.

Dunkley said a dog bite incident he could understand. That was almost as common here in Jamaica as a parking violation in Manhattan, but Dalton Yap fired? For fraud? Try again. That kind of action required the mindset of an individual who had lost his soul. Dalton was the boy wonder who practically wore a cape at the bank. Dalton, former Head Boy of an upstanding high school. A man who actually admitted to listening to motivational tapes, even calling some of them "classics". A generally spirited person, who didn't give a rat's ass if you rolled on the floor watching him do the electric slide at a wedding.

What bothered Christopher Dunkley the most was that, for what he considered to be a highly intelligent man, I seemed to have been taken completely by surprise. Like I'd stumbled into a masquerade party without a mask.

When he walked into Chris Berry's Oxford Road office in Kingston's financial district later that day, Dunkley's almond eyes went almost round at the sight before him. I had come in about four hours earlier, and had turned my brother-in-law's normally neat office into a paper processing factory. Everywhere Dunkley looked, stacks of white paper covered any flat surface; even the seats of chairs. At the centre of the scene was the overloaded conference table at which we now stood. Next to the table, the photocopier purred and flickered.

Dunkley's solid frame remained anchored for a few seconds as he took it all in. We greeted each other by clasping shoulders, his intense eyes now focusing on mine. Even though I stood several inches taller than Dunkley, he was to me at this moment the tallest man in the room. His first words were that of a concerned friend. "Dalton. You okay, man?"

I gave a weak nod. "Thanks for coming so soon, Dunkley." Still reeling from the morning's move, I barely recognized my own voice, devoid of its usual spring. The other two shook hands firmly as Dunkley scanned the scene before him.

Chris Berry answered Dunkley's questioning look. "Getting a head start on the paper trail," he said. "Copies. We're just about done."

Dunkley found room at a nearby table and grabbed a chair as I handed him the dismissal letter. For the next few minutes I trained my eyes on him as if he were a doctor reading my test results, but at that point he had become poker-faced, and I could detect nothing. He'd become the lawyer I needed now.

Finally, he spoke. "Okay, gentlemen," he said. "Good work here. Quick thinking. I suggest we get three piles going under the categories of 'useless,' 'maybe,' and 'definitely.' We'll need two copies each. One set is to be locked up in a vault with the key thrown away. When we know more we'll adjust those piles. After that, Dalton, you're going to tell me everything you know. And I mean *everything*. But make a note. First thing Monday morning, you go back to that bank and get the rest of your personal belongings the hell out of there. And that includes your money."

Our council of war did not end that evening until close to midnight, long after I had gone back to the office to return what I had borrowed.

For hours we sat there huddled in discussion, with no concept of time, hunger or the people in our lives waiting anxiously at home. Both Chris Dunkley and Chris Berry said the evidence looked promising for my defence, but as it was way too early to start speculating, we stopped only when we could push no further. The only other clear image I have of that weekend was of my retreat to Mandeville Sunday morning.

IT WAS A shaken man who stepped into that quiet kitchen, where an elderly father sat alone in the soft light waiting for his firstborn son. I stood there at the door, unsure of how to begin speaking, or how to lift my eyes to his.

And then suddenly, the man I had grown to become left my body. Now standing before my father was the ten year-old son whose favourite pet had just died. The boy who had just had his prized toy broken, the one he'd saved up for months to buy. I was the little boy who didn't make the school football team. I was all of those boys all at once—desperate now for the comfort of his father's reassurance.

On seeing me there was no physical touching, no open tears. Instead, he slowly rose to his feet in silence, holding onto the back of the chair for support. Then, with the hurt etched in his brave face, my father hugged me with his eyes. They were trying desperately to tell me that everything would be okay. That's when he broke the silence, and spoke to me in the tongue of our ancestors.

"Dalton. In many ways we try to be like the tiger—strong and powerful. But when a tiger dies, it leaves behind only its skin. When we die, we leave our name. Our legacy. We will fight this, my son. We will clear your name. We will clear our family's name."

In my father's honour, I fought back the tears.

FOUR

F or the first time ever I did not embrace the morning. The hope I'd been nursing for an abrupt end to my nightmare was growing weaker with each reality check and I had had several that weekend, courtesy of those closest to me.

Among those was Mr. Maurice Berry, Chris's father, and a gentleman I greatly respected. He had called begging me to take this seriously, saying that it wasn't going to end for now. *From my experience*, he had said. A former deputy governor of Jamaica's central bank, Mr. Berry's warning had me even more on edge. He even offered the help of his family's lawyer, but as another close friend had already called with an offer to introduce me to a prominent Queen's Counsel friend of his, I had no choice but to decline Mr. Berry's.

"Dalton," my friend had said, "the bank has Michael Hylton. They're not playing around. You need a Queen's Counsel of equal might. Get the right horse for the right course." He would take me in to meet this highly recommended lawyer for a quick introduction not long after. Meanwhile, fear about our opposing counsel began to creep in. I asked Dunkley about this Hylton fellow. "Well, I can tell you that he's not yet lost a case at the Privy Council," he said with a matter of fact tone. That was the first time my lawyer would utter the name "Privy Council" regarding my situation. I doubt either of us took much notice.

Looking back, I must have been the only one who was still clinging to the notion that the nightmare could vanish overnight. *I just need to make that phone call to the Chairman, I kept saying. Just let me speak to the people at the top. Let me talk to those who know me, and this whole mess will disappear.* I believed that as wholeheartedly as I believed my mother had given birth to me.

At Dunkley's request, I had spent most of Sunday outlining on paper the events leading up to my dismissal. *While your memory is fresh,* he had suggested. I had also spent most of the day torturing myself with images of friends and members of the Chinese community at the garden party, surely wondering why I hadn't shown my face. I was, after all, the association's treasurer—the person entrusted with their money. The same man now being accused of fraud. For a community that did not often hand out second chances when it came to honour, this was not good.

We left Mandeville that Monday morning in convoy. Pauline and I went in the Cefiro, while Afen followed in Pauline's red Honda Civic. This time the road into Kingston seemed to almost tug at the wheels, as if to slow us down. With each mile we cleared, the knot in my stomach grew tighter and tighter. I don't think my wife and I exchanged two words.

Once in downtown Kingston, we parked in the bank's parking lot. Pauline was to come in with me while Afen waited in the car. My brother offered me an anxious glance as I prepared to face a full bank. Later he would tell me that he could see me struggling for breath.

By the time I arrived, most of the staff was already there. Some did double takes at the sight of me in jeans and polo shirt on a Monday. Debbie gave me a troubled look as we hurried past her into my office. The anxiety that swept across her face told me she had already heard something she didn't like. Her eyes held a hundred questions.

Once inside, without waiting to sit, I grabbed the receiver and punched in the extension for the bank's legal counsel, Camille Facey. She answered after the third ring. The call was short. Her response to my request for a meeting with Mr. Danny Williams was guarded. She agreed to call and let me know if it would take place. Her instructions to me were very clear. If I did not hear from her, I should conclude that I would not be meeting with the Chairman. Her call would never come.

As the minutes ticked by, word began to seep throughout the bank about my fate. Pauline began packing silently while I confirmed the news to those members of my staff who chose to come by. They trickled in timidly to give me a brief handshake or touch on the arm without saying much, as if afraid that speaking would make the whispers true. A speechless Debbie joined my wife and slowly started tugging at books on the shelves, carefully placing them in boxes.

Right about then one either very uninformed or very insensitive staff member of mine made the mistake of waltzing into the office in mid-sentence about some business matter—as I stood there amid boxes and emptied shelves in non-office attire. Unfortunately for him, he happened to be a former colleague of Ewart from the days when they both reported to the Finance manager. It was their close connection that launched me into a tirade about the person to whom he should be directing all his frigging questions. My poor unsuspecting visitor pivoted on his heels and made a swift exit as Pauline and Debbie continued to pack. The sting of my bitter reply still echoed in the room.

I owe all recollection of the ensuing scene to Edward Gabbidon. He would graciously save the description for a time much later when I could finally see some humour in it:

"When we first heard about Dalton's dismissal that morning, all clocks stopped turning for those of us who called him our *boss*. For a while we could do nothing that required thought. I swear even our limbs had gone to sludge.

There was no other Dalton Yap. The man was a virtual caricature of 'the hard worker'. This was the person who would cut a vein open for his employer and ask how many pints they needed. We didn't even have to ask if his family suffered for it. A math-impaired idiot could figure it out. He arrived before us, turned out the lights after we'd gone—even broke his sleep on occasion to dial in and check that the system was running smoothly. Because, according to him, if he slept eight hours a night he'd end up sleeping away a third of his life, and who the hell needed that much sleep anyway? A casual observer might have mistaken him for being another people-pleasing whore, but they'd be wrong. The man simply loved what he did. And if you could benefit from that, well he was fine with it. With Dalton, it wasn't about keeping score. It was all about doing his job and the wonderful world of technology.

He didn't even try to be cool about his enthusiasm. We couldn't count the number of times we'd see him literally throw off his jacket and roll up his sleeves to tear open a box of new equipment like it was Christmas, just so that he could be the first to read the manual cover to cover. The rest of us would have to wait for days before we could get our hands on it. No question about it, his constant push for knowledge kept us on our toes—forced us to stay sharp. And he'd never ask us to do something he wasn't prepared to do himself. He'd strip his own damn wires if he had to—while wearing his monogrammed shirts.

Dalton was the kind of boss who led instead of commanded. It was all about getting the job done. He could be cracking the whip one day if he needed to, and lunching with you out of a cardboard takeout box the next. He was the kind of leader who gave you the room to think and execute, and who had your back no matter what. So while Dalton Yap might have been one of the bank's general managers, he was our fearless general. Resent him if you wished for showing you up. Dislike him if you must for usually getting the tools he needed and the toys he wanted. The point was he did the work. The man was a dying breed. And not just in his work ethic. At JCB we had this tired old *we-them* culture when it came to managers and the rest of us. We didn't dare address the suited ones by their first names. Dalton was one of the few managers who comfortably transcended all tiers, without apology. Elon Beckford came close. He would at least stop and chat with you briefly on the steps and so on. But our boss had no problem with you calling him Dalton or 'hey you.' Just as long as there was respect.

When I got to the door of his office that awful day, my legs simply stopped. I could not cross the threshold and become a part of that horrible scene. Inside, Debbie was crying without a sound, carefully moving from shelf to box, like a robot on automatic drive. Pauline was shuffling around as well, also without a word. Her eyes belied her stony silence. They were wide with despair.

Pacing from wall to wall was a crazed man I did not recognize. In one hand he was holding a glass of grape juice, but I did not see him drink. His eyes were red, but no tears flowed. He was muttering in spasms about not stealing anything, and not doing anything wrong to the bank, and asking how they could be doing this to him. His free hand kept flying to his head, as if to hold it in place. I don't think he even saw me standing there the entire time. Never before had I seen my general flustered.

Standing there, watching, I felt my own mortality for the first time."

WITH PAULINE AND Debbie's help I completed my packing, leaving behind a pair of crystal drinking glasses the bank had given to me. I merely shook my head at Debbie, who kept insisting that they belonged to me. I did not walk through my division to bid any final goodbyes. Despite the fact that I knew I was innocent of the allegations, I couldn't raise my head to face the questions in their eyes. I simply didn't have the energy to begin sifting through the rubble to figure out whom I could trust.

Following on Dunkley's orders, I went to close my accounts with the bank. This time I'd call the branch manager in Miami, where the bulk of my money sat. Again a door slammed shut. Like the bank's in-house attorney, his hurried reply about having to wait seven working days before accessing my funds told me that he too was acting under strict orders. They were holding me to the banker's contract that allowed the bank to request notice prior to a withdrawal. I would have to wait it out another week. As much as I tried to convince myself that the notice was standard, I knew in my gut that this was not business as usual.

My opportunity to speak came a day later, when I chanced a direct call to Mr. Danny Williams's office. To this day I still laugh at the surge of adrenaline I felt as his secretary was putting the call through. I convinced myself that help was finally on its way because he was accepting the call. *Please, sir, you have to hear me out* I believe was the desperate plea I blurted out when his distinguished voice emerged from the other end of the line.

Yes, I begged the man. I begged him for a chance to be heard because I was innocent of every single allegation being levelled at me. I begged him for just five minutes of his time because I knew I could clear my name. I pleaded with him as a young man with a family to support.

The Chairman replied with careful reference to the capable executives in whose hands the matter now lay. I couldn't be certain at the time, but I thought I detected an unhappy strain in his tone. I thought about my brother-in-law's words. In the end I decided to believe and accept that Mr. Williams, a man I had always thought highly of, felt he was acting appropriately based on the information presented to him by his senior officers. He was a man caught in an uncomfortable position. At least he had been decent enough to take my call, but I had been clinging to his intervention as my last chance. So when I put the receiver down that day, I stopped hoping. It was at that point that I finally got up off my knees, and turned to stare my future down its long, dark barrel.

That Friday, October 8, I was served with a writ. Jamaica Citizens Bank was suing me for $2 million United States dollars. I am not ashamed to admit it: the shock of just hearing those words almost made me vomit.

MY LAWYER SAT alone in his downtown second-floor office pondering the week that was. Outside, Duke Street was mellowing under the easy afternoon sun.

As much as he managed to sidestep emotion, Chris Dunkley was by now on edge over the unexpected strike against his friend. The nature of the distress call from the Yap clan was not one on which he'd have ever placed a bet. In his practice he'd seen some stuff go down, but this one had no ring of logic to it. In fact, quite the opposite, he thought. It was as if they'd all stepped into a twilight zone. It was what had made the earlier sorting stint at Berry's office all the more of an exercise in the dark. With only the dismissal letter to go by, they could only guess at what was coming next.

Well "next" had just shown its face. The *ex parte* writ was a toxic one by any standard. Dalton, their star systems manager with a flare for international business, was being accused of some reprehensible extracurricular activity—of basically putting his brilliance to bad use. It was a terse shot glass of allegations only four lines long: breach of contract, deceit, negligence. *Fraud.* His client was being sued to the unbelievable tune of US$2 million. Chris understood that this was not a tenuous schoolyard jab resulting from some growing squabble. This was more like a solid fist to the groin, delivered unexpectedly around a dark corner. They weren't kidding around. But there was more.

Christopher Dunkley knew from the age of ten what he was going to do with his life. That's exactly how old he was when Trinidad's famous Malik trial hooked him—a case he continued to follow even as he and his family prepared to emigrate to Jamaica. After completing his degree at the University of the West Indies, he packed his belongings, and headed for England where he went to law school, gorged on junk food, and joined the army as a reservist. The latter was a strong second love, and served as both an outlet and energy source for his particular zest for strategy.

After graduating from law school in 1987, Dunkley returned to Jamaica. He joined the army fulltime, delaying his legal career for a year. After a brief stint with Crafton, Miller and Co., he went on his own in 1989. The move was pure Dunkley; at a time when most of his fellow graduates were comfortably landing positions as highly-paid in-house lawyers in the booming corporate Jamaica of the late 1980s,

Chris was the lone sheep going against the crowd saying excuse me, excuse me. His decision to struggle first would season him well. Becoming the sole legal counsel for Motor General and Insurance Company in 1992, he was handling no less than two hundred personal injury cases and steadily making a name for himself as a tireless lawyer. He'd also establish a reputation for attention to attire, earning the nickname "Angela Channing's lawyer" by his close friends.

By October 1993 he was still laying the foundation, but was nevertheless on a nice roll. He had just established Wright, Dunkley with Norman Wright, both having previously been single practitioners. By then Dunkley had been a lawyer for just six years, a husband for two, a father for three months, and army captain for one. His equally busy wife, Erica, was just about to resume her medical practice after a brief maternity leave. The two were high school friends and eventually sweethearts. At just thirty-one, Chris Dunkley was already enjoying his life and strapping himself in for a great ride.

I harboured no doubt in my choice of Chris Dunkley and Norman Wright as my lawyers. I had observed in Chris's tone of voice and body language the high regard he held for the seasoned lead counsel. And Christopher Dunkley was not someone who was easily impressed.

From the day I was fired I was tied to them by an invisible cord. While up to that point my recommended Queen's Counsel continued to maintain a largely phantom presence, Chris was standing front and centre—patiently taking my every frantic call, handling me with the calm assurance I needed, even if I didn't always feel so assured. So when I got the call from his secretary, Etta, to come down as soon as I could that Friday, I jumped into the car and headed downtown.

When I walked into his office, I saw for the first time, a hint of angst in his eyes. I took a deep breath.

"Dunkley?"

"Come in, Dalton," he said motioning me to sit. His voice was charged but very much under control. I settled in my seat as he closed a file in front of him and pushed it aside. He cleared his throat and clasped his hands on his desk, the way doctors do sometimes when they're about to give you less than happy news. "Okay. Let's get straight into it, shall we? No time to waste. There's more to the lawsuit now. They've just served us with a Mareva injunction."

I nodded. "Okay. What's that?" I asked the question knowing that I wasn't going to like his answer.

It was Chris's turn to inhale. "It's a freezing order of the worst kind, Dalton. They're freezing your assets for up to $400,000."

My Asian eyes widened. "What?"

Again Chris paused. "And, just to be clear Dalton, that's U.S. dollars." Freeze was the right word. Inside I had gone ice cold. Not only was I drowning, but now they were tying my hands. Chris watched my reaction, wanting to keep pace with my absorption of the news.

"Bottom line is you are now prohibited from touching your assets wherever they may be in the world. Understand of course," he said in as close to a business-as-usual voice as he could muster, "that they're probably doing this because they think you've got your bags packed with a one-way ticket to Hong Kong."

I stared at him trying to decide how panicked I should be. "So—you're saying that this is just—standard procedure?"

Chris grimaced. "Ah, not exactly. I'm afraid this one's rougher than usual." I slumped deeper into the chair and put my hand over my clenched mouth. He continued. "Look, it's easy to see what they've done here. They've made an automatic connection between the money they see moving around in your personal accounts and their losses in the telemarketing business. It's unfortunate they didn't even stop to ask where the money came from. Very unfortunate."

I exhaled in frustration. "Easier to assume I took it, right?"

"It sure seems as if they're eyeballing that scenario real hard. Let's face it. To many, you're probably too young to be business-savvy. Too young to be that successful, if you get my drift."

"So I have a head for business! Big deal!" I bounced out of my chair and stalked toward the wall so I could turn my head away for a second and stew.

"The thing is, Dalton, this one has real teeth. Normally such injunctions last for only twenty-one days, twenty-eight at the most. But not this one. This one is until judgment."

I spun around to face him again. "Until judgment." I repeated the words like a recorder.

Chris nodded. "Until the lawsuit is over. Either these people really don't like you, Yap, or they're confident they can pin something on you. They're coming at you with a nuclear bomb as if you're enemy number one. Your own colleague, Ewart Scott, signed the affidavit supporting the application."

It wasn't so much that I didn't like what I was hearing. I didn't like that it seemed to have Chris standing at attention. He was not a man easily spooked. Eventually I found my voice again. "Until judgment. How long is that?"

Chris folded his arms across his chest and leaned back slowly in his chair. "That's the hitch. Unfortunately for us, this isn't England where we could be in the commercial courts in a matter of weeks. Our system is clogged. It could be months before we get to trial. A year, even."

Suddenly Mr. Maurice Berry's words came floating back. This could take a long time, Dalton. Hunker down. "My God, Chris. What can we do?"

"Apply for a discharge. Norman and I are already working on it and we'll have it submitted first thing Monday."

"Okay." I was no idiot and had certainly been exposed to the legal system before, but I wanted to understand every word from here on out. "Will that take care of it? I mean, what are the chances that—"

"Don't worry, Yap." His voice was steady with reassurance. "We're going to do everything we can. Everything."

I wrung my hands together. "What do they have on me, Dunkley? What are they coming with?"

"I don't know," he said. I really don't know, but we'll find out soon enough. Just hang in there."

Chris hoped it didn't sound like a platitude. He didn't want to alarm his client, but something was needling him. He'd have to check, but he was quite certain that this was the first significant application of the Mareva injunction in Jamaica's modern-day history. There had been one back in the 1980s, but nowhere near as serious; it had only lasted a few weeks at most. This plaintiff was taking no chances and seemed to be pretty damn sure of its position—sure enough for its lawyers to be venturing into such a rare area of law in the country. Why was that? Did they even realize the implications? Exactly what *did* the plaintiff have on his client?

MYERS, FLETCHER & GORDON was just about the biggest law firm in the land. Everyone knew that. The contrast between the legal giant and Dunkley's growing but still relatively young practice couldn't have been greater.

Myers, Fletcher & Gordon had an impressive secretarial pool and the latest technology for legal research. Dunkley had one capable assistant by the name of Etta Gordon, who was already at her limit and threatening retirement. Myers, Fletcher & Gordon's offices practically took up an entire city block, and even had its own parking lot. It had beautiful original paintings and exquisite wood furniture. My lawyer was working out of a nice enough but modestly-furnished office with old—but polished—wood flooring, a basic desk, a few four-drawer filing cabinets, and bland off-white walls that would have been bare save for his diplomas. The only reason they were even there had to do with a close call: Beryl, the office attendant, almost tossed out the cardboard box containing the diplomas. Her defence was that she thought her boss had asked her to throw this box away. In actual fact he had asked her to put this box away in the vault. That was Dunkley's significant lesson on the importance of communication. Message sent is not necessarily message received. Thanks to Beryl and the cardboard box incident, from then on he always tried to get feedback on something he had just communicated to someone else.

The mere mention of the name Myers, Fletcher & Gordon was usually accompanied by a blare of trumpets. And they were sending out the big guns for this case—the highly respected and competent Byron St. Michael Hylton, Queen's Counsel, or Michael Hylton as he was better known. He was to be assisted by Patrick McDonald, a young and extremely capable attorney who many considered "one to watch." Our opposing team was indeed a formidable one.

None of this seemed to make Dunkley queasy. If the bank wanted a fight, he'd be ready, he said. All he needed to do now before taking up the gauntlet was to pose that necessary question of his client. It happened one evening at the end of another very long question-and-answer session at his office.

"Dalton," he nudged, "before we take this further and really bring Norman in, you know I have to ask you, for the record. Did you do any of this? Are any of these allegations true? Any one of them?"

I fully acknowledge that my lawyer, and friend, felt pained at having to ask. His eyes told me so, but knowing it was of little comfort. So let me say this. If you ever want to know what it feels like to have the living rage seep out of your very pores and drain you of all civility, just have someone question your integrity to your face when you know you're innocent. Even if it's only for the record.

JUSTICE NEVILLE THEOBALDS heard our application on October 15. That date would mark my first time in any judicial system as a participant. I had served in the summer of 1993 as a juror. This was also the first time I wore a suit since my dismissal from the bank.

I still see that day clearly like photos in an album. Me: at home trying to swallow coffee, my family huddling around me, some calling on the phone to wish me well. Me: walking through the metal detector at the courthouse, my eyes cast downward and fixed on the ground or Dunkley's shoes. I struggled with the humiliation of just being here, and still tried to figure out how this all happened.

We headed upstairs to Justice Theobald's chambers. He was already seated when we entered the long, narrow room and greeted us with a nod. Shelves and bookcases surrounded us. As this was a chamber matter and not a court matter, he wore a jacket and tie without the usual robe and wig.

I'd say everything else was pretty much as I had remembered it from my time on jury duty. In our courts there is no appointed court reporter, no super-speedy typist to capture everyone's every word. The poor judges are left to handwrite everything they wish to capture for review. Everyone who speaks has to slow it right down to a snail's pace or face a quick dressing-down from the judge himself.

I sat silently, glued to my seat. I listened to my lawyer rebuke the other side for the unjust pursuit of an injunction —until judgment no less—against his client. *My client is a man whose*

67

defence the Court has yet to hear, mi Lord! Chris also argued that the basis of the plaintiff's injunction was an auditor's report referred to in their writ; a report they had yet to present to the Court.

It must be noted now that for the entire duration of the trial of *Jamaica Citizens Bank v Yap,* that auditor's report—the very foundation of my dismissal and basis for the bank's lawsuit, would never be produced.

It is nothing short of an out-of-body experience to be in a room with a group of people, mostly strangers, whose sole purpose is to talk about you. To argue about what you did or did not do. Refer to you in the third person. Call you strange names that grate like fingernails on a chalkboard. Names like "defendant" or "appellant." I focused carefully as I tried to follow the legal jargon, and could barely hold my breath in my throat when Justice Neville Theobalds began hurling stinging criticism at our affidavit, calling it a sparse and pathetic attempt to explain certain points—which, by the way, he delivered at a much healthier canter. In the end, Justice Theobalds did what was right and handed down a judgment in our favour, albeit on a technicality, and discharged the Mareva. A dam of air came gushing out of my lungs at that very moment. Dunkley seemed both satisfied and incensed.

That night my entire family gathered at Jade Gardens Restaurant for a celebratory dinner. There were my parents, my four siblings and their families, Pauline and the kids. Dunkley's and Norman's families were there too. We had won our first battle and needed to catch our breaths. His Lordship's ruling was a good sign. It spun a promising aura around our case.

That evening we banqueted with big appetites and pent-up frustrations, unapologetic about polluting the air with noisy conversation, slapstick jokes and a general clanking of cutlery. Ours was the table to be with. Some diners smiled curiously at our hyper bunch. Others looked as if they were wishing us gone.

We didn't care. My two children were seeing their father smile again for the first time in two weeks. They took turns clinging to my neck and squeezing. There may have been dark circles under my eyes, but at least tonight they had a spark. Pauline's shone with relief and happiness. Across the table Afen was imitating the bank being miffed at our winning play. The others cheered as my avid badminton player brother used some sort of a smash shot analogy, hands in the air and all.

I honestly don't remember what I had done to scrape through the long days and nights leading up to this point. My worried family could hardly console themselves let alone help me. I was in a place I had never been before and had no instruction manual for it. In my new world food had no taste. Words came at me in a muffled echo. I could not believe the world was so insensitive that others could continue living while I was left to disintegrate.

Suddenly I had no job to wake up for and drive to. No projects to work on. No meetings to attend. No deadlines to meet. The Chinese Cultural Association had already accepted my resignation by way of a telephone phone call to the President, who did not even offer a polite request to rethink my hasty decision. My own partner in the plastics factory could only scream for his money that had been trapped in the mess. I, Dalton Yap, who had risen at 4 a.m. as a boy to make patties for our shop, no longer had a purpose to my day. My life's entire metabolism had changed.

Seated next to me at the table were Dunkley and Norman. I had noticed that for most of the night they had not been indulging in the belly-busting jokes like the rest of us. I decided to spar a little with the young lawyer. "So, Mr. Dunkley, have you recovered yet from the big ass-chewing?" In truth, I was sympathizing. Part of the profession or not, taking a rap on the knuckles by a judge couldn't be easy for any grown man or woman.

Dunkley swallowed his roast duck with a mouthful of scowl. He had not been at all pleased with Justice Theobald's comments about his handiwork. It was patently clear in his opinion, he said, that the burden of proof was on the plaintiff and not on his client. "That, kind sir, was a deliberate move. Not an oversight." And as the others continued their merriment, my attorney explained the tactic behind the seemingly weak affidavit. Since the other side had not yet filed their statement of claim, our response needed to be as brief as their four-line writ. We were not, he said, going to show our hand and help them tailor a statement he personally suspected they were having trouble stitching together. I would hear the words *trust me* several times from Dunkley throughout the duration of my case.

That evening I let down the hair that I still sported on my head, only retreating slightly when Dunkley finally leaned over and said, "Dalton. You do know they're coming back for us, right?"

I knew he firmly believed that, but I doubt that even he could have guessed what that next move was going to be.

THE FOLLOWING WORK day I returned to the bank for my money, only to be stalled again—this time by the manager of the head office branch. Through Dunkley, I would soon discover the reason for the manager's nervous behaviour. Just hours before my arrival, the bank's lawyers had raced to the Court of Appeal and secured a stay of Justice Theobald's ruling. The Mareva would stick. Once again my hands were tied and the team of Dunkley and Wright got to work. By now, Dunkley was livid.

Days later, on October 23, my brother-in-law's father, Mr. Maurice Berry, passed away unexpectedly. We laid him to his rest on October 30, the same day the news media broke the story of *Jamaica Citizens Bank v Yap* to the nation.

Not wanting to make eye contact with anyone, I wore dark glasses and kept my head down. As I stood by Mr. Berry's grave with my head hanging over my chest, I wished, for one fleeting, selfish moment, that I could take his place.

FIVE

I am a parent. I know the agony of seeing your child in pain. By the time the New Year slipped in, I was also now familiar with the dull ache that corrodes your soul when you're an adult child watching your elderly parents grieve—and you are the source of their hurt and pain. I was adding that to my list of life experiences while everyone else was guzzling champagne and being merry.

My mother and father were by now two very broken people. My siblings Pat, Felice, Terry, Afen—they were agents of fury. They rallied around me like a small army. Ever since word of my troubles had become public information, we'd all been transformed into a public curiosity. My ordeal would prove to be the ultimate friendship sifter. One by one friends and acquaintances slipped into the shadows. My small band of Mandeville friends and a handful of others were the only true believers. Together they buoyed me with the kind of tough fighting words a man needs to hear when he can't voice them himself: This is foolishness, Yap! Don't let them get away with this bullshit! I also received a kind card from Bishop Boyle offering his support, and another bearing words of encouragement from one of the bank's other general managers.

Like Hollywood, in a small community nothing brings you more celebrity than trouble. Wait! Is yuh brother dem talking 'bout? The whisperings always floated back, sometimes with the author's name tagged to it, sometimes not. Boy, looks like Dalton got too ambitious for his own good. What a ting when these young boys tink dem smart! We heard them all. Every hurtful veranda comment. Every oh-just-my-opinion disclaimer. Every personal prediction of the verdict. It didn't help any that I took every word in the news media as a stab at my honour. To everyone else it was just the news, but to me it may as well have been a scouring pad on a fresh open wound.

Mostly it was the immediate silence from the wider Chinese community that stung my family and me. It surprised us. Its sentencing gong echoed for miles. Not once did the phone ring with its caller bearing kind words of consolation or support. Not once did anyone pull up to our driveway on a Sunday for some hot cha and encouraging hand-on-the-shoulder talk. Not once did a wise elder come to give his sage advice—even if it couldn't help much.

I watched my father sink into an old hurt. As a young man raising his family, he had been the financially-challenged half-Chinese who would only receive the attention of the more established Chinese-Jamaicans once his daughters became of marriageable age, and when his big son was a big shot executive driving a fancy car and wearing designer suits. I had, believe it or not, applied for another job in the banking sector after my dismissal, but I was never even called in for the first interview. Years earlier, while still working at JCB, I had been selected to chair the technical steering committee for the Jamaica Electronic Transfer System, or JETS. The purpose of the joint venture by the various banking entities was to enable customers to use their banking cards at any ATM machine. Finally operational, JETS was now looking for someone to run it. I was hardly surprised that they never considered me, of course, but I had to try, if only to make my old man smile again. I would have done just about anything to ease my parents' pain.

My father had met my mother in Hong Kong after his escape from mainland China. They married and soon settled in a village near Tai Po, where my siblings and I were all born in rapid succession in the 1960s. My father worked hard for his young family. When the rumours began floating around that China was eventually going to take Hong Kong back, Dad—who was working for Pan Am Airlines at the time—took advantage of his access to discounted airfares, and returned to Jamaica to scout for a new home. Still unsure about whether to leave, the decision was made for him the day the leftist riots broke out in Hong Kong in May of 1967. Sparked by a labour dispute against the ruling English, the sudden riots were enough to convince my father that it was now time to go.

At the time, a young and stately Hugh Shearer was Prime Minister, and Jamaica felt right to my father. In 1971, he packed up his belongings, took two of his children, and boarded a plane for the West Indies. He, Afen and Theresa at first lived with our grandmother and my father's half-brother, Uncle Sydney. Dad had taken a job at Lenn Happ Supermarket in Kingston packing shelves for $30 a week, and kept an eye out for something that he could do on his own. The two kids began missing their mother in Hong Kong, who was already crying her eyes red for them. Eventually my father borrowed some money to bring Mom and Felice over. Now reunited with Afen and Theresa, it wasn't long before my poor mother started weeping for Pat and me.

We finally joined our family September 9, 1972. We were all together again, all of us under one humble roof in busy Papine near the market. Never mind that the roof covered an adjoining rum bar, which we now operated. As the eldest, I served customers at the tiny establishment. It in turn served as my first introduction to English—and the more colourful side of the local vernacular. Much to my father's dismay, I was becoming particularly good at Jamaican cursing. Less than a year later, however, we were forced to leave our Papine home. Cheated by a sly business partner, my father came home one day and told us to pack our belongings. That night we slept in the garage. The next day we climbed into a truck Dad had rented, and headed for Mandeville where a kind family friend offered us the use of his guesthouse. Four months later, Dad took over a restaurant from a Mr. Lester Lyn. That September, I began classes at West Indies College to study proper English.

Now my father found himself retreating to his garden to silently agonize over what was happening to his firstborn. I could only watch through the window as he tended to his crop with a troubled frown. I wanted to rip my hair out for giving him this pain. I was sick over it.

My mother was also going through her own private battle. A proud woman who had for years successfully run her own ice cream parlour—despite being unable to read or speak English—she now found herself having to decipher the sly double-talk her friends were dishing out whenever they gathered to play "look-fu", one of their favourite Chinese card games. As they played, they each offered their interpretation of what they had read in the papers that day or heard on the evening news about me. Most of the time they'd get it wrong. Inevitably she'd end up tugging at Pauline or the others— always with brave tears—begging them to tell her what was happening, to please tell her what was going on with her son and the people at the bank. The details they would always try to spare her. They were, at any rate, often too intricate to follow. My mother would never let me see her cry openly. Nor would she approach me directly with questions.

The truth is that by now few could reach me. For that I will never stop seeking the forgiveness of my wife and children. I never meant to walk past them all the times that I did. I just could not see them. I could see no one.

Sometimes Pauline would try to tell me about her day. It was a habit she used to enjoy before I had been fired. She'd talk about which products she was thinking of selling, how to improve the space problem she was having, or which employees were showing potential and which needed to move on. Meanwhile I'd listen quietly while changing my clothes or chewing slowly on my dinner. I'd think about what she was saying, and then offer my thoughts at the end.

That was before October 1. Now when she tried gingerly to ease into some kind of conversation, my reaction would range from an unemotional question or two, to a listless nod, to nothing at all. The hurt in her eyes only forced me to face my helplessness. It was made all the worse by the knowledge that she had yet to utter a single complaint.

I think I was secretly wishing that Pauline would ignore me as much as I was trying to block the universe out. That way I wouldn't have to go searching for the words to comfort her, only to admit that I couldn't find them. I began wondering if all this had happened to force me to slow my life down. A sharp and sudden reminder to maintain that delicate balance between working for what feeds my material life and what feeds my soul. I made a quiet promise to myself that if I could get back on my feet again, I would not forget the lesson.

Meanwhile, my lawyer was in his own state of distraction. He was hardly allowed the luxury of indulging in the holiday season that had just passed. Just weeks after my dismissal, he had to fly into court for another client. Motor General Insurance Company had just been delisted, a shocking first for the industry. Suddenly Dunkley found himself taking on the Ministry of Finance and the Superintendent of Insurance. The bundle and reams of paper began to sprout in his office like weeds. He began talking about taking on another secretary or two.

Then there was my case. Ever since the matter of the Mareva, Christopher Dunkley had not been a happy soldier. He would say on more than one occasion that he didn't like the smell of the case unfolding before him. It was bad enough that the plaintiff wasn't satisfied with just suing his client. Why did they feel the need to cut off his oxygen supply?

That they could go in with a four-line writ and secure a Mareva injunction until judgment was a nasty surprise on its own, but then to stand in contention *with* the defendant before Justice Theobalds— *inter parte*—in the lower court, lose that round, and then run into the Court of Appeal *behind* our backs—*ex parte*—to secure a seven-day stay of the ruling from another judge? No, man, he'd rant. What the hell was that? Why not just go to the Court of Appeal, serve the defendant, and give him a chance to fight you there face-to-face, instead of trying to fight it behind the scenes just so you can buy yourself more time? If you're so sure of your position, just fight it in the open— *inter parte*—all the way. To Dunkley it felt more like trial by ambush.

We were scheduled to appear in the Court of Appeal in January of 1994. My lawyer sacrificed most of his holidays preparing for it. By then we were meeting outside of the office, often gathering in Afen's living room or Dunkley's house. Once I even tracked him down in the officer's mess hall by Up Park Camp. I admit that I had all but tethered myself to my legal team. When saving your life as you know it boils down to the expertise of one or two individuals, your survival instincts kick in. And you don't care about being a royal pain in the ass.

Dunkley understood this and pretty much held his door wide open. Still disgruntled over the plaintiff's last move, he was at least encouraged about going before Justice Wolfe in January. We had reason to be confident, he said, while at the breakfast table one morning. Based on Wolfe's stance on past matters, he was hopeful that Justice Wolfe would rule in our favour. Dunkley was almost sure he would be critical of the bank's behaviour— going *ex parte* in the appellate court after having lost *inter parte* in the lower. "In my opinion, Wolfe is not the kind to countenance that kind of surreptitious approach," he insisted again late one evening after going through more documents with me. "I simply can't see how it'll wash with him."

Our court date loomed like final exams. It's not nearly enough time to prepare, and yet you want it to be over with so that the pain in your stomach can stop. And this wasn't even the real case.

I did not have the energy to attend court that day. To be quite frank, I did not think I could sit calmly once more and watch my life being treated as "a matter" through cold, officious documents and statements—when what I really wanted to do was jump to the other side and slam some heads into the concrete wall. Instead, I tore myself away from the couch that had been growing out of my ass, and busied myself with trying to sell plastic drinking straws. They had been manufactured by the same factory I had invested in as a minority shareholder just a year or two before.

It should be said that my two business partners were none too happy with me. With my account in Miami now on ice, a large cheque drawn before my dismissal to one of our suppliers in the States had been summarily returned. Purple-faced and panicked, my managing partner kicked up a cloud of dust just trying to bolt in the opposite direction. The man who had sought me out as a partner, and who happened to be my wife's relative, never once gave me a chance to defend myself. While he signed a letter confirming the origins and the use of the monies in my account, he made sure to maintain his distance by penning his own letter of disassociation to my lawyers. Our relationship would never recover.

So that day, as Dunkley and Norman stood in court for me, I drove from business to business peddling drinking straws, with the boxes bouncing around in the backseat of Pauline's Honda Civic. It was the first and only time I would dare be absent from the courtroom or justice's chambers.

It is said that in the legal world of black robes, wigs and linguistic posturing, there are certain unofficial measures of a successful performance in the courtroom. I know only from hearsay—from Dunkley himself and some others in attendance—that our performance won us such hallowed gestures of approval from the esteemed panel that presided over our appeal.

ELISE CRAWFORD KEPT glancing up from her computer screen to the front door. She was curious about her accuracy. Still just a couple months new to the firm, and to the legal field, she was already learning the signs of victory or defeat by just watching her boss approach the door from a day in court. Little things like how he pressed the buzzer—two snappy zaps, or one long blast? Could she see his cheeks through the frosted glass? If they were puffed up high so you couldn't see his eyes, hold on tight. If he stormed in and immediately slammed his bag down, hold on even tighter.

He was like this for each and every matter. That was part of the reason she was beginning to love her job. Her boss loved his even more.

Today he was representing Mr. Yap, fighting to get the Mareva injunction overturned. As was always the case whenever her boss was gearing up for a day in court, the weeks leading up to this day had involved her fair share of working lunches and late nights. It was her sacrifice of time and energy as a single working mother with a two year-old daughter. So Elise couldn't help but consider the case's outcome partly hers. If her boss was going to start spewing at the walls today, she might very well join him instead of just nodding in agreement. This time the client was a person. Not just a big company with a fancy name and letterhead. She had looked into this defendant's eyes and had seen the worry and felt the pain.

Elise says that the first time she met me the words that came to her mind were "boss-like". She'd later blame her first impression on the frozen look on my face:

79

"At first I wasn't sure about this Dalton Yap. Nothing about the man was, well, ordinary. For instance, he was tall for Chinese, and had that funny Chinese-Jamaican accent. That kind of thing you normally see with the older Chinese folk, and yet his English was smooth. Then whereas most other clients never really took the time to worry 'bout your name, not once did he set foot in the office without greeting me or the other secretaries. True, you didn't see many teeth in the beginning, but the words were pleasant enough and sounded real nice in his deep, reverent tone. *Hello, Paula—Hi there, Elise.*

It was only when I finally got up to speed with his file that I understood how very serious his case was. That's when I realized that his greetings, and even queries about our weekends, were real. Very real, and extremely generous, under the circumstances. That's when I knew that Mr. Yap was just a pretty nice man having a really bad time.

I remember one night when we were working late and had tons of documents to produce. When my fingers finally got sore, he jumped on the computer so I could take a break. Then when the time came to print, the printer started acting up because the default had been set on letter size. Each time we printed on legal paper the machine jammed, forcing us to feed it page by painful page. We must have done about thirty like that before he started cussing. *What kind of nonsense is this, man? Elise, I'm going to see that you get a decent printer!* And so said, so done. From then on whenever he called the office, he'd ask if everything was working okay, because if it wasn't, he was going to straighten out Mr. Dunkley for us. That was how Mr. Yap was throughout the entire trial. A real person."

THAT DAY DUNKLEY zapped the buzzer twice. As her boss burst through the door, his eyes glimmering like twin laser beams, Elise leaned back in her swivel chair, biting down on her lips trying to conceal her grin. "Elise! I think we did it, Elise! Mr. Wright was barely half way through our defence when Mr. Justice Forte started giving him the *okay, Mr. Wright, point made, Mr. Wright, we don't wish to hear from you further, Mr. Wright.* Lord, even the other side seemed to know the Court was with us. Now we just have to wait thirty days for the Court of Appeal to hand down the judgment. How you doing? What's going on with you, Miss Paula? Everything okay? Miss Elise, I could really put down a good oxtail lunch about now. Get Mr. Yap on the phone for me, would you please?"

Thirty days later the President of the Court of Appeal handed down the official judgment on behalf of the panel that had presided—Messrs. Justice Wolfe, Justice Forte and Justice Downer. To this day, just about everyone who sat in that courtroom quietly acknowledges that it was a clear and obvious victory for the defence—but the Mareva injunction was reinstated. Inexplicably, we had lost.

No one could have known then that that judgment in the bank's favour would make Jamaica Citizens Bank v Yap the landmark case that it was to become.

I ALMOST HAD to temporarily shelve my own despair the day the judgment was handed down. The last thing my lawyers had expected was a defeat.

By now I was an expert at recognizing the look of devastation. For a brief moment Dunkley had disappeared into his own black hole. I think that was the day I got a better glimpse of the man. I now understood what he wanted his legacy to be—a lawyer who delivered justice on behalf of his wronged clients.

I was there at his office the moment he surfaced.

"Dalton," he began, "I'm just speculating here, but the only theory I can come up with is that the panel opted for a protected position."

"You want to say that again? In English this time?" Hang around lawyers long enough and you learn the jargon fast, but sometimes you need it plain and straight. No fancy rhetoric.

"Sorry," he said as he straightened up in his chair. Outside in the lobby an irate phone had just started ringing, demanding to be answered. "Okay. We're up against a major bank. Right? And you know banks and bankers. In this country, they can do no wrong. They're royalty."

"Go on," I replied folding my arms.

"Okay. Keep that in mind as we put ourselves in the judges' uncomfortable shoes for a minute," he continued. "Now, if the panel discharges the injunction and it turns out that you are the kind of person for whom the injunction was rightly placed, then that would forever stand as a criticism against them. Again, remember, we're talking about the country's oldest Jamaican-owned bank. But if the panel decides that Justice Theobalds got it all wrong, and goes with preserving the status quo until your substantive case—the lawsuit itself—and you are eventually exonerated, then all they'll have done is maintain the situation a bit longer. So basically what they're doing is playing it safe until the substantive case. You follow?"

I gave a reluctant nod. "I suppose it makes sense, but I still don't feel any better about it."

Dunkley continued. "In fact, for them to do anything else would mean taking an exceptionally brave but potentially disastrous stride in the face of a possible technical defence. Add to that the fact that they know we can apply for variations on the injunction for at least your major living expenses, like school fees and so on. Yes, it will mean a bitch load of work and expense to have to be constantly submitting applications and all that, but—" Dunkley clasped his hands firmly on his desk.

Again I nodded, this time with a heavy sigh. "Got it."

"Dalton," he said. "Look, I know this is like hell for you right now, but try to keep it together. We're not finished yet. Far from."

I looked up inquiringly. "You know something I don't?"

And a cautious confidence came over his face. "Well, yes, actually. I wasn't sure at first, but I've been doing some late night research."

"And?" I was both hopeful and impatient.

"Seems as if our pain-in-the-ass injunction could be a rainbow in disguise if all goes well with the case."

"Meaning?" I leaned forward.

"The extent of the Mareva's jurisdiction, which has its origins in the United Kingdom, is, shall we say, extensive. There's a nice flip side to it. If you win your case, it allows for an automatic undertaking as to damages once you're cleared. We just have to get you to that point. Now, either they're truly confident of their position, or they don't quite understand the gravity of this new area of jurisdiction." Dunkley pressed his lips together for a second. There was a curious energy about him now. "And I'm going to say it here and now, I honestly don't think anyone fully appreciates what this could mean down the road."

By now he had my full attention. "Go on." It sounded like good news and I was determined to get my share of cheer.

"The Court of Appeal upholding the injunction against you, freezing your assets—it could well be the plaintiff's biggest regret. Because if we can clear you, Dalton Yap, we can go after them for all your expenses, all lost income, and loss of reputation. I'm talking full damages here. Do you understand what I'm saying? Full damages."

I went silent for just a moment, daring now to savour the thought. "*If* you can clear me."

Suddenly he stood up and shoved his hands in his pockets. "Dalton," he said locking his knees back, "I don't really know what happened here. I know how to read the behaviour that comes with a favourable judgment, and I can promise you that thirty days ago they were with us in that courtroom. But today—today really threw me for a nasty spin. I'll give you that. I did not see that coming. I really thought they were going to box the Mareva away, especially when we kept hammering the plaintiff with the fact that they still haven't filed their statement of claim against you. And yet here they are, trying to tie up all your money. And then there's something unsettling about the way the judgment reads— like they, I dunno, saw a ghost and panicked or something. I can't quite put my finger on it. But, look, it really doesn't matter. We're just going to have to fight them and make this whole nightmare disappear."

I pounded a fist on Dunkley's desk. "What case do they have on me, Chris? *What?*" My lawyer would hear this question from me several dozen times throughout my trial.

It was his turn to complain as he began to pace the floor. "God alone knows and I wish He'd tell me."

"Chris, I have to ask. The internal auditor's report. Obasare's."

He stopped to face me. "What about it?"

"Isn't it strange that they haven't presented it to the Court?"

"Very."

"What do you make of it?"

He let a small smirk escape. "That maybe there's something in there they don't want anyone to see?"

"Like?"

"No clue at the moment. Could be nothing more than just sloppy accounting that they're too embarrassed to show. I really can't say."

"Can't we court-order a copy?"

"We could," he said, obviously humouring me.

"Then why the hell don't we?" It was a question that would make for a longstanding point of contention between us.

"Dalton," he said leaning forward, his palms flat on the desk. "You're a man of logic. Why would we deliberately take on more of a fight?"

"Because I can defend anything and everything they're accusing me of! I want to clear my name of all their accusations!"

Chris held up a hand. "I know, Yap. I know. But just trust me on this one, okay? They have every reason, one would assume, to want to show it. Yet they haven't. Believe me, we like it just the way it is. It makes their case seem all the more—ridiculous. And that," he pointed a finger at me, "is what we're banking on."

"Dunkley?" I said with a raised eyebrow.

"Mm?"

"No cheap jokes right now, okay?"

"Sorry, man."

We got down to more work right after that, our stamina temporarily bolstered by a 12-piece comfort box of spicy chicken wings. Chris washed it down with an ice-cold grape soda.

A few hours later I returned to the parking lot. There I discovered a small but curious late-afternoon crowd gathered around the red Honda Civic. I didn't even have to ask. The broken glass on the dirty sidewalk was evidence enough. My eager eyewitness was a plump fruit vendor with a colourful scarf tied around her head. She dished out the details in rapid-fire patois: a young boy had smashed the back window with a rock, taking off on foot with the boxes.

Moments later I stuck my head back in Dunkley's office. "Chris," I said. "Make a note. When we're tallying up my damages at the end of all this, throw in something for two boxes of drinking straws."

THE JANUARY LOSS in the Court of Appeal had sent my financial situation hurtling to the ground. Like a kid on allowance, I was now relegated to submitting my basic living expenses to the Court for relief payments. Chris began filing applications like loaves of bread coming off a conveyor belt. I watched anxiously as my wife's savings from her small business began to dwindle along with some of my male pride. I had always been a good provider, and I was not terribly comfortable with the sudden shift in roles. An immediate and generous loan from Pat and my brother-in-law helped ease the growing pile of legal fees. I struggled to ignore the debt I was incurring. I tried hard not to worry about the mortgage payments. I tried not to notice what needed to be repaired in the house or purchased for the children, but I was failing miserably.

We had always pulled together as a family in every way. That included the businesses we'd sacrificed to build. One of those sacrifices included sharing the same roof with my parents.

That was the real glue for us—a lot of work, resourcefulness and a ton of humour. We had lived it ever since we could blow our own noses. Like the time my mother had no fresh vegetables in her kitchen with which to feed her family for dinner. We were still young then, and absolutely had to have our daily serving of greens. I don't recall whether my father had agreed to it or not, but that evening my mother served us the baby shoots she had harvested from his young potato plants in a tasty stir-fry with a healthy dose of garlic. While we never messed with Dad's potato plants again, I must say— the meal wasn't bad at all.

The only thing I could do now was prepare for my trial. Dunkley warned of a long wait before we could be given an available date. I was told, and I have no reason to doubt it, that by now the only subject that could get me to focus my eyes on someone and put more than two sentences together was the trial. Friends were subjected to all the details of the preparation, even if I was running into them for the first time in weeks or months. I'd simply cliff dive into the facts and details, without the usual conversational warm-up. Most were kind enough to just let me ramble and pretend to follow the information I was spewing out.

Dunkley and Norman fell into that category, but in a worse way. They had to listen to me on almost a daily basis as I began to wear the matter of my honour and my vindication like a prosthetic arm. Even Elise was getting used to seeing me fly into their offices with a quick wave hello to her and the other secretary, while closely guarding under my arm a folder containing new notes I'd just put together in the middle of the night on a particular point.

The following month Dunkley went to see my Queen's Counsel. My friend's suggestion to secure one was, of course, quite valid. Both Chris Dunkley and Norman Wright understood the need to find an equal match for the plaintiff's powerful Michael Hylton.

In the British Commonwealth, a lawyer pretty much becomes a Queen's Counsel the way one became a member of a private country club. A seasoned lawyer of a certain professional calibre ascertains, through the whisperings and invisible nods of colleagues, that he or she would likely be accepted as Queen's Counsel in England. That lawyer, if so inclined, then submits a request to the Chief Justice and his committee of seven; himself, the President of the Court of Appeal, the Attorney General, the President of the Bar Association, President of Advocates, President of the General Legal Council and a leading Queen's Counsel. The committee in turn deliberates and offers its recommendation to the Governor General, who then makes the appointment official. Once lawyers have achieved the rank of Queen's Counsel, they must take on a junior lawyer in their practice. For some, the attainment of such rank is worth the expense. Physically demarcated by the silk gowns they wear, Queen's Counsels are considered the profession's elite—"the silks".

Chris was not thrilled with mine. The truth was I felt as if I'd been left to tread in cold water. Following our court appearance in January, and in anticipation of a date for the substantive case, Chris had arranged to sit with the senior lawyer to brief him. It was an incensed Dunkley who returned from the meeting, got me on the phone and yelled into the mouthpiece, *we are not using him!* Apparently the gentleman, upon reviewing my dismissal letter and other documents, offered Chris his honest albeit not so encouraging opinion that went something like: *but your man not looking so good!* And as much as the gentleman was entitled to his own professional opinion, those were not quite the words we wanted to hear.

However, as he came highly recommended by my dear friend—the gentleman, to his credit, was the lawyer of choice for many a large company—I'd make another personal visit not long after. It was only then that I understood Chris's stubborn insistence that we find another silk. Sitting in this lawyer's office, I was just another file—another patient with a serious illness who would likely become just another sad statistic. Worse than that, I did not feel he believed in my recovery. And I needed one who did. After what felt like a disappointing level of commitment by the esteemed lawyer, I would soon terminate his services with a polite but honest letter. I received an equally balanced reply several weeks later.

Chris would immediately go hunting for a replacement.

BY NOW MY moods and emotions were no longer mine to control.

They pretty much belonged to whatever cosmic force was helping me crawl out of bed each day, or send down my throat whatever meal had been made for me by my mom. Sometimes she'd manage to settle me down with some plain boiled chicken, or *pak-jam-guy*, one of those Chinese-Jamaican favourites you won't find in restaurants. Since my dismissal, the petite woman had taken to shuffling around me, cleaning everything in my vicinity two or three times just so that she could keep an eye on her son.

The change is most visible when depression comes to one who has never really known it. In the life that was mine before being fired and humiliated, everything had a solution. My sentences had more verbs than adjectives. Everything was logical, and nothing insurmountable. You just needed to sit, think about it, make a plan of action, and then implement it. But I was no longer at the steering wheel. I couldn't veer away from the phantom waves of despair that sat around the corners waiting to pitch me over the precipice.

Instead, I now sat for hours playing the scene in Ewart's office over and over in my head, reliving the injury to my spirit until I could literally feel the hurt in my neck and back, and sometimes in my legs. This was not an exercise in self-pity. It was an attempt to exorcise the sick feeling of betrayal that now festered inside of me, eating away at the very cells that held my body together. I felt that if I could stare it in the face, then maybe I could control it, and with some effort, banish it.

Almost overnight the borders of my world had been reduced to my house, my family, and a small group of believers. I was cut off from the world. Suddenly I was aware of everything that I was *not* doing, like not waking up at dawn to drink coffee and not jumping into my car to head for Kingston and my career.

Those around me played a constant game of "watch and see." Watch Dalton's mood. See if you can talk to him. It is a sad truth that sometimes, when you're in pain, you treat strangers better than you treat loved ones. Perhaps you assume or hope that the history and love you share will automatically secure their understanding, their forgiveness. Throughout the months of waiting for my life to be given back to me, I projected warmth and consideration to no one in my family. I answered questions only when I wanted to. Each time I assumed they'd bounce back unscathed from my explosive comments and sharp dismissals.

My brave wife, hiding her own hurt, would occasionally make gentle suggestions to try and ease me back into my children's life. "*I need someone to take the kids to school today,*" she would mention while pouring me a cup of tea. or, "*I think Jeremy needs someone to check his homework.*" But I was no longer up to the fatherhood role. Now there was no reading, no playing board games, no silly jokes with my daughter while proudly running my hands through her long, silky hair. And yet I had all this damn free time.

I honestly don't know why Pauline didn't leave me. For a while after October 1993, her husband had retreated into a dark hole no one dared enter. I was beyond unbearable. Without a word or argument, she had become mother and father to our children. I will be forever grateful for my wife's determination to hold our family together. And I will be forever grateful for her commitment to me.

As for Kimmy and Jeremy, they might have been too young to understand their father's problem, but not too young to sense the turmoil and confusion coursing through my veins and into our family life. They acted on their instincts and spoke quietly around their now unpredictable father. The effect that the case had on them is, to this day, my biggest regret. The unwanted ordeal may have been mine, but in the end my children picked up the tab. Kimmy still remembers the evening the laughter left our house:

"Before Daddy lost his job, my little brother and I used to light up whenever he stepped into a room with his broad smile and Santa Claus laugh. Daddy was always busy working, but he'd make time for us most Sunday afternoons. He'd pack us up in the car and whisk us off to the south coast for some family adventure while belting out some Sinatra or Earth, Wind & Fire tune. He'd always remember to make a roadside stop to buy soup and corn, which he knew I loved. If we didn't go driving, he'd play tennis with us after his morning with the 'big boys' to cool down. That's when he'd patiently keep after me to perfect my backhand so that I could be as good as he was.

I was his little star and loved nothing more than to make my daddy proud. For me, his opinion was the one I held my breath for. No matter how much praise I got from others, if I didn't have his seal of approval, I had nothing. Mom was usually the one who would whisper to me how impressed he was with something I had done. Those words were magic stardust to me.

I was only seven when I met the other side of my father. We had just gone back to school after our holiday in Toronto. Suddenly Jeremy and I were beginning to see a lot more of Daddy around the house. At first we were thrilled. What could be better than having more of Daddy at home? Then one evening I did what I had always done. I ran to sit at his desk so he could help me with my more difficult homework. But I guess I shouldn't have bothered him that night with long division.

I remember sitting there for awhile bent over my exercise book working on a practice problem he had set. I was finally making progress when all of a sudden a terrible noise shot out from the room where my parents had been talking—but the shouting was in Cantonese so I couldn't understand. Soon the shouting turned to a loud sobbing followed by a door slamming with a deafening bang. That was the first time I had ever heard Mommy cry.

I straightened up in my chair with thoughts of rushing to her to tell her that everything was okay, even though I didn't know what was wrong to begin with. But before I could complete the thought, I was suddenly confronted by a strange man who was demanding that I tell him what seventy-nine divided by six was, and what the remainder would be. I sat frozen, too scared to even know where to begin as the numbers danced in my head behind my blank stare. After three failed attempts, the angry man finally stormed out of the room muttering something about raising a fool.

That was the first time Daddy had ever walked out on me. He seemed so sad. Tears began to fall on my math exercise book, and soon the numbers began to wash away on the page. Slowly, I slid off the chair with my exercise book in my hand, and headed for the room Mommy was in. But when I turned the knob, it wouldn't move. Behind the door I could hear faint sobbing. 'Mommy?' I called to her three times. But she never answered. She had abandoned me too.

From that day on Jeremy and I lived knowing what it was like to feel knots growing in our stomachs whenever Daddy was approaching. He was like some outlaw arriving in town to terrorize its residents with his verbal pistol. Overnight my goal changed from trying to make him proud to trying not to upset him. 'Daddy coming' was the phrase we adopted, which meant you should find a room to sit quietly so that you didn't catch his eye or rage. Those days it didn't take much to make his nostrils flare—a shoe that hadn't made it back to the closet, a toy left on the ground, too much talking at the dinner table, or grammatically-flawed speech. It wasn't long before we started to not love our daddy so much. It was harder for Jeremy who could hardly look at him now.

As we got a little older, Mom started telling us little bits and pieces of what had happened to Daddy. Soon I began to understand that his work had hurt him. No wonder all the flashy suits were gone. He hadn't gone mad after all. We secretly forgave him and started giving him good luck kisses whenever he'd tell us that Daddy was about to have a 'big day.'

It would be nine years before I could feel comfortable in my family again."

MY MORE PLAINSPOKEN doctor sister, Pat, was the one to yank me by the collar whenever I had careened too far off course. It wasn't long before she decided that I needed to see a psychiatrist.

"You're not looking right, big brother," she said one day at one of our Sunday family dinners after pulling me out of earshot from the others. She told me I looked like hell and that she didn't like the way I was handling the children. She ended her lecture by telling me that she'd arranged for me to see Dr. Thessiger. I think she even asked me if "everything" was functioning okay in the bedroom.

The truth was, I had no idea if I was in complete working order or not. It was the last thing on my mind, quite frankly. As for Thessiger, while I had long been familiar with the good doctor's excellent reputation as a psychiatrist, I just never pictured myself a patient of his. For many Chinese, just visiting your general practitioner for the common cold was a sign of weakness. Seeing a psychiatrist for mental issues was simply way beyond our comfort zone. Naturally, I protested. Pat, of course, ignored me.

A week or two later I found myself in his office, bristling with resentment for being there. The anger was not aimed at him, but at my former employer. The hour I spent with Dr. Thessiger, in fact, proved helpful. We talked about compartmentalizing my problems, a strategy that helped ease my severe insomnia. I would thank my sister later on for her well-timed intervention.

My siblings were my coaches, my life jackets, sometimes even my voice. They took their particular strengths and shored me up with them. The baby of the family, Felice would use her business background to patiently take in the details of the case whenever I needed someone to share them with, and generally kept pace with Dunkley and me on the intricate matters. Afen and Terry hovered around, called and checked up on me. Did I need anything, did I need to get something done, go somewhere? See someone?

And then there was Pat. We were the closest in age, I being older, and yet she had taken over as if she were my big sister. Those who knew her at the time of this incident were no doubt privy to her feelings on the grave injustice that had been done to her brother. My sister would recall her assessment of our family's new struggle:

"The maddening thing was that I had always been the trouble maker in the family. I was the natural fighter, not Dalton. He was always the quiet one who absolutely abhorred trouble and confrontation – like the time he defended me against those boys back in Hong Kong when we were walking to school. He did the brave big brotherly move and beat them off, but then he was upset afterwards, while I was still jumping around as they ran away, my fists in a ball calling them back for more.

I think maybe in a way God picked up on his most dreaded weakness to test him. Okay, so now he was being tested in the worst way. I knew the only thing we could do was let the law of the land take its course, but I was too furious to see straight. They had no idea what a decent man my brother was. I mean, this was Dalton who used to wake up in the dark of morning as a school kid, ride three miles on bicycle to the shop, and use his bare hands to make patties before going to school. The rest of us would go to half-day school and then head for the shop to help Dad sell the patties Dalton had made. After school he'd go home to do his homework first, rest up a little, and then return to the store to make dough so that he could start the process all over again the next morning.

But that was my big brother. Always hardworking, easygoing, jovial. Always trying to keep things smooth and peaceful. It's true that sometimes we'd get a little embarrassed for having to work on a Saturday when our friends were going to the Tudor or Odeon movie theatres by our shop. We'd duck behind the counter when they passed by. But he never once complained or fussed to our parents.

And that trait of not putting up a fight, not whining about his woes, stayed with him. Case in point was the night his car was stolen. We were rooming together in Kingston while attending university in 1980. The Ford Cortina he had bought after a series of summer jobs was our transportation. It was a used car—a 1973 model—but it was his very first and he treated it like it would be his last. Kept it cleaned and waxed. He was so proud of it.

At that time he was big into badminton, and had entered a tournament at the national arena. One night closer to the end of the tournament, he came home but this time much later than usual. I remember he had this strange look on his face. It was an odd, almost embarrassed expression. So I inquired about his game. Oh, he'd won the match, he said, but still the look remained. So I pressed some more. And that's when he told me that his car had been stolen. He was trying so hard to hide his disappointment from me, and from himself, but I could tell he was crushed. That's why it hurt me so badly when the bank turned on him.

Before the lawsuit I would have described my brother as loving and affectionate. Always busy, but always caring. Because of the dismissal and the lawsuit he became withdrawn. Because of their attack he woke up several times each night pacing the house in the darkness on the cold tile floor. He even lost his hair in the process. The whole nightmare changed his appearance inside and out. It sent his sense of humour into hibernation for a while. He'd sigh involuntarily all the time—a heavy, hopeless, sad release that had become a part of him. I don't think he even realized he was doing it, but we heard him each and every time.

The whole experience of being betrayed like that by people in your own camp—it practically ripped the skin off of him."

My former boss had done well to teach me about not going it alone—about not playing hero. I could never have made it through without my brothers and sisters.

MY LOWEST POINT came unexpectedly.

It is midday, and I'm sitting in the living room in Mandeville, in old cotton shorts and plain white t-shirt. I am alone, holding a cup of hot broth between my hands. My wife is at work, the children are in school, and my parents are out on some errand. The sound of a jackhammer rattles the air, signalling some sort of construction on a nearby house.

I guess for a fleeting moment I have forgotten my woes, because the next thing I recall holding is not a cup of broth, but the karaoke microphone which is now pushed up to my mouth. And I'm singing into it. The karaoke room is about six months new. I had built the extension so that my family and I could have some fun entertaining ourselves in sleepy Mandeville. I can still smell the fresh concrete around me.

I don't remember the exact song. It was most likely a Sinatra number I used to sing while learning English. I'm craning my neck toward the ceiling, eyes closed, and I'm acting like a minor pop star on stage because I think I can actually carry a tune fairly well. The singing is lifting me to a comfortable place. The colours are creeping back up the walls now. The air feels fresher. The blood begins to flow to my cheeks. Suddenly I'm in a world where there is no room for business suits, jobs, lawyers, newspapers or bills. There are no problems, no hurt, no ugly words or looks. Only music and a cheerful mountain breeze. I can feel the joy seeping into my soul again, filling the crevices.

Suddenly I'm interrupted by a loud knock at the gate. My head pulls back and turns. It's one of the chefs from our restaurant, looking for my father. I can see him peering in through the grille with his eyebrows furrowed as he shifts from leg to leg. He turns away quickly when I catch his eye. I shut the music off and go to greet him. He has this uncomfortable look on his face, like he's shown up accidentally at a black tie reception in full khaki.

And then he says in Cantonese, "Oh, I, I um—I guess you don't have much to do right now?" The question slams me to the ground. The chef stays only briefly, saying anxiously that he needs to hurry off because he's busy. As I used to be.

When he leaves I shut the karaoke machine off, sink into the folds of the soft couch, and sob hot, angry tears.

Six

Thomas Powell bit down on his lips as he left the manager's office. Yet another requisition for computer hardware material stalled with a patronizing *we'll get back to you on it.*

Tommy ignored the secretary just outside the office who was trying—quite unsuccessfully—to stifle a mean grin. As he walked past her desk he pictured himself trashing her neat little desk before pitching it out the window.

Then he shook his head in frustration at the shameful thought. The work environment had changed just a bit too much since his boss's dramatic departure, and it was starting to get to him. With no replacement general manager installed, the Technology and Operations Division was without senior representation, and had since been forced to turn to surrogate senior managers. It seemed to Powell that the foster care executives didn't, well, *care* about getting the work done. In fact, if he didn't know better he'd swear they were determined to inflict a case of severe constipation on the recently orphaned department.

Since that day in October 1993, the entire division had been frozen in an uneasy silence. Months later, they were still numb over the bewildering dismissal of their popular general manager. Of course, the tabloid-style allegations had swept like a forest fire through the bank and its branches several times over, courtesy of the very healthy corporate grapevine.

The rumours showed no signs of withering. In fact, they had gotten so bad no one knew where to cast one's eyes anymore. It was being said that Dalton had gone out on a limb and single-handedly started the whole scheme without approval, even writing up the documentation for the bank and the telemarketers. Then when asked to cease and desist, he refused, causing the bank to lose a lot of money. And what were the rumours saying now? That Dalton had been getting kickbacks? *Kickbacks?* That kind of extraterrestrial shit was simply too much to hear, Tommy would say, admitting that even so, no one had publicly offered a single word in their former manager's defence. "It wasn't that we didn't want to," he said. "It was that we didn't dare to."

According to Tommy, however, there was much more behind the staff's diplomatic silence. "It had a lot to do with shattered notions," he said. "Nothing is more frightening than the dark side of human nature. We were in plain old-fashioned shock." It was as if they had come to work one morning and, after years of knowing their lives the way they knew the feel of their favourite pair of sneakers, were suddenly being told to abandon all prior experiences, because in this new world one plus one no longer makes two.

Tommy Powell was also barely in his thirties at the time, and was just getting cozy in the corporate world. He recalls the division staff's immediate reaction following that pivotal day in October:

> "When we first heard the news the day it happened, we all said, 'impossible' and assumed it was just a huge, horrible mistake. But when we realized it was really true, when we heard that he had actually packed his things and left, we immediately turned our attention to Mr. Wiggan the moment the man returned from Singapore. Because if Wiggan was the roof, Yap was the walls and hurricane straps.

But when we heard that the Managing Director was on the 'other side,' that's when the real shock grabbed us by the ankles and shook us upside down. In no part of this universe was it possible that Mr. Wiggan could turn against Dalton.

It had never happened before. Certainly not in the workplace. Not even when his lead technician, Edward Gabbidon, ended up drilling a hole in Wiggan's spanking new mahogany desk—to accommodate his specific instructions that no wires be seen dangling from the back of the computer. And of course, he wanted the computer positioned at the front of his desk and not at the back against a wall. Word had it that after the incident, Wiggan would only stew silently as Dalton sheepishly pointed out to him the perfect roundness of the neat hole Gabbidon had made, for which the eager and innovative technician had gone out on the road and purchased a brand new drill bit.

So, no way. A blind man could have seen that if Wiggan itched, Dalton scratched. Something was not right here. Even if the man had sincerely thought that Dalton had messed up, lost his mind or just gone rotten overnight somehow, his reaction was off. In that case you'd hope that he'd pull his faithful wingman aside, buy him a cold beer and a jerk pork dinner and have a heart-to-heart. Ask him, *Hey, man, what's going on with you and all this crap? What are you thinking?* I'd say that that would be the thing to do.

But what happens instead? The man boards a plane for a destination halfway around the world leaving Dalton to face the music. Now I'm not saying that he absolutely knew that Dalton was about to be fired. Lord knows stranger things have happened. But you could not convince us that a managing director would not be informed at some point or another by phone or mail that one of his top guys was about to get the axe. And that's what we couldn't accept. The man who had interviewed Dalton fresh out of college, who had groomed and worked with him for ten years, was not there at the darkest hour of his career.

For the staff of Dalton Yap, that was a day of baptism. We witnessed firsthand that the confidence can indeed be shaken out of a strong man as fast as you can snap a dry twig in two. We learned that trust is a notion only the foolish dare embrace. From that day on we withdrew into shells constructed in a mad hurry, and pulled the door shut behind us. Many of us who once worked for him would agree; nothing was ever quite the same again. No more innocence. No more security blanket. No more lofty corporate dreams of long service, loyalty and reward. We'd been ripped a new one good and proper."

IN THE WAKE of my departure, the young division had been forced into a paradigm shift. Suddenly, everyone was looking over their shoulder and selecting their confidantes with greater scrutiny now. Discussion about the surgical dismissal was eerily non-existent. Staff morale was gone. The steam had finally evaporated from that wonderful cup of coffee.

Now it was just about work, which was being dutifully executed under the competent guidance of Systems Manager, Lesley Hew. Now the staff watched the clock. Few lingered after office hours to socialize. No one gathered over a beverage or the latest edition of the evening *Star* newspaper to gossip. Not a soul bothered to ask if someone needed help on a project. There was none of the follow-up queries about your stubborn headache from the day before, or your family's weekend plans. Gone was the usual interaction that makes the work environment a more pleasant, human experience.

Instead, several began studying the employment section of the newspapers during lunchtime. Lesley would cocoon herself with a wall of silence as she attempted to fill her former boss's shoes while constantly checking the path ahead for landmines. She would eventually make a quiet exit from both the bank and the island, and head for safer shores. Debbie Brooks, my former secretary, would also find her way to Toronto where she'd eventually earn herself a college degree and find a husband.

Tommy kept a cautious eye on the other managers. He was wide awake now and not about to risk even a blink. The atmosphere surrounding the executives was not exactly an openly festive one, he would observe. No one was drinking champagne, or waving huge victory banners or anything like that. There was, most certainly, a subtle hum of satisfaction piping through the air—an undercurrent of smugness that filtered through the corridors. You could see it in their stride, in the way they confidently shoved their hands in their pockets while standing alone or in small groups. You could hear it in their muffled chuckles through doors left ajar. It was there. No doubt about it.

One day out of the blue, I called Tommy at the office. I had just received a huge sympathy card from my old division team members, filled with handwritten messages about courage, faith and perseverance. I had been reminded that I still had friends. Good friends in key places.

I remember thinking how strange it felt to be calling the main switchboard number. The only bank numbers I had ever dialled were private line numbers and I could have, in fact, called Tommy on his, but I decided that if any of the phones were bugged, it would be those instead of the PBX models. The latter were harder to tamper with.

I think I only stopped sweating when his voice came through the receiver. We had not spoken since my dismissal, and I had an important favour to ask of him.

"Powell here."

"Tommy." There was an immediate silence. I could almost see him at the other end literally dropping whatever it was he had in his hands right onto his unsuspecting foot.

"Dalton?" he whispered. "Is that you?"

"How you doing, man?"

"Me?" he gasped. "Never mind me, chief. How are *you*?"

I managed a chuckle. "Hanging in there, thanks. Is it okay to talk right now? You alone?"

"Yes, man. Don't worry. We're behind you, boss. Hope you know that."

"I got the card, yes. Please thank the team for me. Tell them it meant a lot to get it. More than they'll ever know. I should have called before but—"

Tommy saved me from having to find the words. "Relax, man. We're cool. You just get yourself out of this mess."

"Thanks, man."

"By the way, I don't mean to rub it in," he said starting to chuckle. "but guess who's sitting in your sweet Cefiro these days."

"Oh, God," I moaned at the thought of someone else in my old dream car. "Okay. Who?"

"Dalton Fowles."

I grinned. "Don't joke."

"Seriously! They sold it to him. But Dalton number two is not a big manual reader like Dalton number one. It took the poor guy a little longer to find the secret brake release." This time we howled together.

"Well I'm glad. Hope he enjoys that car as much as I did. But, tell me. How are things with you guys? And the staff—you all holding it together?"

"Lesley's doing a great job. You'd be proud. But boy, it's not the same. Harder now to get what we need. All of a sudden the damn branches can't schedule us in at our usual times, requisition orders take forever to arrive, *if* they get approved to begin with—shit like that, you know? If you ask me I'd say them bastards are on a power trip. They're enjoying this just a little too much."

"Well, Mr. Powell, you're probably not asking nicely enough," I jabbed, touching on an old joke of ours and a personal belief I had always shared with my team.

"Aw shit, Yap!" he snapped, pretending to be annoyed. "You know damn well I'm not brown-nosing anybody! Meritocracy! That was your word? Remember? Take me on my merit or frig the hell off?"

"Can't forget," I laughed. "Can't forget." And then I made my move. "Listen, Tommy, you have a minute? There's something I need to ask you. A big favour."

HE CHOSE A quiet night on which to do the deed. The few who were there would not see him slip quietly through the door and up the stairs. The lone security guard who met him at the door was barely interested in seeing Tommy's company identification and asked no questions.

Just days after our conversation, he was still battling a nervous stomach, and with good reason. The favour I had requested of him was not a small one. I had asked would he help me secure some documents I needed for my defence? Would he be able to go into the bank and get them for me? My brave friend did not hesitate.

The computer he needed to access sat in a secure area on the second floor in a remote part of the building. In it was stored certain credit card transactions that had taken place during the period in question. As we had rightly guessed, it had been left there as if completely forgotten. Tommy slipped into the room easily enough. Once inside, he worked quickly and copied the transactions on floppy diskettes. The following morning he handed them over to Afen and Felice at the family's meat processing shop on Dames Road near Vineyard Town.

Tommy summed up his decision to step up to the plate for a friend in this way: "The whole damn thing taught me that belief is a powerful fuel. When you truly believe in someone, you'll do just about anything for them. Especially if they've been there for you in the past."

THE REQUEST MADE of my friend and former colleague did not come without serious thought. I will forever remember the show of courage and loyalty that came from this man who offered no hesitation and yet had much to lose, including his job. Before this, I had never known what it was like to impose on others, much less to ask them to stick their necks out for no other's benefit than mine. Before this, I never much understood confrontation, preferring always to compromise or even step away if I could, but I was now learning that sometimes you just need to hold your hand up and ask. Sometimes, you just have to muscle up and fight back.

I would, on one other occasion, benefit from information coming from within the bank's walls.

TWO YEARS IS a long time to wait for your life to return to you.

My trial had been set for September 1996. The date flashed in my head like a massive billboard. It was my only focus as we prepared for the serious work on my substantive case. And that time had now come. Following the January 1994 Mareva appeal, the much-anticipated plaintiff's statement of claim at long last appeared. This was the statement that officially laid out in detail the allegations being thrown at me. The other side was finally showing its hand. The timing of its arrival in relation to the trial would not go unnoticed by my legal team, and supported Dunkley's earlier gut instinct that the plaintiff was not having an easy time stitching together a position.

Fourteen days after we submitted our statement of defence we received the plaintiff's amended statement. Chris was pleased and so was I, but I could tell that something was bothering him concerning the judgment and the original statement of claim. Throughout the duration of the case, Chris would go silent on me a handful of times while his brain churned, leaving me alone with my layman speculations. This was one of those times.

It sounds terribly cliché, but preparing one's case really is like preparing for battle. You say goodbye to your family and promise to return when your tour of duty is over. Dunkley, whose own kids began calling me "Uncle Dalton", had the added pressure of asking Motor and General Insurance Company— perhaps his largest client at the time—to temporarily take a backseat while he focused on me. It is no small measure of his human decency that the company's CEO, Winston Murray, graciously agreed. It is also to the young lawyer's credit that the Trinidadian insurance giant did not swap him for another. One by one he began turning down new cases. The truth is that Christopher Dunkley ran the very real risk of killing his successful law practice to save my life, even if we won. If he wasn't careful, by the time it was all over he'd have no more clients patiently waiting in line. His gamble humbled me.

My lawyers and I settled into war mode, with many of the weekend sessions taking place at my brother's house just down the road from the Dunkley residence. Together we sat and planned our strategy. We threw out possible lines of attack by the plaintiff, listed its weak areas, decided which weapons to arm ourselves with, sifted through the material, learned the details and practised our attack over and over again until our proverbial knuckles were raw.

We began to meet almost daily, gathering every single piece of evidence acquired up until this point. We pored over every single page without exception, dissecting each one until we saw them in our sleep. By then I had decided to make use of my computer skills and developed a cross-reference chart to aid us in making the necessary links in our defence chain. We practised using it to show which document could be used to tackle which allegation: we attached dates, points of significance and easy-to-remember titles to each document. We plotted the timeline of events and the players, whether they were significant or not.

In the meantime, Chris's office and meeting room were transformed into an auto body shop for *Jamaica Citizens Bank v Yap*. Crudely made signs of coloured cartridge paper helped us to categorize and quickly locate the batches of documents we needed whenever that time came. Even floor space had also become premium real estate. Our engine was beginning to purr smoothly.

Chris's secretary kept pace and joined us as we shoved artery-clogging meals down our throats when even a half-hour break was out of the question. Only on one occasion did I have to resort to begging the petite workhorse to give us some of her time on a weekend—after she had already made plans with her toddler.

It was an understanding Elise who eventually sighed a seemingly cross "okay" into the phone. I could almost see her gritting her teeth as she agreed to join us early that Saturday morning, but her decision did not come without some amount of admonishment. "Listen here now, Mr. Yap," she had lectured. "I want you to know that it's only because you've managed to fix all the half-dead photocopiers and fax machines in our office why I'm even agreeing to this. Because let me tell you. This girl Crawford here tired! Tired, I tell you! I need to recharge my batteries too or you won't be getting much more out of me! So, okay then. Have a good evening and I'll see you in the morning."

I had to admire her for her honesty and took note of the lesson. Let others get their way a few too many times and eventually you have to put your foot down. Elise Crawford was in the right profession and the profession was lucky to have her. I took the sharp reprimand with a big gulp of gratitude and thanked her profusely for her understanding. At the end of the day, Elise knew that we acknowledged and appreciated the value of her work.

Dunkley and Norman had by this time secured the esteemed Mr. Dennis Morrison as our new Queen's Counsel. Even though I didn't know Mr. Morrison from a hole in the wall, Dunkley, Norman and I shared no debate or moment's hesitation over his selection. I completely trusted and accepted my legal team's choice. I also appreciated that Chris cared more about winning my case and clearing my name than covering his ass. He could have played it safe and gone with my initial choice, leaving me to suffer the consequences with only myself to blame after the judgment had been delivered. I was, after all, his paying client. I have no doubt that many other lawyers would have opted for the safer route. I could be stubborn too.

Throughout the case I learned a few things—like the fact that sometimes you absolutely need to let the professionals do their job for you. I'd also learn that Christopher Dunkley did not worry about making unpopular decisions, especially if they were for his client's good.

The statement of claim had just delivered us a severe blow. According to the bank, I had been up to a lot of no good.

In a nutshell, they painted me as a man huddled in my office, pretending to be busy with the bank's work, when all along I'm conspiring with foreigners to steal from the bank through a new credit card processing business—a business they claimed I started without their approval. And I pull this off by vetting legal documents, coercing my superiors to sign them, and opening accounts on my own—even though JCB had one of the largest in-house legal departments in the country.

The bank had lost money and it was throwing everything at me, including the kitchen sink. Dunkley and Norman called it panoramic. I called it pathetic.

By now my techie mind had begun to turn legal. No longer able to just sit back and watch the whirlwind around me, I regularly marched into bookstores and the university libraries in search of material that would bring me up to speed. I needed to better understand definitions. I wanted to know more about certain rulings and principles. More than anything, I wanted to understand the language that came out of lawyers' mouths so that I didn't have to slow them down with requests for the layman equivalent. I threw myself at those books with the determination of a toddler who no longer wanted to just crawl.

Meanwhile my own babies were seeing less and less of their father. My daughter was just at that age when dragons, fairies and unicorns ran through her cotton candy-filled dreams at night. Pauline had already hinted a few times that Kimmy was asking about going to Disney World, but all I did was offer some kind of rambling response that we couldn't afford it and promised that we'd go as soon as the trial was over. In my own warped world of post-October 1993, that's how it would have worked out. Except that by the time the trial was over, my little girl was not so little anymore, and had already outgrown cartoons, fairies and Disney World. I think it is also safe to say—and I could not blame her—that by the trial's end my daughter was also no longer interested in any of my promises.

My legal team was now in full throttle. Our strategy was straightforward. Know our case better than anyone else did. We were to learn the details of every letter, every contract, and memorandum. We were to know who scribbled which hand-written note on which document and on what date, comma, period and question mark. Given the prestige of our opponent, we had no choice but to put down a defence so incredibly airtight, it would squeeze the breath out of them. We had underestimated the system before. We would not do it again.

The bank was claiming a financial loss due to my supposedly fraudulent and negligent actions. Through intense study of the paperwork, we were beginning to slowly put the pieces together on the matter of the missing funds. There was no question that as part of our line of attack we were going to lead the Court's attention to where the problem really lay—or with whom—once we knew for sure, but that matter would take care of itself.

THE CALL THAT came from inside the bank was anonymous and brief.

The information was a surprise box of fireworks. JCB was apparently going after one of its earlier associates in their credit card business—someone who had nothing to do with the telemarketing fiasco. They were chasing Ken Palmer of the Chicago-based FTA Card Services Inc.

I don't think I even waited to speak to Chris. I immediately called my brother-in-law Leo, and asked him for his sister's number in the United States. Lisa just happened to be an attorney. I was putting my hand up again for another big favour. And this time I wasn't hesitating.

SEVEN

We had agreed to meet over an early dinner at Felice's place.

She and Leo had offered their dining room for what was to be an intense session of evidence crunching. A hot meal, comfortable chairs and a large dining table would ensure a relaxed night of work for us and our boxes of documents. The venue would be one of many but also a regular one for us. We decided to work as we ate.

"Okay, Yap," Dunkley began. "Let's take it again from the top. The summary of activities you did for me last October when the shit hit the fan is now just a guideline because at that time we didn't even know what we were looking for."

I nodded, not wanting to break his stride. Felice began laying the plates and food on the table with as little sound as possible. I gently tugged at her elbow in appreciation. She had cooked one of Dunkley's favourites; Oxtail and beans.

"Let us recap that first summary you did," he continued. "After that we'll address the allegations now that we have the statement of claim. We'll break down the evidence into pieces and keep hammering away at it until we're satisfied. After the discovery session with the other side we'll know better what they're coming with so we can hone our argument accordingly."

Again I nodded without a word.

"Okay then. The very first time you're hearing about the credit card telemarketing business is in mid-1991. Elon Beckford, still Managing Director at the time, comes to you after a senior management meeting—you're not an executive back then so you're not part of that meeting. And he tells you that there's this Floridian with a bank in Antigua, a Mel Reaume, who's interested in doing offshore transactional processing with JCB. They need JCB to process the credit card paper generated by their telemarketing customers because Antigua has no VISA principal member. Beckford asks you to make contact and find out what it's all about and so on."

"Yes. He says to me something like, 'Dalton, just work with Reaume.'"

"Okay. And, incidentally, when did Beckford leave the bank?"

"Elon? That would be 1992." My voice softened a bit. I had coincidentally run into the former JCB executive in Mandeville just a few weeks before, while he was attending a United Way meeting at the Alcan Sports Club. I recalled feeling surprised at his warm greeting and words of support. The gesture did more for me than I let on, but inside I was smiling. "Elon left to start his Horizon Merchant Bank," I continued. "Wiggan took his place, and I eventually got promoted to General Manager of the Technology and Operations Division."

"Okay. Beckford tells you to 'work with Reaume.' So you telephone Reaume, he introduces you to a Bill Todd of South East Caribbean Trading Company—SECT for short. Todd becomes the contact person from that point on and acts like a coordinator of sorts—putting the bank in touch with the technical people and, eventually, potential merchants. Yes?"

I swallowed the first mouthful I'd been chewing. "Yes."

"Okay. Next thing Todd does is to put you in touch with James Lattimore of Ceridian Corporation. Ceridian is a huge credit card paper processing company out of the States.

The two of you begin to work on setting up the processing system, but it drags out and nothing much happens between 1991 and the beginning of 1993. That's when Todd and Reaume bring in Richard McGranahan of World Transaction Services—or 'WTS.' His involvement on the technical side finalizes the set-up, and by the end of February 1993, JCB is in a position to process electronic credit card transactions for telemarketers."

"Meanwhile, Ewart Scott, who is now General Manager of the Retail Banking and Marketing Division, has taken over from where Elon Beckford left off and is having dialogue to get the business off the ground. We know this, because by mid-March—March 17 to be exact—there is a Trade Secret Information Agreement with a company by the name of Universal Bancard Systems Inc., a Mr. Charles Sapp of Ceridian, Richard McGranahan of WTS and Ewart Scott of JCB. The following day, March 18, Scott signs a tri-party Letter of Intent with Ceridian and WTS. On March 25, McGranahan sends you a draft merchant agreement termed 'Market and Service Agreement' prepared by WTS and SECT, which you pass on to Ewart Scott. Shortly after that, JCB begins processing transactions for one telemarketing merchant by the name of Travel Connection. Others follow subsequent to that. The entire operation comes to a grinding halt in late August when Mr. Scott orders the termination of all merchants introduced by WTS and SECT. That's essentially the bare bones version. We're good with that?"

"Good," I said.

"Okay. Now, before we get into the details, humour me while I feed my face and walk me again through the whole credit card paper processing business and how it works. Then tell me why the bank, if it was already processing regular credit cards transactions, needed to set up differently for telemarketing transactions."

"Okay, let me answer the first question. Say you're a VISA cardholder. You, Chris Dunkley, are on the phone buying a coffee maker from a telemarketer, which we'll call 'the merchant'. You use your VISA card to make the purchase. The merchant then submits the resultant sales voucher to its designated acquiring bank. This is the bank the merchant uses to process the voucher. In this case, the acquiring bank is JCB. JCB then pays the merchant the amount of the transaction less its processing fee. JCB then goes through VISA's network system to recover the funds from your issuing bank where your VISA account is held. The issuing bank is the bank that originally issued you your VISA card to begin with. VISA gets its fee too, of course."

"As for the technical difference between processing for brick-and-mortar merchants versus telemarketers, one produces an actual paper voucher. The other produces only electronic information. We have to accommodate for the latter technologically. That means we have to set it up so we can interface with the systems of those we're dealing with and capture the information we need."

Chris nodded. "I follow, I follow. Tell me about chargebacks."

"Okay. In a perfect world, the cardholders are happy with their purchases, everyone gets reimbursed and makes a little money for their troubles. However, chargebacks are the common exception to that scenario. Let's say Miss Jane Doe makes a purchase with her card. If for some reason she has a problem with the item or service purchased, or perhaps just changes her mind, she can essentially get her money back— provided she makes a claim within six months of making the purchase. The bank sits in a position of potential liability for the sums of the paper processed, until the recourse period has passed. To cover that potential exposure, we are required to place a security deposit with the company processing our paper. Once the cardholder is outside the period of recourse, we're no longer liable for anything. And even if the cardholder acts within the period of recourse, reimbursement is *not* automatic. Okay? We'd still have to conduct the necessary investigation to ensure that the claim for the chargeback is in fact valid."

"So if everything is legit, meaning the cardholder's complaint and the merchant's integrity, and all parties act within the provided recourse period, everyone gets his money back. Right?"

"Yes."

"Even the acquiring bank?"

"Correct. JCB would get its money back from the merchant to whom it paid out the sum of the voucher."

"But if the merchant turns out to be bogus, the bank gets screwed."

"Which is why those background checks are crucial before signing them on."

"Okay," Dunkley said, a fork of rice headed for his mouth. "Understood. Now tell me how you first met our Mr. Ken Palmer—the person you're being accused of conspiring with and the man JCB is chasing on the sly."

"I met Palmer through my old boss," I replied. "That same year, 1991, Wiggan came asking me to help them deal with a problem. Now at the time he was the executive in charge of the entire Credit Card Centre. That was a new division set up and established by Alarene Wong, who reported to him. He had recruited her not too long before to set it up for the bank."

"His position then?

"General Manager of Technology and Operations. I was his Assistant General Manager."

"And Wong's background?"

"Credit card experience with National Commercial Bank's Keycard centre. She was brought in as the expert on credit card centres and all that. Well," I held up a cautionary hand, "that's what we were told, okay?"

"You question it?"

"No. Not at all. I'm just telling you that I was not privy to her résumé. Anyway, my boss came to me saying that the bank had acquired some US$140,000 in MasterCard paper that they couldn't process. So he asked me to go find a processor to deal with the paper for us right away. It was an urgent matter because they only had the one hundred and eighty days in which to get reimbursed before they entered the stale-dated period."

"After which—"

"After which reimbursement might be a problem."

"So the bank had accumulated that much in MasterCard vouchers and didn't have the capability?"

"Correct."

"And they had already paid out the money to the merchants, so they were out of pocket for that much. Yes?"

"Correct again."

"What made them think they could process it to begin with?"

"Like I said, Alarene was running the Credit Card Centre at that time and was in charge of both marketing *and* operations. Clearly she was under the impression that VISA's VICAPS software system could process MasterCard paper too. VICAPS is the software system VISA provides its principal members, like a JCB. Anyway, unfortunately she went and told the merchants—this is regular brick-and-mortar merchants now—that JCB could also process MasterCard paper. She did this before realizing that this was *not* the case. The real problem was that the VICAPS system was sort of buggy at the time and couldn't handle it."

"Okay, go on."

"The point is that the bank had to scramble to find a processor to deal with it. So the first thing I did, of course, was to call our MasterCard representative overseas and ask her where to find such a company. The representative gave me a list of six or seven names and phone numbers. Some I couldn't get through to. Others couldn't or wouldn't handle the volume of the transactions we had. The only one that indicated they could handle the volume of paper we had accumulated was a company out of Chicago by the name of FTA. Their chief person was Ken Palmer."

"So this is the first time you're talking to him. First time meeting him, so to speak." By Dunkley's tone I could tell that this was important.

"Yes."

"What happens next?"

"Palmer and I discuss JCB's situation. And he sends me an agreement for the bank to look over and a signature card to fill out, because we needed to open an account as part of the arrangement. I hand the document over to Wiggan, and Wiggan sends it on to Legal for vetting."

"How do you know he did that?"

I frowned defensively. "Well, he said he would. He must have, because Legal mentioned to me later on that they wanted a few amendments made to it, which I in turn communicated to Palmer."

"And what did you do about the signature card?"

"Wiggan said the Finance Department had responsibility for that, so he directed me to Neville Parkinson. At the time Parkinson was already General Manager of Finance and Administration. So I went to him and explained that we needed to open this account overseas with Southwest Suburban Bank in Chicago, so that FTA could process our MasterCard paper. That's when I asked him what the procedure was in this case."

"So you did not know what the procedure was?"

"To open an account for the bank? Rass, man. No more than Parkinson knew how to write software programs."

"So Wiggan didn't refer you to an internal procedures manual that covered the matter?"

I blurted out a scornful laugh. "The only manuals I knew to exist in that bank were the computer manuals on my shelves!"

"Okay." Chris said.

"At that point," I continued, "he signed the card and then —"

"Sorry," Chris interrupted as he began looking through a box of files near him. "Need to ask you first. Did Parkinson sign it in front of you?"

"Yes, in front of me. He signed the card and then sent me to Ewart Scott for his signature as well."

"Why Ewart, you think? As opposed to someone else?"

"Well, Ewart was his Assistant General Manager at the time, so that must be it, I guess?"

"Okay," he continued, holding up a document for me to see. Chris was in full lawyer mode. "Since we're dealing with the allegation that you opened this account by preparing and issuing a document which you falsely represented to FTA to be a Resolution of the bank's executive board, let's deal with the actual document in question."

I shifted irritably in my chair. Just hearing the asinine statement alone brought hot blood to my face. I glared at Chris but he didn't flinch. "This," he said, ignoring me, "is one of the documents that Palmer couriered along with the signature cards after your telephone discussion. See here where it reads: *'I further certify that the named persons are officers of the said Corporation duly qualified and now acting as such.'* How did your signature end up on it?"

I nodded slowly. "I remember this one well. I had actually noticed that this particular document required the Company's seal, and therefore the signature of the Company Secretary, who is the keeper of the seal. But when I pointed it out to Neville, he said that it wasn't everything that needed to go to the Board. He said that if we had to go to the Board each and every time an account needed to be opened, the bank's work wouldn't get done. And in this case, since the matter was urgent, we needed to hurry. And then he told me that I should just witness the signatures. So I did as my Finance Manager asked and that is all I thought I was doing— witnessing signatures. Look," I said, pointing with my index finger. "You can see where I crossed out the word 'Secretary,' and handwrote my title next to my signature. And right there is Scott's signature."

Chris frowned. "So you're telling me that Parkinson just decides arbitrarily that this does not need to go to the Board of Directors?"

"Arbitrarily or not, I can't say. But that's the call he made. Okay, maybe he thought it was the practical move under the circumstances. I mean the bank *was* on the verge of kissing off US$140,000! To be honest with you, I didn't even think to question Neville. He was the finance man and the bank's most senior general manager back then. I felt safe under his guidance and assumed he knew what he was doing. But that kind of make-it-up-as-you-go-along culture was very JCB. No real procedures documented. Nothing written down that you could follow so that you knew for sure you were okay. You had to go on people's say-so. Imagine me now as the newest kid on the block, fumbling around trying to get all this done. Tell me. Who the hell was I to question them?"

Chris nodded. "Fair enough. Well, while we're here let's deal with the allegation that you caused or allowed this document to be signed by two other officers of the bank. Did you, Dalton, coerce anyone into signing the FTA agreements?"

"No. I'm charming, but I'm not that good."

"And did you cause the document to be completed in such a manner as to allow Ken Palmer to withdraw funds from the account only on his signature?"

"How? By literally handing the contract to Neville for signing? And I sure as hell didn't write the damn thing."

"Okay," he said. "Back to the contracts. Did you read them? The terms and conditions?"

"I might have to some extent, but I can't say I studied them much since that wasn't my area. The only thing I know I read for sure, in its entirety, was the cover letter where Palmer talked about coming to Jamaica to meet us in person."

"So you never examined the other documents closely."

"No. I figured that was Legal's job."

"So this clause here that says, *'the Bank hereby grants FTA the limited authority to debit or credit the Daily Settlement Account as appropriate for or with the net daily settlement transactions or other debits or credits resulting from the operation of the Bank's program'* —you never saw this clause before they signed it?"

"No. I didn't. You think that's the one that got the bank in trouble?"

"Where Palmer is concerned, possibly. It sure leaves a lot of room for misinterpretation—or mischief—if that was his intention. Okay. So after everything was signed, what next?"

"I then popped the signature cards and documents into an envelope and sent them back to Palmer. After that my mission was accomplished, and it was all back in Alarene's hands again."

"And Palmer? Did he eventually come to Kingston to meet with the bank?"

"Sure! He met with Wiggan, Elon Beckford, Alarene and me."

"Okay. So as far as you're concerned, you've solved the problem, that's the end of Ken Palmer for now, and you go back to your own work."

"Yes to all the above."

"And the bank gets all its money back."

"Not quite."

"Oh?" Chris raised an eyebrow.

"Long story short, FTA didn't do the actual processing, but brokered the arrangements for us with another company. But we were well aware of that, so that's not an issue. Anyway, I guess our particular situation meant a longer search time, but eventually they located a company that agreed to do it. By the time everything was put in place between JCB and FTA, almost a year had passed, and so had the one hundred and eighty-day window of opportunity. So the bottom line was that the bank still ended up losing some forty or fifty grand."

Chris raised his eyebrows. "Oh? Guess they were pretty irate about it."

I paused. "You know, I couldn't really say, to be honest."

"Meaning?"

"Maybe they were upset, but quite frankly I don't remember anyone getting in trouble over this one."

"No?"

"Nope."

"Wiggan wasn't upset?"

"From what I remember, Wiggan was pretty quiet."

"He was?"

"As far as I can remember."

"No one else made a stink over this?"

"Not that I recall. If someone did, then I was not aware of it."

Chris tilted his head but said nothing. He paused for a few seconds. "Okay, Dalton. What's the next logical dot we should be connecting here?"

I tapped my finger on the table as I took a moment to think. "In 1992 he comes to me with another problem, again coming out of the Credit Card Centre. This time it's an operational issue—things like a serious backlog of credit card applications, backlog of queries from existing cardholders, and so on."

"Because by now the bank is also issuing credit cards, right?"

"Right,' I said. "We were both an issuing bank and acquiring bank. Essentially we were a VISA Principal Member. So Wiggan now wants me to actually take over the operational side of the Credit Card Centre."

"Because—"

"From what he was telling me, it needed the help."

"The Credit Card centre was still under Alarene Wong when Wiggan came to you for help?"

I nodded. "So they're now splitting the credit card department into two. Essentially Alarene would bring the business through the front door, while I would handle the operations side of things."

"Sounds okay."

"Sure. Not a problem."

"What next?"

"Well, the first thing I did was to request an independent consultant to come and assess the department's operations side."

"And why'd you do that?"

"Let's just say I thought it prudent to get an objective opinion on the state of the department I was about to inherit."

Dunkley smirked. "What's the matter, Yap? Don't you like surprises?"

I scoffed, "No more than I like lawsuits."

"Alright," Chris chuckled as he stretched across the table for another file. "So Wiggan lets you seek outside advice. That was good of him."

"Look. I always said he was intelligent and practical. Can't take that from him. He always knew what needed to be done. So anyway, we get a Mr. Oscar Molina from a company out of Florida called Systematic Control Inc. Molina visits us April to May of 1992 and then makes his observations and recommendations in writing. It was a pretty thorough report. Excellent recommendations too."

"Ah," Chris said rifling through a file. "Here we go. Molina's report to you. Let's go through it again. First he mentions the need to develop a General Ledger interface necessary for balancing VISA transactions. Then he talks about observing a work flow problem, lack of discipline with regard to routine operational flow, questionable performance on the part of the operators and questionable distribution of reports to the various branches. He identifies the VISA operations as the biggest concern, shows where the lack of discipline and job assignments compromises the productivity and desired accuracy. And this is a good one. He says that the team members carry a heavy load and that the combination of functions lends itself to error and increases the bank's potential for liability. And he cites an example of the problems. And I quote. *'I restored a tape labeled April 30, when in fact the date contained in this tape belonged to April 20.'* Sounds like pure chaos in there!"

"You have no idea," I said with a grimace.

"Makes you understand why these multinationals are so hooked on written procedures."

"Precisely."

"Okay. So you get Molina's recommendations. What happens next?"

"As soon as the new division is officially handed to me, I fly to Chicago to meet with Palmer so that we can discuss the recommendations and agree on the procedures to be followed."

"And your reason for meeting him in person?"

"Well since the division was now my responsibility, I wanted a firm understanding of how things were to run with zero misinterpretations. I'm talking about things like frequency of reports from FTA, details of reports and so on. I had met Palmer before when I first got him to deal with JCB's MasterCard problem. But now as the person in charge of the credit card operations, I needed to know more about the correct flow of the paper trail and so on. I didn't think a telephone conversation was going to cut it."

"So you meet with Palmer and then—"

"When I return from Chicago, I start implementing the recommended procedures. I even begin holding regular meetings with my own managers, just to make sure that the old problems don't happen again."

"And minutes are taken at these meetings?"

"Yes."

"Okay. After you implemented the procedures, did you check to see that they were being followed?"

"Other than meeting with my managers? Yes. I mean, I'd randomly check that the requisite statements were coming in from FTA and all that. I can't say that I was in the habit of reading them line by line, okay? I was not a one-man show."

"They clearly thought you were."

"Then I was being severely underpaid."

"So," Dunkley said. "Dalton Yap saves the day. Again."

I shook my head slowly. "See where it got me?"

"So it's early 1992 and you're now in charge of the operations side of the credit card department. You're learning the ropes and ironing out the wrinkles. What about Ken Palmer? What's our friend up to?"

"Okay. Of any significance is a letter he sends to me early 1993 with billing details covering the period from June 1991 to January 1993. As the person in charge of the operations side of the credit card centre, I am now his main contact. In this letter he talks about the bank's need to establish a larger security deposit with FTA because the volume of our transactions has increased. He was moving it up to US $100,000."

"Up from where?"

"If my memory serves me well, I think we started out with a mere US $5,000."

"And it kept inching up?"

"Along with our volume of processing, yes."

"Now, the billing, Dalton. Were those based on the terms and conditions which were all a part of the arrangements made back in 1991, when Wiggan asked you to locate a processor?"

"I presume so. I certainly never had discussions with him about that. The charges were for miscellaneous administrative expenses like training, couriers, telephone, processing and stuff."

"And those charges would be debited out of which account?"

"JCB's Daily Settlement Account. The same account Parkinson was rushing to open that day without the company seal so that FTA could start processing the MasterCard paper for us."

"And you sent this FTA bill and all other FTA statements to the Accounts Department?"

"Every month."

"So there was no hiding of anything."

"For what?" I was pissed and my tone made it known.

Dunkley didn't ease up. "You know, I have to ask, so humour me."

"No. There was no hiding."

"What did you do about the security deposit issue?"

"I sent a copy of the letter to Ewart Scott for him to deal with it."

"Why him?"

"Well for one, that's the business side and I don't know about negotiating such things. I'm just in charge of technology and operations. Since Ewart was in charge of the business end, I sent it to his attention."

"And?"

"And I never heard from him."

"So you interpreted his silence to mean what, exactly?"

"That the man was dealing with it, of course."

"Fair enough. Let's put Mr. Palmer aside for now and look at part two of this case—the new telemarketing side of the credit card business. Let's start by going back now to Ewart Scott. We said in our summary earlier on that while you're busy getting the technical side of things ready for the bank, as per Elon Beckford's 1991 request to work with Reaume, everything continues as planned. Scott is busy tidying up the business end and has all these drafted agreements ready by mid-March 1993. Yes?"

"Yes."

"Now. They are saying that a decision was taken by the executive board to cease pursuing the telemarketing business. Talk to me about this."

"Yes, there *was* a monthly executive meeting before that. It was in February, I believe. It had to be February because Scott and I had met with Bill Todd and Richard McGranahan in January. By then Elon Beckford had left the bank, and Ewart Scott had taken over the Retail Banking and Marketing Division as General Manager. Anyway, this monthly executive meeting was one of those all-day marathon killers. Well at some point, and I can't say exactly when, the issue of the telemarketing business is briefly mentioned. I won't even call it a discussion—it was more like brief ramblings. Basically they were just bouncing around questions about the risk factor. But in my mind, it was nothing more than the standard attention to caution. I mean, which business doesn't carry some level of risk that must be at least addressed?"

"I follow. So what then? A decision is taken to drop it?"

"Absolutely not. I would have definitely remembered something like that, especially since Scott and I had only just met with the other parties. Okay? But we can always check the minutes. The only thing is, I don't have them."

Chris went silent for a few seconds as he scribbled. "I'll request copies," he said. "At any rate, Scott's subsequent decision to sign all these agreements with the various parties shores up the logical argument that the bank had *not* changed its mind about pursuing telemarketing."

"I would think so. I mean, really. Don't let my Chinese accent fool you. I do have a strong command of the English language. All Ewart or Wiggan would have needed to do was just tell me the bank wanted to drop the whole damn thing. End of story. I would have complied."

"You would have?"

"You're really asking me that, Dunkley?"

Chris nodded and continued scribbling for a few minutes before pushing another sheet of paper in front of me. "Okay. So you and Scott meet Todd and McGranahan in January. The meeting is followed by all these agreements. Let's talk about this March 18th Letter of Intent that has Ceridian's signature missing."

I waited a few seconds allowing the scene to come back to me. I pictured myself in my cozy office with the wood paneling.

"Ewart comes into my office with this letter and shows it to me. I remember seeing Bill Todd's signature, Ewart's and McGranahan's. But I also notice that Ceridian's is missing, and I remember specifically asking Ewart why. He then tells me that Charles Sapp, their owner or manager—I'm not sure— couldn't fly down for the meeting, and so Bill Todd would take the agreement back to Sapp and have him sign. After getting Ceridian's signature he'd then return the signed document back to us."

"Go on."

I exhaled loudly. "At that point Ewart says to me something along the lines of 'just run with it, Dalton, and work with Bill Todd.'"

"Just run with it?"

"Just run with it."

"Okay, Dalton. This is important. What did you understand Ewart to mean when he said to *just run with it?*"

129

"Put them on line. Hook them up to the system. Get things going so that they can start processing for us."

"In your mind why could it be nothing else but that?"

"Simple. By then I had pretty much completed the technological set-up. All the software had been written. We'd already met with the people involved, so there wasn't much else for me to do. At this point it was just a matter of flicking on that final switch, you see. The bank was ready to start doing business with these telemarketing merchants."

"Okay, so Todd and McGranahan begin introducing potential merchants to the bank."

"Yes, through the Marketing Department. So now we're beginning to do business with Travel Connection, Floral Exchange, International Concepts, LMP Marketing, Universal Bancard System and all these wonderful people."

"So based on Scott's instructions to *run with it* following the signing of the Letter of Intent, you do what exactly?"

"A few days later on the 22nd, I write Ceridian—yes that's the letter—I write to provide them with the final information they'd need to work with us. As you can see, just basic things like our address, contact names on the processing and operational sides, our identification numbers for our VISA and MasterCard systems. These are just the last few bits of information Ceridian needs in order for their software system to interface with ours."

"So would you say this is *the* turning point?"

"Pretty much. We had turned the ignition. Engines started. We could now process paper for these merchants."

"Accounts were now opened—by your staff, your division—for these telemarketing merchants. Do I have that right?"

"Yes, sir."

"Did Ewart specifically tell you to provide them with the information that you did?"

"Not in so many words, no, but—"

"Then why did you do it?" Chris cut me off.

I threw my hands out. "Look, Dunkley. I was the manager in charge of technology. Like I said, if the man tells me to *run with it*, providing Ceridian with that information was the technology manager's way of *running with it!*"

"Easy, Yap, easy," he said in a calm voice. "I just wanted to make sure you really believed that."

"Yeah? I was beginning to think you don't believe *me.*"

"Just giving you a taste of the courtroom. They're going to come charging after you. Get used to it. Okay. The accounts are now open. Did you do any kind of background checks on the merchants?"

I shook my head defiantly. "Not for me to do. That's all Marketing's responsibility."

"Fair enough. So off you went doing your job, assuming that Ewart was dealing with marketing."

"Ewart or his staff, yes."

"And shortly after this you get the massive Market and Service Agreement from McGranahan. Why does he send it to you, by the way?"

"And not to Scott, you mean?"

Dunkley nodded.

"It was a huge document being sent by computer and I had a modem. Scott didn't."

"Ah. Okay, and upon receiving it you do what?"

"I ask my secretary to copy it and pass it on to Ewart. I wrote a note on it with those specific instructions."

"And did you and Scott subsequently have a discussion about it?"

"He didn't call me or anything. I mean the details of this agreement were pretty clear and straightforward. So there wasn't really anything to iron out at that point."

"So you—?"

I shrugged. "Just continued going, based on his instructions to *run with it.*"

"Okay. Let's move on to another allegation concerning your supposed breach of contract. This one that says you established accounts without the authority and knowledge of the bank. You established them without doing the proper credit checks, and contravened VISA International's license conditions by entering into credit card relationships with merchants outside of the bank's region. One at a time. One, who was responsible for carrying out background checks before accounts were opened?"

"I just told you. That was Ewart Scott's division. Remember that he assumed duties as General Manager for Retail Banking when Elon Beckford left."

"So when Todd was bringing in these merchants and so on, you had no knowledge of the nature of their business. You were not the bank's policeman, so to speak."

"No and no."

"Next allegation—the one about bringing in merchants outside of the bank's region. This has to do with that 'local paper rule.' Let's go to this letter over here from Luis Soublette and Joe Dawson of VISA. It says that their investigations show that one of the telemarketing merchants, Travel Connection, is laundering sales drafts and violating their local paper rule. In this same letter, they tell you to terminate Travel Connection's account and freeze whatever deposits they have with the bank."

"I remember the letter," I said. "For a while I was fuzzy on that whole paper rule issue."

"Explain."

"Okay. This goes back to 1991 when we first bring in FTA to process the same US $140,000 worth of MasterCard paper. That's when I first realize that the bank is actually sending out paper to Chicago. Based on the little I had gleaned earlier about VISA's 'local paper rule'—the one that says you can only process paper in the region where you acquire it—I'm thinking to myself that this seems to be in violation of that rule. But then, since MasterCard isn't saying anything about it, I'm left to assume that they either have a different rule, or that I just didn't understand it very well. You follow?"

"Yes."

"So I didn't focus too much on getting my brain clear on the issue, since it wasn't my division's responsibility anyway."

"Okay. In terms of VISA's local paper rule, Jamaica is categorized as what, exactly?"

"Latin America and the Caribbean. This meant that if there was an island in the Caribbean that didn't have a VISA principal member, like Antigua at that time, then a merchant in Antigua could have their stuff processed by a Principal member on another island but within the region."

"Like a JCB in Jamaica."

"Exactly."

"Did you know where these merchants were located as they were coming in?"

"Again, that would have been Marketing's job. I never got involved in the compliancy part, including their addresses. For my purposes, all I needed to do was assign them a number for the system."

"And what did you do upon receiving this letter from VISA complaining about Travel Connection, in early May?"

"I forwarded it to McGranahan since he was the one who had brought in Travel Connection."

"What came about as a result of that?"

"A letter from McGranahan where he suggests having all their merchants go through an office Bill Todd either already had, or would eventually have, in Jamaica."

"And that sounded okay with you?"

"Sure," I said with a shrug. "I knew that Bill Todd had other business in Jamaica. He was on the island a whole lot. So it didn't sound suspicious to me, if that's what you're asking."

"That's what I'm asking. Did it sound like circumvention to you?"

"Not at all. I mean, an address is an address. A business can have branches anywhere it chooses to, right? In my mind it was a mere technicality. To be honest, I saw it the opposite way. I saw it as them trying to be compliant."

"So did you end up closing the Travel Connection account as ordered by VISA?"

"No!" I flinched with surprise at the question.

"Why not?"

"Chris, I opened those accounts *under Scott's instructions.* It only made sense therefore that any instructions to close them should come from the same person. I didn't know that VISA or MasterCard could tell us who to shut down just like that. That didn't sound correct to me. I thought that if we were to shut these accounts down, surely there was a process we had to follow."

"Reasonable. June 29. We have here a fax from VISA querying LMP and its activities. July 2. A letter from Dawson to Alarene directly. In it, he sends her a Fraud Transaction Screening Program report concerning LMP, International Concepts and complains that he hasn't heard from you since the facsimile of June 29." Chris looked up and raised an eye. "He's in a hurry, eh?"

"I tried, but it was impossible to check out everything overnight."

"Dawson gives the bank a report deadline of July 6, at which point they want to hear what JCB plans to do. And here we have a note to you from Scott in what I can only presume is his handwriting. *Dalton. Please note and take action.* So these complaints in general from Dawson and Soublette about other telemarketing merchants, saying that their activities seemed questionable. What did you do with them?"

"Communicated with the source. McGranahan. Asked him to investigate VISA's concerns and get back to me. Made whatever checks I could."

"Did you call, write?"

"Probably both."

"But at some point—July 6 to be exact—these accounts for Travel Connection, Floral Exchange, L.M.P. Marketing, International Concepts, Universal Bancard and so on. They were terminated. Yes?"

"Yes. That happened when Dawson decided to contact Alarene instead of me, expressing VISA's concern over the telemarketers. I happened to be out of the office that day. Incidentally this is just before my vacation too. I'd like to think that Alarene merely panicked. I guess it's not every day you get a hot letter from the Vice President of VISA International. Dawson was a former FBI man hired by VISA to sniff out any kind of fraudulent activity, so it's his job to keep his radar up. Anyway, I guess she saw the urgency, decided to act on it and took the letter to George Lumsden of the Retail Marketing division. Lumsden, you'll remember, reported to Ewart Scott. Lumsden then sends a memo to Lesley Hew of my division ordering the immediate closure of those accounts. By the time I return to the office, it's already been done. So all I can do after that is write a letter to Dawson confirming the closure of the accounts for *new* sales—but also advising that the accounts remain open to accommodate chargebacks only, should they arise."

"Okay. And I see here you take him to task for writing to Alarene."

I chuckled with a sheepish grin. "I was pretty peeved."

"Why? "

"For one, he is going to someone junior to me. Okay? Yes it's true he'd been dealing with her from before, when she was in charge of the whole credit card department, so he was used to communicating with her. But I was handling it now and should have been kept in the loop. Two, she was the same person I twice had to help out before, so I felt I had reason to feel a little uneasy. Three, I had been dealing with Dawson's queries up to that point. Whenever he raised a concern, I'd check back with McGranahan, request explanations from the merchants, after which I'd confirm my findings to Dawson."

"But clearly he wasn't satisfied that things were really okay, and that's why he went in search of someone else to fire his complaints to. I suppose he had reason to be concerned since VISA had in fact been uncovering telemarketing fraud in the States. I guess he was ready to pounce on anything that looked remotely odd. And I understand that. I just couldn't understand why he didn't go to my boss if he was that concerned, know what I mean?" I paused for a moment to think. "Well okay, I think Wiggan was on vacation around that time." I paused again, this time stretching my head back. "Yes, yes he was away part of July. Hell, that was a crazy month. Anyway, the other problem I had with Dawson changing his line of communication was what happened as a result. And by that I mean the immediate reaction by the bank to close the accounts without any thought to the consequences. Look at what happened next."

"Frantic merchants threatening legal action."

"Exactly," I said slapping my hand on the table. "All of a sudden we're being bombarded by calls and letters by confused merchants who can't understand why we're not only closing their accounts, but also freezing whatever monies we have due to them—especially when they haven't done a single thing wrong. I mean, not only did they go to the pains of pointing out their good track records with minimal chargebacks, some even offered to set up Letters of Credit to ease our fears of potential chargebacks! I mean, does that sound like fraudulent behavior to you?"

Chris nodded and continued to write. "Okay. I see your point. These accounts we just mentioned are closed on July 6. Then shortly after, on July 19, there is a meeting concerning a sort of new potential telemarketing merchant called Worldwide Marketing. In attendance are George Lumsden, Alarene Wong, George Beckford, Maria Green and you. Beckford and Green report to you."

"Correct."

"The merchant is only sort of new, because this new company is owned by the same person who has Travel Connection."

"Yes."

"So what was all this about, and what happens in the meeting?"

"A Mr. Greenlese of Worldwide Marketing makes a presentation to us about their business, and hands out brochures and stuff. In the meeting it is agreed that there is good potential for business with Worldwide."

"And that," Chris continued, "led to this memo to you from Lumsden. In it he refers to Worldwide Marketing's proposal as an attractive source of new business, and one that could utilize the bank's credit card technology and capabilities."

"Yes."

"So it is decided in this meeting that it's okay to open an account for Worldwide Marketing."

"Yes, because in addition to which, they were complying with the local paper rule by establishing a local address."

"And again, this sounded okay to you. It sounded like the real deal."

"Well sure! We had no reason to think that it was not going to be a real brick-and-mortar office with actual desks and chairs and all that. No one else in the meeting saw it as circumvention. No one even questioned it!"

"Okay, let's move along. Here's this allegation that you authorized payments to the companies to the tune of some US $800,000 without maintaining a reserve. Was the whole issue of reserves your division's responsibility?"

"No. Authorizing payments and maintaining reserves had nothing to do with us. Remember. I had passed on that letter from Ken Palmer to Ewart Scott when Palmer raised the issue of increasing the security deposit and all that."

Chris nodded. "Yes, I remember. And as for the allegation that you caused the account to be opened with the understanding that account statements in relation to FTA would not be sent to JCB's accounts department. Your response?"

"So what, now I'm in control of accounts too? Neville Parkinson was the one who signed the agreement with FTA as the head of our finance division!"

"Hold on tight now. Coming at you with the worst of them. Did you conspire with various persons, including Ken Palmer and the heads of those companies, to defraud the bank and cardholder customers?"

"No."

"Did you receive any personal benefit out of these transactions?"

"*No.*"

"Did you conspire to cause bills to be rendered to the bank for goods and services supposedly ordered by cardholders over the phone from the merchants, when in fact those goods and services had not been ordered, delivered or supplied?"

"I did not."

"Did you conspire to have the relevant cardholders invoiced for said goods and services?"

"No, Chris. No!

"Did you set up a fictitious office or offices in Jamaica for one or more of the Companies so as to circumvent the local paper rule?"

"What—like these fictitious allegations?"

"Answer?"

"No, I did not."

"Here's another one. Did you attend an Audio Text convention in California with a view to learning how to circumvent the system?"

"Ridiculous! Wiggan sent me to that convention! He signed the authorization letter!"

"He could say he didn't know what it was about."

"Chris, all the information on the convention was right there! And how could I force him to sign what he doesn't want to? And that's not even the point! Why the hell would I suddenly want to circumvent the system? Why? I mean what the hell is wrong with these people? What are they really trying to say? That after five years of priding myself on giving outstanding service, I suddenly turn into a bad seed overnight and start screwing them over right under their noses?"

CHRIS LOOKED IN his rear view mirror. His son had finally fallen asleep. Erica, also tired from her day, had handed the crying toddler over to her husband as he stepped into the house that night. It was an old trick the new father was happy to use. He decided to take one final drive around the neighbourhood to ensure his child was in a deep, peaceful slumber. He waved back at a neighbour just pulling into his own driveway. *We work too hard sometimes,* he thought, and tried to remember the last time he'd had a chance to do some laps in the pool at Up Park Camp.

Chris kept his eyes on the dark road and let his mind run a bit on his career, and on human nature in general. As grave as the charges against his client were, he at least knew that I had an amazing family with enough combined wherewithal and conviction to see me through to the end. Because that was where we were determined to go. The very end.

What if his client had been some poor soul just collecting his monthly pay with barely any spare change to buy that new pair of pants, much less money to hire a lawyer? Where would he turn? What are his options if he doesn't have some rich uncle he can call? Who will hire him after such an unresolved stain on his record? How is he to function with such a cloud hanging over his head? And how can it be that an employer can just up and decide one day that *hey, we need a scapegoat and guess what, you're it, boy.* What really happens to the life of the person who, after counting his savings and checking his humble network of friends, simply cannot come up with the money or connections it takes to fight an opponent who has access to all the money and influence in the land? Does he simply acquiesce and move on with his tail between his legs? Is that what an innocent person is left to do?

For the first time, Chris felt a nagging uneasiness over the darker side of his profession. And then he turned his focus on the session we'd been through that night. He thought it had gone well, even if by the end of it everyone was drained and not in the mood for small talk or even dessert. Answering ridiculous charges like the ones I faced was a lot like trying to argue with an idiot. Eventually logic seems to take a jump out the window and you don't know which way is up. Over the months leading up to my trial, we would wrestle through several sessions like the one we had that night. Some would be rougher than others depending on how tough Chris got— and on how much sleep had eluded me the night before.

BY THE TIME the painful one-year anniversary of my dismissal arrived, I was still trapped in the nightmare I'd fallen into. People, places and things I once considered familiar still seemed distorted. Twisted. Menacing. My lack of interest in the world and its tragedies, both natural and man-induced, had not changed—there was simply no energy left for any of it.

Now, more than ever, we had real reason to feel hopeful. The surprise tip about the bank going after Ken Palmer was pure manna from heaven. Just waiting for the news had turned my lawyer into an excited school kid.

So when we finally got that phone call in the early months of 1995 from Los Angeles, we could hardly contain our jubilation. The bank had not only sued Ken Palmer, it had won.

EIGHT

By the time we rang in 1995, my former employer had already undergone some corporate reshuffling to become Citizens Bank. Whether by design or coincidence, certain senior members of the bank left at about the same time. Among those were Neville Parkinson and Ewart Scott. Alarene Wong and George Lumsden would also depart sometime after. By then Elon Beckford had already moved on to his new Horizon Merchant Bank.

For my legal team and me, the changes were mildly humorous, but mostly incidental. Our attention was now wrapped up in the astonishing fact that the other side had not yet shared with us a single word about the Ken Palmer suit. Their "dear Chris" letter my lawyer was now checking for daily—the one that would amend their statement of claim on that particular item—still had not arrived. The bank had nailed its man. Surely they had to tell us. It had gotten to the point where Elise could anticipate the question with marksman precision. "Sorry, Mr. Dunkley, sir," she'd say, cutting him off as he opened his mouth to ask. "No letter as yet."

For weeks Chris kept insisting it would soon appear. "No, man Dalton. There's no way they're not going to tell us. They *have* to," he'd assure me whenever I asked about it.

I knew he'd finally come to terms with the other side's surprise play when he started muttering under his breath with eyebrows furrowed. Elise knew it too, when he stopped asking her about the statement. I gave my lawyer some room to take the blow in private.

Now the case was taking on a different kind of feel. Suddenly the atmosphere around it felt thicker. It was at this point that my lawyer ripped off his tie and rolled up his sleeves. If that's how the other side was going to play, he said, well that was certainly their prerogative and he'd have to accept that. All it meant was that we'd have to come up with our own fun and games. And Dunkley had already cooked up a plan. We were going to spin their silence into gold.

In a litigation suit, there is a cooperative phase that requires all daggers to be put aside in the interest of the proper management of one's case. Called the "discovery process," this often-lengthy pre-trial preparation phase brings together, through correspondence and face-to-face meetings, the opposing lawyers for what is ideally meant to be a basically polite and orderly exchanging of information—without prejudice. This is the period in which the two sides are expected to iron out amongst themselves those details that need not be entertained in court. The premise is that precious judicial time and citizens' tax dollars should be reserved only for those issues that absolutely cannot be agreed upon.

The result is usually several bundles of relevant documents neatly arranged and properly labelled and indexed for use in the actual trial. While neither side is expected to divulge how the presented material is going to be used, each is expected to deduce what it will and build its presentation accordingly. Each is also expected to use the opportunity to ask of the other whatever material it's interested in, as no surprises are entertained in court once the trial has commenced. I fully admit that the concept of being civil before putting up your dukes was a strange one for me to grasp. In reality, discovery was often messy and contentious.

By this time we were well into the discovery phase. Our opponent's material non-disclosure was both surprising and significant, and would soon send my legal bills soaring. I thought about the bank and wondered what level of the stratosphere their bills had reached.

Chris was pissed. He carefully buried into one of his list of requests the docket number of the bank's case against Palmer. Hoping that he had, in effect, planted a ticking sleeper, the energetic lawyer went about the rest of discovery doing what he would become well known for in this case—making a whole lot of noise about everything under the sun. He ranted about any and everything. Everything—except the Ken Palmer case.

Almost a year and a half later, just months before the commencement of the trial in September 1996, he made one final query about it to ensure that we would not be caught in a non-disclosure position in front of the judge. This time the exchange was a verbal one with Patrick McDonald, the junior lawyer who was still assisting the plaintiff's Queen's Counsel at the time. According to Chris, his deliberately nonchalant, *so, whatever happened with that Palmer case* query was met with little more than a good-natured chuckle, head thrown back and all. Chris made sure to chime in with his own hearty laugh. The move was a big gamble. He needed to raise the issue so that the plaintiff could not say he never asked. At the same time, he didn't want to tip his hand before the trial commenced.

When I questioned him about not blowing them out of the water right then and there, he calmly assured me that whether before or after, the revelation would have the same result in terms of a reduction in the scope of their allegations. It was the difference in impact that he was after. But he wouldn't tell me more. For the time being, I could only wait and see how the game would unfold for my lawyer. He continued to keep his cards close to his chest.

Discovery confirmed what we already knew. The bank was throwing everything at us. It was almost impressive what they were bringing to the table. I pictured the judge being delivered his bundles by forklift. This was far more attention than I ever thought I could generate.

Despite the mountain of letters and memos and documents, still missing were the two documents to which the plaintiff's argument should have been fused by inches of glue, if they in fact held the fatal blow—the 1993 minutes of the monthly executive meeting in question, and the internal auditor's report.

Chris knew full well they couldn't produce minutes to a decision that was never taken, but happily went along with the game. "I never ever come out and call the other side a liar," he explained to me one day while taking a break with yet another boxed lunch. "I just ask them for the document in question during discovery. When they don't produce it, I merely ask for it again in the hearing, and watch as the poor judge sits there, waiting while they search."

The absence of the two pieces of evidence continued to plague us with curiosity. If not those, what then was the plaintiff's ultimate weapon? Meanwhile, Dunkley was casting a curious eye on the island's finance sector. A long-favoured local merchant bank had just closed its doors that July amid cocktail circuit allegations of "mismanagement". The demise of Century National Bank had caught the nation with its pants down, and would signal the start of the near-collapse of the country's booming financial sector. It was a fall that would soon force the Government to jump in and attempt to save it. Dunkley said he smelled a spicy cauldron brewing.

The timing couldn't have been kinder to me. Just months before my trial, it was an unexpected gift, as unfortunate as it was. Perhaps now the judge would be more inclined to consider a different view of the almighty banker.

The news helped to further ease the knot that had long lodged itself in my stomach. It was still there, just not pulling as tightly. My steps back into life were feeling more sure-footed now. By then I had already started helping my wife sort out some of her administrative woes at her haberdashery. We were once more acting like the team we used to be, and in more ways than one. By the spring of 1996, Pauline became pregnant with our third child.

With the court date in full view, we settled into the routine of playing devil's advocate, and stripped to the skeleton any new angle or questions we could think of. As usual, everyone's kitchen, living and dining room became fair game for our work. It was in one of these sessions that I asked Chris about another document he had opted not to ask the other side for—the chargeback reports. Once again, his penchant for strategy came to the fore.

"Simple," he began. The ice cubes in his glass of Pepsi rattled as he took a swig of the still fizzling drink. In front of me sat a white tea pot and cha cup. "Very simple. We know they have them. But we don't want to shine any attention on the reports right now. We don't want to alert the other side to the fact that we know that after a few months, the potential liability from chargebacks would automatically be reduced from several hundred thousand dollars, to a much smaller percentage—depending on the complaints, of course."

"You're talking about the recourse period of six months," I confirmed, pouring some hot tea into the empty cup. At the sight of steam rising from the spout, my shoulders relaxed.

"Right," said Chris. "They're coming in all hot and foaming at the mouth about their losses, right? But look at what they're really talking about here—*potential loss!* They're focusing on the recourse period in which they were exposed for a few hundred thousand US dollars. So either their banker clients haven't explained to them that those weren't actual losses, or they think we're stupid. In this case I'd guess the former and sympathize with my fellow opposing counsel. They don't know the credit card business. Their clients have to want to take the time out from their two-hour long lunches to sit down and explain everything from A to Z to them. Anyway," he said with a dismissive wave of his hand, "whatever the reason, that point is for *them* to pick up on, not us. I'm thinking that if this goes undetected until the trial begins, we could do some real damage to their case by literally standing up in court and pointing out that the plaintiff is suing us precipitously and erroneously based on potential liability, because those chargeback reports will support our position that the bank only ended up having a 10 percent attempt at recourse, or whatever the actual percentage was. And just to make my point, Dalton—if there were zero chargeback claims, there would be zero exposure on the bank's part. You follow?"

I shook my head in amazement. Every word had made perfect sense. "Man. It makes you wonder if the bank really understood the telemarketing business to begin with."

"Trust me, D. Yap," Chris said. "I've given careful thought to what documents we're asking for. If we do this right, we'll have them exactly where we want them. Now. Let's go through these bundles step by step."

"Ready," I said, already bracing for the onslaught of dates, names, times and details Chris would require me to recall. He had made it clear from day one that we were to know the case better than the plaintiff did. I was prepared to deliver.

"Okay," he began, holding up his index finger. "First thing Norman says we're going to throw at them is your stack of irrefutably outstanding annual performance evaluations. He wants us to include every single one of them."

"Every one?" I asked.

"Every last one."

147

I sipped some tea and thought for a second. "But won't that frustrate the judge—irritate him, even?"

"Worth the risk," Chris said. "He doesn't know you. You're being charged with issues that speak to your track record as a worker. So we need to establish your character. Show them that your actions have always reconciled with your motives— to do a good job. We need to show the court that you were, by JCB's own admission, a model employee." Chris grabbed the bundle that contained the glowing professional report cards. "I mean, listen to them gushing about you—'Dalton demonstrates strong leadership, selflessness, determination—excellent team player—has a strong commitment to customer service— communicates effectively—accepts additional responsibilities readily—works assiduously— has achieved this, has achieved that—continues to be an outstanding member of the team— represents the bank with dignity and professionalism'. All signed by your old boss, of course. And then there are all the increases in pay and merit pay that they felt you deserved. We can even reach back to your Citibank days and lick them with your performance there. Let's see them try to refute all that."

I pressed my middle and index fingers at my temples. "They'll say I coerced them into writing nice things about me."

Chris shook his head as if contemplating how ridiculous things could get in the courtroom. "Okay," he said, "I think we've already dealt with the Ken Palmer issue sufficiently for now. We have all the documents we need, including those agreements allowing FTA limited authority to debit or credit the bank's account without notifying them. And they're all signed by Wiggan, Scott and so on just as you said. But as the conspiracy allegations tying you to Palmer are about to become a moot point, we no longer need to worry about him where that is concerned. Let's focus now on the whole telemarketing mess chronologically."

"Hold on, Chris. I know we're happy about the fact that they nailed their culprit. But now I'm wondering if we should be worried instead."

"Why should we worry?"

"If they found Palmer guilty, maybe they think they have something to make the conspiracy charge against me stick."

"They can try all they want, Yap. Bottom line is, no such thing happened. You know it, I know it, and they know it."

"Then why the silence?"

"No idea, but don't worry about it, Dalton. Like I said, it's a dead issue. Now, let's go back to examining the telemarketing nightmare."

"Okay."

Chris studied his notes for a minute. "Let's begin with these letters from VISA called 'Risk Management and Security'. This one here dates back to December 1991, but makes reference to even earlier bulletins. Seems as if they'd been issuing them from as early as 1990, before you were handed over the Operations side. Essentially these are general alert bulletins from VISA to its principal members about the rise in fraud through telemarketing activity throughout the Latin American region. And they're addressed in memo format to Centre Managers and Security Directors." Chris looked up. "Were you receiving these love letters back then?"

It was my turn to shake my head. "No. They were probably still being sent to Alarene since she used to run the whole Credit Card Centre."

"But she never passed them on to you or shared the information?" he asked. "Same for these alert bulletins from MasterCard. You never got those?"

"No, sir."

Chris continued, "In fact, it seems as if a lot of the correspondence concerning the whole telemarketing business continued to go to her even after the department was split in two. Like this one from FTA dated August 30, 1991, asking her for information on merchant categories and things like that."

"That's right. In her defence, I didn't get the feeling that JCB had apprised all the relevant external contacts of our internal changes. It's entirely possible that that's what happened. The truth is, however, those concerns were marketing-related anyway. So it was right that the bulletins be addressed to her."

Chris nodded in agreement as he continued sifting through. "Which just supports our position that Marketing was being a sloppy security guard. Now, over here we have correspondence from VISA to Wiggan in May of 1992 about the same VICAPS system you mentioned before. He was still General Manager of Technology and—hold on now," he said suddenly, looking up with his index finger pointing to a section of the same letter. "Is that a list of problems with the system?"

"Yes," I said, leaning in to get a better look at the letter. Any mention of technology still had the ability to perk me up. Once upon a time it had been my passion. "VICAPS was pretty good, but it still needed some work. But why would this be relevant?"

"You never know, but at least we can show that the system VISA itself provided was imperfect. Just in case they use that to try and shift the blame on you even more. Okay. May 29, 1992. Oscar Molina's letter to you after his independent investigation on Wong's department. Then we have all the minutes covering your meetings once you took over the operations side—" His voice morphed into a mumble as he quickly scanned the minutes to the meetings I used to look forward to each Friday morning. "Okay, very detailed, very well-written. That's good. Requests for better accuracy, better checks and balances, requests by you that all incoming data balance with outgoing reports and so on. Excellent, very good." Chris chuckled. "Quite the demanding boss, were you, Mr. Yap?"

I waved him off. "Just trying to do the bank's work."

"Again, more bulletins from VISA still addressed to 'Centre Managers and Security Directors'. Now Dalton, if these had come to you, whether directly or through Alarene, would your staff members have stamped them as they did all other correspondence?"

"Of course! That was standard procedure for my division. Everything else coming to me is stamped with day *and* time."

"Already noted," he confirmed with a nod. "The mere fact that we got these bulletins from the other side proves that *someone* in the bank got these first—someone other than you. So that cannot be disputed. Hell—just about everything we have here comes from them anyway! Okay. Let's move into 1993. I see here some correspondence from Ceridian in March about something called Quasi Cash." Chris laughed. "Sounds like the Jamaican dollar. What is it?"

"Well, Ceridian had all sorts of products the bank was considering at the time along with the telemarketing. Call it new business possibilities. Quasi Cash was one, but we never got very far with it. Never materialized. Essentially it involved getting a cash advance from your credit card."

"And this is the same Ceridian from our telemarketing business?"

"Yes."

"Okay—just to repeat the sequence of events, we're in March. Scott and the others sign the Trade Secret Agreement and the Letter of Intent. This is when he tells you to *just run with it.* Yes?"

"Right."

151

"And then, based on that directive, you provide Ceridian with the information they need for computer interfacing. McGranahan sends you WTS's sixteen-page Market and Service Agreement soon after that. This is when they bring in Travel Connection and so on. I see your note to Debbie telling her to copy it to Scott. This is your handwriting. Yes?"

"It is," I said.

"And did she in fact send it to him?"

"Unless she decided to suddenly become a slacker, I can only assume she did as she was asked."

"Did you hear from him on it?"

"On that specifically? No, I don't think so."

"So you thought what, exactly?"

I shrugged and slumped against the back of my seat, finishing his sentence. "—that he was doing whatever he needed to be doing on the Marketing side. I didn't take his silence to signal anything odd, if that's what you mean."

"He never came to you and said 'Hey, Dalton, don't you remember that we're nixing this telemarketing business?' He didn't call you saying to hold off until further notice. Nothing like that?"

"No, sir."

"Okay," he said with approval. "So business begins. A couple months later—on May 3, to be specific—Luis Soublette of VISA International's Security division writes Alarene Wong and George Beckford a memo in which he refers to a prior telephone conversation between them. He goes on to talk about a Central Deposit Monitoring Report showing merchants that VISA thinks might be involved in fraudulent transactions. He goes on to single out Travel Connection and mentions ten transactions that are being queried by cardholders. That same day Alarene memos Ewart Scott on the matter. She says she can't find any merchant agreement with Travel Connection, and then refers to you as the person who opened the account." Chris looked up. "How do you respond, Mr. Yap?"

"Maybe Ewart didn't hand over the agreement to her? Maybe their filing system was lacking? Maybe someone used it to wipe up a spill on the floor?"

"And the point about you being the one to have the account opened. Are you disputing that?"

"No," I returned, my arms folded across my chest. "The opening of accounts absolutely fell under my division—once we had the go-ahead from the Marketing Department."

Chris pressed. "Okay, Dalton. What exactly was that 'go-ahead' moment for you?"

"What the hell, Dunkley?" I shot back. "The Merchant and Service Agreement! Look," I said leaning into the table, "Hear me again. This agreement arrives from the gentlemen with whom the bank's executives and I have been having ongoing discussions. At that point I'm assuming that Marketing has already done its check on the merchant named in the agreement. I hand the document over to the man in charge. He says nothing, and certainly gives no indication that I should put on the brakes. So you tell me. What else is a logical man to conclude?"

"And on that basis—? "

"On that basis," I broke in, "I instructed my staff to open the damn accounts!"

"You understand why I'm digging you on this one, Yap. *This* is the crux of the matter. This is about who really initiated the opening of these accounts. This is about who brought those merchants through the front door."

"Yes, sorry. I know," I said running my hand over my mouth.

"But the fact of the matter is that Mr. Scott's signature is all over these agreements."

"Exactly. So how are they going to refute that?"

"We'll see that in court, I'm sure." Chris continued his unbroken record of absolute patience with his sometimes irritable client. I was growing tired and could feel my legs going numb. I needed to get up and stretch but remained seated. "Okay, Dalton. After a few months of business, Ewart Scott gets that May 3 memo from Alarene, in which certain transactions are being questioned. These are transactions by merchants for which she says she cannot find agreements. So at that point did he order you to close the accounts?"

"No."

"Would he have had the authority to do so?"

"Absolutely."

"Did he, whether by telephone, in person, in the middle of the hallway, men's room or by written form, ask you where the hell these people came from, and how the ass did they come to be in business with the bank? In other words, did he show surprise in any way?"

"No."

"Shock? Anger?"

"Nope."

"Veiled reprimand?"

"Nothing."

"After the May 3 memo, did Alarene come flying into your office demanding information on these merchants so that she, or someone in Marketing, could conduct due diligence on them, now that she was aware of their existence?"

"Not to me, no. If she went to someone else in my division, I wasn't aware of it. But I wouldn't necessarily have been told, okay?"

"Because that was the sole responsibility of her department and it would have been normal for her to do so?"

"Exactly. *Unless,*" I said, holding a finger up, "unless there was a problem. In that case, I'm pretty certain I would have been told."

Chris did a combination of nodding and shaking his head while he scribbled. He chuckled again before continuing. "Three days later you get the same memo from Soublette in which he refers to a conversation between the two of you. So you had called him at some point?"

"I guess I did." By now I had leaned into the back support of my chair. Somewhere outside a playful dog was barking at a gate. It rattled every time he pounced on it. Chris's voice broke my momentary distraction.

"May 7. You write Mr. McGranahan about Soublette's complaints and list the cardholders disputing charges. McGranahan replies the following day—May 8. Now, his letter is a strange one. Before addressing the transaction disputes, he talks about WTS working on establishing a banking relationship in Mexico through some private banks, and talks about the possibility of JCB opening a branch in Mexico. He says he has attorneys in Tijuana who can 'make this happen virtually overnight' if JCB wants to continue." Again my lawyer looked at me hard. "Sounds like something out of a movie, Yap. What the hell is all this about? What's with this overnight business?"

I cocked my head up for a second in an effort to jog my memory. "I think it has to do with the same VISA local paper rule issue. McGranahan was trying to encourage us to expand our reach so that we could facilitate telemarketing transactions in South America. The 'more branches, the more business' kind of thing. I didn't think there was anything suspicious behind that, though. You?"

Chris shrugged. "It just sounds odd, you know. Like there's some mad rush. One thing's for sure. These fellows certainly seemed to have a firm grip on the credit card system."

"Yup." For the first time I wondered about what might have really been going on in the minds of the others. I asked Chris whether he thought the bank had been caught unawares in a potential scam.

"My gut says *no*. I don't think these guys set out to do any harm to the bank. At the most, they might have been trying to get cheaper processing done. But that's a VISA issue and this is not their trial." I reflected on Chris's assessment until his voice broke my thoughts. "Moving on. In this next paragraph he says, 'As we discussed, all our existing business will originate in Jamaica at the office where Mr. Todd will be housed.' Again Chris glanced up, seeking my reaction.

"Like I said before, all I knew was that Mr. Todd had business here. He was on the island more often than not. So again, it did not give me any cause for concern."

"May 13. You receive a letter from Ms. Bell of the same disputed Travel Connection. In it, she refers to your letter to her of May 11, in which you list VISA's complaints and in which you ask her to provide details of the transactions under scrutiny. She then goes on to address each case one by one. So you *did* make an effort to satisfy VISA's concerns. You *did* investigate."

"Well of course," I said. "And quite frankly, Chris, I thought her response was pretty solid. She went through each complaint and wasn't skimping on information. You read it and tell me."

Chris was silent as he went through Bell's letter. Each paragraph referred to the cardholders by name, openly offering careful details of a cardholder who had simply changed his or her mind about a purchase, or some other scenario that seemed completely logical, even mundane. At the end he simply shrugged and nodded.

Satisfied, he continued. "Well what counts here is that you were making the effort to satisfy VISA. May 17. Soublette writes again asking you to hurry please with the information on Travel Connection. You respond five days later with the details. So, I have to ask you. Any particular reason for not writing him immediately?"

"You mean like the very next day?" I asked. He nodded, his eyes fixed on me. "Honestly, Chris, in the back of my mind I was satisfied that all was well with the merchant in question— and I still had other work to do running my division. Believe it or not, telemarketing was not the only work I had on my plate. Okay? Some days were busier than others. On top of which I think, and I'll have to check my notes on this, but I'm pretty sure that that was the month I got called in for jury duty. Ironic, I know. And I also had to go to Arkansas on JCB work as well."

"So it would be reasonable to say that you were busy in May trying to cram in your workload into a shorter time to compensate for your upcoming absence."

"Yes. It was a crazy month."

"You weren't trying to stall your reply to VISA for any reason then."

"No stalling, man. No reason to! As far as I'm concerned I got back to Soublette within a reasonable time frame, especially considering that I had an entire division to run."

"Okay. We're into June now. We have here communication to your secretary from the nice folks putting on the Audiotext forum in California."

"Oh yes," I scoffed with a jerk of my head. "This is where I'm supposed to be learning how to circumvent VISA's system, right?"

"We won't belabour this one. Wiggan's signature is on your authorization memo, so this is another no-brainer. But what exactly is Audiotext anyway?"

"Essentially the sale of information by telephone."

"So another form of telemarketing?"

"Right. Say your service is to provide cricket test scores."

"Uh huh."

"I phone in, give you my credit card number and you give me the service I want. And that's it. But I can't believe they're having a fit over my attendance! Did I remember to tell you that VISA and MasterCard had their own representatives on the presentation roster at the same convention?"

Chris looked up in surprise. "No, you didn't."

I flipped over to the second page of the memo and stuck my index finger on the sheet. "There it is on the schedule, in black and white."

Chris chuckled in disbelief. "Like I said, we won't bother to flog this one. So you're out of the office somewhere between the eighth and the eleventh over in California, soaking up technology fun. Meanwhile, Soublette sends you another memo on the eleventh, again about Travel Connection. This time he's complaining about some nine transactions that he feels look suspicious. Eight of them are for the exact same dollar amount. He then writes on June 17, with more details about transactions that had taken place the week before on the eleventh and twelfth that also raise a red flag in VISA's eyes. Thing is, I don't see any correspondence from you to him in between his memos of the eleventh and seventeenth. Do you remember what you did?"

"Not sure. I'd have just returned from California. So between trying to catch up with my backlog and figuring out what's going on with Travel Connection, I probably just called Soublette as the faster option to say I'd be on it as soon as I could. I'm not sure. I think Wiggan had also just left for vacation, so that would have meant added pressure for me."

"Alright. June 21. We have two letters from VISA International—one from Mr. Dawson, their Vice President of Security, and one from Soublette. Again they're bawling about Travel Connection, and this time Dawson demands that the bank close the said account. Next day, June 22. Another letter from Soublette, saying that he's tried to reach you, but has been unsuccessful. He's now saying that he has suspicions about another merchant. This time it's Floral Exchange. He claims that they're showing deposits of the same amounts as Travel Connection. June 23, he writes about LMP Marketing. Same complaints. So let me ask you, Yap. You've already explained why you didn't close the accounts as he directed. I get that. But at this point what's going on in your mind? VISA is having near cardiac arrest here and they're not letting up. What are you thinking?"

"I'm thinking that while it's Dawson and Soublette's job to be on the constant prowl, even to err on the side of caution if you will, I'm thinking that it's also JCB's job not to screw up. I'm *thinking* that we need to make sure we're not overreacting hastily to the detriment of our merchants. These are people we've struck up a business relationship with. Okay? And keep in mind, please, that all along I'm stupidly acting on the assumption that Marketing has done its job and has checked these people out thoroughly. Now, I'm not saying that I totally dismissed the possibility of suspicious activity. There's always some asshole out there looking for a free ride. I'm just saying that clearly many of these transactions had logical explanations behind them as we saw in Bell's letter. So I'm *thinking* that we simply need to do as we've been doing all along—conduct the necessary investigation and make the right decision based on our findings. Chris." I wanted to shout my next sentence out. Instead, I forced my tone right down. "I am a logical man. You've said it before. I'm sorry, but I do not react to hype. That's just not how I operate."

"I hear you," Chris replied. "Understood. Now things start to snowball. June 28. Alarene memos Scott about a telephone conversation she had with Dawson concerning the merchants in question. She cites the concerns and potential loss to the bank through excessive chargebacks, if these transactions are indeed bogus. Again she claims that she sees no evidence of merchant agreements with these people and points to you as the person who opened the accounts, and yet we see the agreements in the bundles. Okay, mind you, some of them only look half completed, but they're here."

I let out a frustrated sigh. "I guess she was being very specific by saying she had not seen them with her own two eyes. Maybe they got lost in her department. I really don't know."

"Alright," Chris said. "Like you, she too is not a one-woman show. So we'll give her that."

"Agreed."

"But the fact of the matter is, yes, here they are. Like this pre-compliance form from Floral Exchange addressed to Alarene herself."

I folded my arms indignantly. "That's what I've been trying to tell you. Those accounts weren't opened on a whim. Okay? There was paperwork. Someone generated the requisite paperwork."

Chris held up his index finger. "Okay, we're gentlemen. But even if we give her the benefit of the doubt, the point is *someone* in that department messed up."

I glowered. "In a big way."

"Okay, July 2. This time Dawson writes to Mrs. Wong, and 'strongly recommends' the termination of accounts for LMP Marketing, Floral Exchange and Travel Connection. He also suggests investigating International Concepts, another telemarketing merchant he suspects is up to no good. He also asks for an update by the sixth. Alarene most likely passes the letter on to Ewart Scott, because he then scribbles a note to you on the face of the same memo saying *Dalton, please note and take action.* Which you did?"

"Which I did," I confirmed. "This is where I closed the accounts in question so that no new sales vouchers could be processed, but left it so that we could accommodate credits. And by that I mean process transaction reversals or chargebacks."

"Why?" he asked. Again he trained his eye on me.

"*Why?* JCB still needed to honour its end of the transaction arrangement. So that meant remaining available to accommodate a customer's genuine complaint and request for a chargeback. That's why."

"The software could accommodate this distinction?"

"Absolutely."

Okay," Chris continued, turning to another document, "But I guess this doesn't please our friend, Dawson. Because on July 6 he writes Wong again, practically screaming this time that LMP is to be shut down. He refers to steps VISA plans to take against JCB should these accounts remain open. This time Wiggan gets a copy of the memo, we can only assume from either Wong or Scott."

"Right," I said.

"Now," Chris said straightening up in his seat, "this is important, because this is the first time we're seeing any evidence of Wiggan on paper concerning the accounts."

"Good point."

"A few days later, Wiggan scribbles a handwritten note to Alarene on the face of the same memo. His note is dated the fourteenth and says *Alarene, I understand from Dalton that all six A/Cs have been closed.* Signed LW." Chris paused. "So that's *all* Wiggan says?"

I looked at him, puzzled. "I don't know what you're trying to get at here."

"In other words, he's not nailing you to the cross for opening the accounts. Like Ewart, he's not showing any surprise or rage. He's not draping you up and asking what the hell is going on here and how did we come to be involved with these people. Was there any of that?"

"Well, no. No reason to be, right? The man works at the bank like the rest of us. He knows what's going on. Nothing's a secret."

"Nice," Chris said with an almost sly grin. "Their individual reactions are sure as shit not meshing with the allegations. Okay. Let's return to July 6 and that memo from Dawson to Alarene. You just happen to be out of the office that day. Alarene gets this stinging letter from VISA. So she and George Lumsden jointly sign a memo to Lesley Hew in lieu of the absent Dalton Yap, ordering her to close the accounts in question. You now return to the office on the seventh, to find that all this has taken place. You immediately write Dawson that same day confirming a few things. One, you confirm the closing of the named accounts for new business, but state that they'll remain open only for credit situations. Two, you confirm that you're investigating International Concepts, which remains fully open. And three, you state that the bank is planning to implement internal policies to certify new merchants. You also take the opportunity to express your displeasure at Dawson going directly to Mrs. Wong. *And* just to tidy things off, you copy the letter to Scott, Lumsden and Wong."

I nodded indignantly. "Damn right I did."

"So VISA has now been told of the status of all the merchants in question, and knows full well that not only will JCB continue seeking new merchants, it even plans to implement internal policies. In other words, what you're saying to VISA is that the bank intends on trying to improve the system of certification."

"Exactly."

"And, for the record, there was no correspondence from Scott, Lumsden, Wong, Wiggan or anyone within the bank correcting you on the issue about JCB taking on new merchants."

"You see any?"

"Yes or no, Yap."

"No," I sighed. "There was no correspondence."

"No one stopped you in the corridor, by the water cooler or parking lot after that. No one came to you and said, 'Look here, Dalton, there's a *new policy* in effect. We are no longer taking on any new merchants, period. So please cease and desist.' No one said or wrote or even hinted anything like that to you."

"Correct."

"Are you absolutely certain?"

"Rass, man!"

"Are you absolutely certain?"

"I'm positive!"

"Alright. Now here's a bit of a knot. Dawson replies to you on July 9, providing a Fraud Transaction Screening Program report on LMP Marketing Ltd, which he says has shown activity up to July 8—even though you had said that the account had been shut down. He urges you again to ensure that there are no further deposits made for LMP, Floral Exchange or Travel Connection. And he reminds you to please let him have the results of your investigation on International Concepts. He copies this letter to Wiggan."

"Right."

"What happened there? Why do we still have an active LMP account?"

"Honestly, Chris, I can't answer that one. I mean, unless I literally stand over my staff, I have to assume for the most part that they follow orders in detail. That had to be a legitimate oversight. I don't know."

"LMP was being processed by Reaume's bank in Antigua, right?"

I nodded. "And please understand that there was never any trouble with Reaume. None."

Chris paused, deep in thought. "This might be a sticky one. All we really have is the fact that they have no evidence linking you to whatever may have caused the LMP account to remain open—or to be reopened, if that's what happened."

"Is that lack of evidence good enough?"

"Under normal circumstances, probably. But the real question is this. Even if you turned out to be the kind of employee they're painting you out to be, why the hell would you reopen the account if its detection was just a matter of time? How would you benefit, exactly?"

"Precisely," I said. "If I'm going to be a crook, I'm going to be *smart* about it. Not sloppy."

Chris laughed in agreement. "Even that flies in the face of your track record of attention to detail. Okay, Dalton. At some point around then, Wiggan asks you about the status of the named accounts, which leads him to jotting that note to Alarene on the fourteenth."

"Right. I believe he had just come back from his two-week vacation, which might be why his note comes no earlier than then."

"So the accounts are now closed. We're now at July 19. This is when you, Mr. Lumsden, Mrs. Wong and Miss Green meet at JCB's offices with a Mr. Greenlese. This Greenlese fellow makes a presentation on behalf of Worldwide Marketing. He's a potential new merchant making his pitch to come on board. He makes his presentation with brochures and all. In the meeting, it is confirmed that a local address is to be used this time. It is also made known that the person who owns Worldwide Marketing is the same person who owns the recently closed Travel Connection—Ms. Bell."

"Correct."

"Now," Chris said carefully, "let's imagine that the other side asks you in court if that didn't raise a red flag for you."

I frowned. "What did? The fact that the same person owned both companies?"

Chris nodded.

"How is that unusual in any way? She wouldn't be the first person to own multiple businesses."

"Agreed, but her Travel Connection had just been cancelled, had it not?"

"Yes, but on a technicality about the foreign address. This time she was setting up her business locally—trying to be compliant. And as for VISA's queries about Travel Connection's transactions, remember that she had defended them rather well, as far as I was concerned. So, no, no red flag for me. And clearly none for Marketing either, based on the reaction of those in the meeting and Lumsden's memo."

"Fair enough," he said. "We move on. Lumsden memos you two days later saying that Worldwide looks like 'an attractive source of new business', but suggests asking them to put more security measures in place, like a Letter of Credit. You respond with your own handwritten note to him on the face of his memo, essentially agreeing with having Worldwide Marketing establish a Letter of Credit."

"Right."

"And so, as a result of that meeting and Lumsden's memo, an account was opened for Worldwide Marketing."

"Yes."

"And once more so that I have it clear, Lumsden would have been there in the capacity of —? "

"Ewart's second in command. And Ewart was away on vacation at the time. So Lumsden would have been the most senior person in attendance representing the Retail and Marketing side of things."

"So as far as you were concerned, Marketing had given its thumbs up. Not even a single complaint from Mrs. Wong?"

I folded my arms, fighting the annoyance brewing inside me. "*Again,* based on the fact that no one on Marketing's side raised any objections in the meeting, and based on Lumsden's subsequent memo, my impression was that yes, Marketing was more than okay with it."

"That very day, July 21, Mrs. Wong memos Wiggan. She tells him that while they have not processed any new sales vouchers since July 2, the same six accounts still remain open to facilitate credits. And she repeats VISA's demand that they be completely closed on the bank's books. Wiggan then scribbles a note to Lumdsen on the face of the memo dated the twenty-ninth, saying simply *George, please follow up on this.*"

I frowned. "He should have been hopping mad, right?"

"Exactly. Once again, Dalton, remember the premise of their attack—you're supposed defiance. If we are to believe the bank's position that you had opened these accounts behind their backs, in blatant contravention of a Board decision, then Wiggan's reaction would seem to be way off course. Much too, anemic. He should have been tying you to the stakes by now."

I blinked and hid a smile as I marvelled at the thought process of the legal mind. "Yes, Mr. Dunkley. I see what you mean."

"Meanwhile, on July 26, you write Dawson confirming the closure of another merchant, International Concepts."

"By then we had done our investigation on International Concepts and agreed that they needed to be shut down."

"Okay excellent. So you concurred with VISA's suspicions on that particular merchant."

I held up my index finger. "*After* investigating, yes."

"Weren't you about to go on vacation around then?"

I nodded once. "The very next day, actually," I said. "That memo to Dawson on the twenty-sixth was probably the last thing I did on telemarketing before packing my bags."

"So as of July 26, you're no longer around for almost a month. We can assume that Lumsden gets his handwritten note from Wiggan three days later, because on that day he memos your George Beckford ordering the accounts completely closed. Again this is for the same group that VISA was upset about—Travel Connection, Floral Exchange and so on. But by now you're up in Toronto with your family—"

"—running up and down the CN Tower—"

"—meanwhile back at the ranch, the correspondence from VISA continues. On the twenty-ninth Soublette writes to you. I guess he didn't know you were on vacation. He writes complaining about Worldwide Marketing. These are the same people who you all met with on the nineteenth, and for whom you ordered an account to be opened. On August 9, Scott instructs Lesley Hew by memo to shut down Worldwide with immediate effect. He copies it to you and George Beckford. August 10. Dawson writes another scathing letter, this time addressed to Ewart Scott. In it, he refers to a telephone conversation they had just had that same day, and reprimands the bank for acquiring VISA merchants that have been laundering for other merchants in the States. He also confirms that they're in violation of the local paper rule. He goes on to advise that several of the merchants were *not* in the business they purported to be in, and raps the bank on the knuckles for not carrying out the requisite background checks." Suddenly Chris stopped reading and stared at the letter.

"Dunkley?"

"Hold on. Something's not—" Two seconds later, he released a near-delirious whoop. "Look at this, Yap! See this letter dated August 10 from Dawson to our friend Mr. Scott?"

"Yes?"

"On August 10 he blasts Scott first by telephone. *Then* he puts his complaints in writing the very same day. And guess which merchant is included in the list." My eyes followed his index finger to the name he'd just mentioned not a few minutes before.

"Worldwide Marketing? But hadn't Scott ordered that account closed the day before by memo to Lesley?"

Chris folded his arms across his chest almost beaming. "Looks like that's what they want us to think."

I leaned forward slowly. "Go on."

"Well, you were still on holiday at the time. But check your original stash of correspondence. The set you copied when you were fired. There's a good chance that the memo dated the ninth is not in there. It's not in there, Yap, because it was most likely written after August 10, and backdated. That has to be what happened."

Suddenly I was following his train of thought. "So what you're saying is, why else would Dawson be ranting and raving about it on the tenth, unless the account was still open up to that point."

"Precisely."

"Son of a bitch! Who do you think did it?"

"We can't say who, and it really doesn't matter. Look at the surrounding content. Look at what is *not* said in their correspondence. There is no reference anywhere by either Dawson or Scott that Scott had already ordered Worldwide cancelled. It gives no hint of Scott taking steps to rectify the situation. What's more, one just doesn't get the feeling from his letter that Scott considered the opening of any of these accounts to be a rogue act by you. See what I mean? Because if that had been the case, believe me, Mr. Scott would have been well within his right to cry foul."

"He'd have probably started giving me hell about it from then." I stared at Dunkley, still reeling from what we had just uncovered.

"Yap? You understand now what we're looking at?" Dunkley was almost smiling now.

"Yes, sir," I said with the tone of someone who had just discovered a dirty little secret.

"Good. Okay, the letter ends with a suggestion that the bank freeze any deposits held for these merchants if the local law so allows. August 13—more correspondence from VISA. Meanwhile our Mr. Yap is still on holiday."

"Enjoying my calm before the storm."

"This time a VISA Security Director, a Mr. Schetinno, writes to a Ms. Bond of JCB." Chris glanced up. "We even have a Bond in the mix? You don't say! Who is she?"

"Assistant Manager of the Credit Card Centre."

"Mr. Schetinno claims that, despite previous assurances from the bank that Worldwide had been shut down, VISA is still seeing activity on their part. Schetinno asks Bond to contact him immediately as they've been trying to reach her 'to no avail,' it says here. He closes by advising that VISA will take appropriate action if the situation is not corrected."

"Funny. That's the same complaint they made of me. Can't reach me. Can't find me."

"When someone's in a hurry nothing moves fast enough. Now," he cleared his throat. "On August 17, Scott confirms to Dawson by memo that the same merchants in question have been closed 'in our books'—with the exception of World Wide Marketing, although he goes on to say that no further transactions have been processed on the latter account. I presume that means processing of sales vouchers. What does all this mean exactly?"

"That there is now zero activity from the debit or credit side. So this means the accounts are dead. Nothing can be processed now. Not even a legitimate chargeback. Iceberg city."

"Understood. Now the real fun begins. August 17. A severely pissed off Ms. Bell of Worldwide Marketing writes to the bank, specifically to the attention of you, Ewart Scott, George Beckford and Lesley Hew. Again, you're still away. In a nutshell, Bell is furious that Worldwide's account has been suspended without notice or cause, and is asking that the account be reinstated so that the transactions already authorized and captured can be settled. In the body of her letter she hurls threats of taking legal action through VISA, MasterCard and the court system if necessary. Finally, she closes off by stating for the record how unprofessionally and unacceptably the closing of the account was handled by the bank's staff."

I gave a smug nod. "She took the words right out of my mouth."

"August 19. A clearly jolted George Lumsden writes Dawson attaching Bell's letter, and highlights the fact that she's threatening legal action. Here's the part I like: *We require from you information which would enforce our action other than the speculation which it appears has been used in support of the suspension of this account.* So now they want something more substantial. Anyway, VISA seems to have provided him some evidence, but after that there seems to be nothing further on the matter. We move on to August 25. Soublette writes Bond asking her for information on the same six merchants. Bond complies the following day."

"I had returned from vacation just before then."

"Rested but clueless?"

I squeezed my eyes shut for a second. "Not quite clueless. Wiggan had made that call to me in Toronto, remember? The one where he's asking me how I could bring in these people? That kind of told me that something was going on in my absence. And then—" My voice dropped at the memory of returning to the cold shoulders and unsettling glances of my former colleagues. Somewhere inside of me a small flame ignited. I could feel the burn in my stomach.

"Dalton?"

Chris's voice echoed. "Sorry, Dunkley. Lumsden was the one who came into my office to update me on what had happened while I was away. That's when I first learned that the whole thing had crashed."

"Not even Scott himself, huh."

I merely shook my head.

Dunkley continued. "Okay. The first post-vacation action we see from you in terms of telemarketing is a memo you wrote to Mr. Reaume on August 27. In it, you advise him that Ewart Scott will be calling him on the following Monday to discuss Reaume setting up a Letter of Credit so that JCB can release 50 percent of the funds frozen in his account. Can I therefore presume there was some sort of earlier telephone conversation with you and Reaume?"

"Oh yes," I said raising my eyebrows at the memory of a most irate Mel Reaume. "He called almost as soon as I returned, frantic and angry because his business had been caught in the net when JCB decided to freeze everyone's accounts across the board."

"His merchant bank, yes?" Chris confirmed.

"Right. In Antigua. They were involved in telemarketing over there too, but they needed us to process their paper since Antigua had no principal VISA member. That's how it all began, remember? They couldn't do it alone, and so they needed to look within the region for a principal member."

"Right. Okay. September 2. One month to go before your dismissal. This time Wiggan gets a letter from a Mr. Ramirez, a VISA Vice President. Mr. Ramirez claims that repeated requests by VISA for information from JCB on their merchants' accounts have been ignored. That's a strange statement given Bond's reply the week before in which she furnishes the information. But anyway, Ramirez goes on to say that due to the now certain exposure to VISA, JCB will have to increase its guarantee to VISA from US$100,000 to $500,000 by September 7." Chris whistled.

I laughed. Not my usual boom but it felt good. "Uh huh. A lot of money to have to cough up in five days."

"A nasty little sum indeed. The bank could not have been too happy with that one."

"No, indeed."

"Well, our ever polished Mr. Wiggan replies to Ramirez on the sixth, apologizes profusely, announces that he's going to order an internal audit, and asks that Ramirez reconsider the amount of the guarantee. He copies the letter to you, Ewart Scott and the internal auditor himself, Emmanuel Obasare. Meanwhile on the seventh, Reaume writes Scott, most likely pursuant to their telephone conversation, demanding that the bank release the funds due to Reaume's merchant bank for credit card transactions processed by JCB. His two-page letter cites all sorts of problems he's had with JCB from June

172

to July, including the fact that he wasn't advised that the bank had stopped processing VISA and MasterCard transactions in July, and confirms that to date his percentage of chargebacks has been less than a percent." Chris raised an eyebrow and paused for a second. "Is that right? Just one lousy percent?"

I shrugged. "Like I said, Reaume's bank was never a problem."

"Okay, he also details the status of LMP's processing and chargebacks. He ends his letter with a stern '(. . .) *to refuse to release any of our funds for no apparent reason while you continue to deny us processing leaves us no recourse but to request an investigation by VISA International or recourse through the Courts.'* Well clearly he's unhappy. And he sounds genuinely bewildered."

"Boy, Chris." This time there was ice in my tone. "I don't know these people, okay? I wasn't the one who introduced them to the bank. But if there were persons up to no good in this whole scheme—and it now seems there might have been some shady characters out there—I am pretty sure Mr. Reaume was not involved. He got hurt like some other innocent people."

Chris nodded slowly. For a few seconds the table fell silent. He released a sigh that was just barely audible. "Let's press on," he said, clearing his throat. "September 9, Palmer writes your George Beckford a short letter discussing the deductions made to cover the security deposit being retained by FTA. You scribble a note at the bottom for Neville Parkinson's attention, basically just forwarding the letter to him." Chris looked up. "Seems like business as usual. But whether it was or not, the man does end his letter by saying that the bank should call if it had any queries."

"And that would have been up to Neville," I snapped. I reached for the teapot and poured. This time there was no more steam. I stifled an expletive.

"Exactly. September 13. You get a letter from LMP Marketing and wait now. They're based out of Antigua? Well then, if they're in the region, how are they breaking the VISA local paper rule?"

I shrugged and shook my head. "Like I said, I was never perfectly clear on it but as that was not my area of responsibility, I didn't spend much time on it."

"Okay," he replied. "We'll make a note of that. Anyway, this Peter LeMay of LMP refers to a telephone conversation you had with him on the tenth. What was the call about? You remember?"

"I was most likely investigating some transactions that MasterCard was querying."

"Yes," Chris said, already midway through the letter. "LeMay is protesting any insinuation that LMP has processed fraudulent or counterfeit transactions, and welcomes any investigation by VISA, MasterCard or JCB's internal audit. Oh, now *this* is interesting. He questions openly whether MasterCard is aware that LMP is in the *Audiotext* business, which he says can generate thousands of transactions per month. He even encloses a file printout of the transactions being questioned, showing all the nitty-gritty details you could want and more." Chris glanced up. "Doesn't sound like he's trying to hide anything either!" He continued reading. "He then ends with an equally bitter '*it is indeed both unfortunate and frustrating that such detailed explanation are required for such minor situations when the major problem of not releasing funds due us has still not yet been addressed. We have been extremely patient while your Bank has been attempting to resolve this problem, even offering to issue a Letter of Credit for the total amount of funds held.*' Another unhappy customer. The plot is really thickening now."

"And we're getting close to termination day. Look at this next letter," I said sounding somewhere between confused and anxious. While Chris was reading LeMay's letter, I had pulled out the next document that came after it in the bundle. "It's from LeMay again, directly to Obasare, dated the fifteenth."

"So Wiggan is making good on his promises to VISA of an internal audit? Not wasting any time."

"Seems so," I said, now reading the letter. "LeMay is providing Obasare with correspondence between Reaume and Scott on the seventh, correspondence between me and him on the thirteenth, and his Company's articles of incorporation and so on. But further on he says something interesting. And I quote, *'Unfortunately numerous requests on our part went unanswered due to the fact that we had no direct contact with JCB. The Ceridian software furnished to us for processing came from Richard McGranahan, not Ceridian. Bill Todd informed me that Richard McGranahan worked for the Bank assisting new clients in processing and giving technical support. Richard McGranahan described it as bootleg software that would enable us to start processing.'* And then he repeats his frustration at not being told that JCB had ceased processing transactions."

Dunkley frowned. "What's all that about?"

"Not sure, not sure," I mumbled, still reading.

"Well, we already know that Marketing had not been advising these merchants about the closures, so—"

And then I interrupted. "Oh, God."

Chris stopped. "What's the matter?"

I could feel that familiar surge in my stomach. "Listen to this. LeMay then says that he made repeated calls to Bill Todd, who could only tell him that Dalton Yap was on vacation, and that he should not be talking to other people at JCB because the situation would be resolved once Dalton Yap returned." I looked at Chris. "What the hell?"

Chris grabbed the letter and continued reading. "*I feel that my business has suffered because someone made a*

*unilateral decision, without investigating the facts, to suspend
the transactions of several businesses because of the actions
of one (. . .). I find it hard to believe that a bank of the size
and reputation of JCB could allow this to continue for months
without ever issuing one piece of correspondence to me offering
some form of explanation.* Hmm."

I pushed my chair back with a loud scrape and began pacing
on my side of the kitchen table. Part of my shirt stuck out at my
waist. I just left it there. "That part about not talking to anyone
else in the bank. What the hell is that, Chris? Even worse, Todd
tells the man not to worry because as soon as Dalton Yap returns
he'll take care of it? Do you know how that sounds, man?"

Chris remained seated but raised his palms at me. "Hold
on, Yap, hold on. Relax. It could be one of several things,"
he said. "It could just be that Todd thought you were the
most competent one in there. Or maybe Todd was just more
comfortable with you since he'd been dealing with you from
the start. We get that way sometimes, right? We go to the
same bank teller we always go to, that kind of thing."

"Maybe," I shot back, turning squarely to face him, "but
if you're the opponent trying to pin this whole mess on me,
this kind of shit is just what they want to hear, right? I mean,
come on!"

"It's a sick comedy of errors. Don't worry about LeMay's
letter, Dalton." Chris was genuinely calm and I mentally
latched on to that. "The evidence is still in our favour, and far
outweighs Todd's impression of who's in charge at the bank
or his motives for wanting to keep Reaume at bay—if there
are even any. But let me ask you this. At *no* point was there an
emergency meeting called by Wiggan or Scott concerning this
whole mess? Not before or after your vacation? There was no
big meeting in the boardroom or someone's office at which
all parties involved were present and asked to flesh out the
details or figure out where it might have all gone wrong? No

meeting was called with a VISA representative? None of that ever happened?"

Mentally exhausted, I sank back into the chair and stayed in a slouched position. "No. Nothing like that. Not even close."

"Now that I find intriguing."

I threw my hands open in frustration. "That's what I didn't understand at the time. I still maintain that if the bank had made a graceful exit, it could have all been okay. We were all educated, intelligent professionals. All we needed to do was sit our asses down at one of those expensive boardroom mahogany tables and think it out like rational, intelligent managers. That was all we had to do."

Chris shook his head. "Yap. You don't get it. If I didn't know better, I'd say that someone *did* sit down and put on their thinking cap. That's when that someone realized that the last thing they needed was a meeting that would expose the blunders. Maybe it was too far gone by then."

"So, what? In desperation they go after someone else?"

"It's the whole jungle theme, my friend. Self preservation. It's an emotion that will drive the best of men to places they never thought they could go."

I conceded with a weary nod.

"Okay," Chris continued. "Let's wrap this up. September 22. Ken Palmer and George Beckford communicate concerning activity on JCB's accounts—meaning, the transfers and withdrawals and so on. Two days later on September 24, George asks Palmer to provide details of the almost half a million dollar security deposit held up to June 18, 1993."

I raised an eyebrow. "First time I'm seeing those, actually."

"Anything unusual here?"

"No, I guess not."

"So nothing in here alarms you. If you had seen this before you left you wouldn't have thought anything of it."

"*Alarm* me? Hell, Chris, I'd have praised Beckford for taking the initiative. I was his manager for God's sake. I damn well expect such details to be brought to the fore."

"Good answer," my lawyer replied.

Tired and no longer willing to even feign patience, my eyebrows crinkled over my burning eyes. Sometimes during these sessions, my sense of the normal and the ridiculous often merged, and existed in my mind as one giant, irritatingly blurred line.

"It's a good response," Dunkley continued, "because we want to show the Court that you, Dalton Yap, walked into that bank every day with no other intention than to just do your job as efficiently as you could. We want to show them that you always had their interest at heart, and acted accordingly. We want to show that you have nothing to hide." My young lawyer leaned back in his chair, folded his arms and smirked as if he'd just thrown a royal straight flush. "Dalton, my friend and client, it is my opinion that you're an unfortunate victim of corporate sloppiness. I'll admit it. It is downright frightening to see how someone's life can trip into mayhem because of a handful of undocumented decisions. My *God*, is it ever frightening. I can't even begin to imagine how many out there have unknowingly come close to standing in your shoes. But mark my words, Yap. You can't see it now, but we'll be the ones laughing in the end. I promise you that."

NINE

DAY ONE OF THE TRIAL. MONDAY, SEPTEMBER 17, 1996

SUPREME COURT OF JUDICATURE OF JAMAICA

I don't think I uttered two words the first morning of my trial. I couldn't.

I dressed carefully, with the attention of an army cadet preparing for inspection. The dark suit, one I had worn often before, surprised me with a loose fit that forced me to go one hole back in my leather belt. At least I no longer had that pot belly to complain about.

Dunkley ascribed to the notion that it mattered how you presented yourself in the courtroom. He said that while the facts cannot be disputed, your spirit inevitably helps to paint the picture of the person that you are, even if all you're doing is just sitting there. "We may be judges and lawyers," he had lectured me during one of our final preparation sessions, "but we're still emotional beings. If you feel you want to show them what you're going through, Dalton, don't try to be a tough man and hold back. Just be human, but always be real." A seasoned judge, he warned sternly, would know when it was just an act.

Pauline went with me that morning to Chris and Norman's office, where we were to meet before all walking together to the courthouse. The rest of the family would be waiting for us there.

179

I have taken hundreds of thousands of steps all over this globe. Few come to mind as clearly as the short walk I had to make that September day. After the first few reluctant steps away from the safety of Dunkley's building, my wife fastened her arm onto mine. I clutched her nervous hand and shielded my eyes from the bright sun with a hard squint. I wanted to be ill right there on the sidewalk.

Scenes from my dismissal began flashing in my head as cars hurried by without concern. Dunkley said something to me, but I was unable to focus. I only heard utterances, not words. I frowned at him, my mouth dry, my voice barely stronger than a whisper. Around me the shabby two-storey buildings swayed and rocked like passers-by waving me on. My eyes gripped onto each one searching desperately for a sign of what was to come. We finally turned the corner to see the courthouse waiting. Pauline flinched. I looked down at her arm to see that my fingers had been digging into her skin. Just ahead of us the opposing team was entering the building. Minutes later, after a numb exchanging of social pleasantries—as was expected in our modern-day field of engagement—we were walking into our assigned courtroom.

My skin prickled as I stepped inside the sleepy room with its dull white ceilings and dark wood benches. The sound I remember most clearly was that of my heart pounding in what seemed to be my ears, not my chest. One by one my family took turns hugging me, each seeming to squeeze tighter than the other, giving me their energy, feeding me wishes in both English and Chinese for victory and vindication. It was hardest to let my father go. He could not speak. Instead, he squeezed my shoulder before stepping back to the spectators' bench.

When the doors closed, we were all locked away from an entire universe. For the duration of my trial I would live in another. I would not care about what was happening beyond those wooden doors. The weather, the winning lottery number, the hottest restaurant to eat in—they were all murky, watery images with no meaning to my life now.

The clerk of the court began the proceedings on time.

Please stand!

Day one and the other side looked ready to pounce, confident of victory. Fighting for the plaintiff were Nicole Lambert, Patrick McDonald and Michael Hylton, Q.C. Giving evidence against me were my former boss, Lloyd Wiggan; the colleague who fired me, Ewart Scott; Alarene Wong who had since become Alarene Knight; and the bank's former legal counsel, Camille Facey. The plaintiff would also be calling Maria Green, a member of my former Operations Division, and George Beckford, who also once reported to me. Strangely enough, neither Neville Parkinson nor Emanuel Obasare was listed to take the stand for the plaintiff.

Over in our corner, we sat ready in order of rank—my Queen's Counsel in the first row, followed by Norman and Christopher in the second, while I sat in the third alone. Our relay team was in place. At Dunkley's suggestion, we had also secured the services of a court recorder. He did not want anything to go missing in the notes of evidence.

Presiding above us all in his elevated platform was the Honourable Mr. Justice Seymour Panton, bespectacled, robed and wigged. As he walked in, my thoughts flew to the job that lay at his feet. He was, I reminded myself, a man who had once been a lawyer. He, too, was once on his feet required to present just one side of a case. Now he had the task of hearing and assessing two well-honed arguments, at the end of which he was to come to a decision—a decision about a stranger's future. In the time that it would take for us to make our respective cases, he would have to dig into the recesses of his mind and intuition, hand down his judgment and feel confident that it was, in fact, the correct one. As much as I hated mine, his was not a position I envied much either.

For a while, I could only feel the numbness as I wandered through the corridors of my memory, still bewildered at how I had managed to fall into this nightmare.

It's 1976 and I'm a spirited, lanky teenager in shorts and a t-shirt, heading for the Mandeville market in my father's white Subaru. I am the vehicle's sole occupant and am enjoying the thrill of the two-minute ride between my house and the market on a sunny Saturday afternoon. As I near the round-a-bout in the town's historic and motley centre, I suddenly come across a crowd angry with its politicians and the world. Before I can maneuver the wheel, the vehicle is engulfed by the mob, which is now literally rocking it side to side and off its small wheels, chanting "Chiney man! Chiney man!" By the grace of God I manage to pull away without harm to myself or the people around me. My nerves are shaken on the outside, but as I scramble for home clutching the steering wheel, I know that everything else is intact. I am still the person that I was when I climbed out of bed that morning. The incident was the last time I'd really ever experienced, firsthand, the ugly side of human nature.

Twenty years later I find myself a 36 year-old husband and father, sitting in an old courtroom in a dark suit defending my honour. My honour. That was the difference between this and the market incident. The mob, as angry as it was, held no personal poison for Dalton Yap, the man. This time the attack was personal. This time it was not about rattling my nerves or attacking the colour of my skin. It was about challenging my integrity. My credibility. This time the assault came not from strangers, but from those who once sat across from me at elegant tables, shared meals with me, and knew the names of my wife, my children, and my siblings. They had once been like family.

Jamaica Citizens Bank versus Dalton Yap!

And then it came. Dunkley sprang to his feet before the plaintiff could utter the first word of its opening submissions. "Mi Lord, we are *not* going anywhere with this case until someone tells me what happened in the matter of Jamaica Citizens Bank versus one Ken Palmer in Chicago!"

With that he took his seat and pulled his head up as the scrambling began on the other side. I'd have paid millions— okay maybe just two—to capture on film the look of surprise on the faces of the opposing counsel. I remember someone from the other side jumping to his feet assuring the defence and Justice Panton that they'd be duly filing an amendment to their original statement of claim, *immediately.*

The apology did little to counteract Dunkley's well-delivered upper hook. My defence team had quickly exposed the first fault line in the plaintiff's argument—literally within minutes of the trial's commencement. Now sullied was the plaintiff's pristine image of a noble bank filled only with individuals of pure integrity. Suddenly saddled with an unforeseen credibility issue, the plaintiff now had the added pressure of working uphill to persuade the judge, who suddenly had reason to look at them somewhat askance. Within minutes court was adjourned. Day one was over.

Chris's strategy had paid off. The next day we eagerly marched into our battleground and began with the plaintiff's hurriedly amended statement of claims. It led to three allegations out of nine being dismissed, and a much-reduced lawsuit against me from US$2 million to US$1.2 million. My burden was almost half gone, and so was the plaintiff's wind. Among the six allegations left standing were the more obscene ones, including the establishing of credit card relationships with the telemarketers in question without the authority or knowledge of the bank, delaying compliance with VISA and MasterCard, delaying communication to the executive on the problems arising, and failing and refusing to terminate the contracts with the telemarketers when instructed to do so, while facilitating the opening of an office in Kingston in order to circumvent the regulations. Thanks to Chris's move and the resultant shift of power on day one, I could ease into a cautious level of hope, despite the grave charges that remained.

It would be unbearable to recount every moment of the trial. What remains in my memory are the salient points of evidence that would lead to Justice Panton's judgment, as one by one we took turns on the witness stand claiming, confirming or conceding.

A cool and seemingly distant Wiggan was the first to take the stand the next day on Wednesday, September 18. I braced myself. It would be the first time I'd hear my former boss speak since October 1993. He was offered to sit on the chair provided, but he declined and remained standing.

His back remained perfectly rigid, boardroom style. For a few seconds he looked like my old boss and none of this was happening. I admit that the issue for me was probably one of ego. I needed to convince myself that I wasn't a bad judge of character—that I had not been that naïve all along. I wanted to believe that I was correct in my initial assessment of the person, even if he did do something completely out of character. For the entire time that he stood there, my old boss would not once glance in my direction.

The first part of Wiggan's evidence was the easiest to hear. He would confirm in his most business-appropriate voice what the performance evaluations would not permit him to deny—that up until the period in question, he had considered me an outstanding employee. He explained the chain of events that brought FTA and Ken Palmer into our lives back in 1991, and agreed that it had been the responsibility of the Marketing Department to acquire and screen new merchants for the bank.

At counsel's table, Chris's pen was kept busy as Wiggan proceeded to make claim after claim in the most concise and flawless language I had ever heard him use. In that regard he kept pace with the lawyers, who had to be excruciatingly accurate in their word selection. For a fleeting moment I was almost ready to applaud him for the performance, but that moment passed the minute the contradictions began.

He insisted that a decision to stay away from telemarketing had been taken at a monthly executive meeting in early 1993, and named March as the month in which the decision had allegedly been made. He said that if Ewart Scott was indeed involved in the telemarketing business from March, he, Wiggan, had no knowledge of that—including the signing of the Market and Servicing and Trade Secret Agreements.

The former Managing Director then testified, much to my disbelief, that it was not until much later in July that he became aware that the bank had entered into the telemarketing business. With respect to FTA, he claimed that it was not until in December 1993 that he realized FTA had access to the bank's Daily Settlement Account, although he conceded that the bank's legal department had vetted the document to which he eventually affixed his signature. With regard to the Audiotext conference, my old boss would at first say that he didn't know if my attendance had been approved by him or not. However, upon being shown his signature on the approval form, he then said that he had assumed the conference would have been about legitimate business.

Wiggan's testimony against me was one of his last acts as an employee of the bank. His resignation, which he had handed in earlier that summer, would take effect just before the trial's end. I would not see him again for many years.

We returned the next day feeling even more relaxed. The plaintiff's first witness had not done any damage to our

185

defence. We were ready—almost curious now—to see what else they had to throw at us. Surely there had to be something more. Something we missed.

A more unsettled Ewart Scott was the second to be sworn in and take the stand, which he did just minutes after ten that morning. Once again the session began with the courtroom formalities and mode of language that had little resemblance to what was being used just beyond its doors on the hot and dusty streets of Kingston:

Mr. Michael Hylton: "Mr. Scott, would you like a seat?"

Mr. Ewart Scott: "Yes, thanks."

Mr. Michael Hylton: "Mi Lord, may the witness sit?"

His Lordship: "Yes."

Mr. Michael Hylton: "I ask you to keep your voice up and in that position."

Mr. Ewart Scott: "Yes. I will."

By then the man who had kicked me out of my corporate life had moved on and up the ladder, now as President of the then-new Horizon Merchant Bank and the group of companies to which it belonged. As he was also the plaintiff's witness, Michael Hylton examined him first, beginning with the telemarketing issue. Seated behind my legal team, I made my own notes as Scott stitched for the court his almost patchwork version of the telemarketing fiasco:

"When were you first aware of the issues as to whether the bank should become involved or not?"

"In January 1993 when I took over the role of General Manager, Retail Banking and Marketing. It was at that stage that I first met the telemarketers, or whatever you call it."

"At this time when you first met them, was anyone else present?"

"Yes. It was at a meeting that I attended at the bank, which would be Mrs. Knight, Mr. Yap, and myself and I think two of the opposing parties. I cannot remember their names at this time."

"Did you know those two gentlemen before?"

"No."

"I am assuming they were gentlemen. Were they?"

"They were men."

(*Laughter.*)

"Was a decision arrived at, at that meeting?"

"The result of that meeting—we decided that further investigation would be done. That is, essentially, what was decided."

"Was the issue raised at any subsequent meeting?"

"The issue was raised at an executive meeting, which I think occurred in February where the overall idea of a business plan or business idea was put forward to the executive. The decision taken at that meeting was that it was too risky. The risk was not worth the effort."

It did not escape the defence that Scott and Wiggan did not seem to remember exactly when this most pivotal executive meeting had taken place. Sitting above on his platform, Justice Panton listened intently as Scott verbally weaved and bobbed, insisting under Hylton's examination that he only first realized the bank had gone ahead with the telemarketers on May 3 when Alarene showed him the letter of complaint from VISA. I caught myself snorting bitterly through my nostrils as the incredible story continued to pour out of the mouth of my former colleague:

(Hylton) "Between the February meeting (. . .) and your receiving this memorandum in May, did you ever see those two men again?"

(Scott) "Yes, I did. I saw—I am not clear as to the exact date, but I had a meeting with Mr—I think his name is Todd, in Mr. Yap's office. We were discussing—"

(Hylton) "One second! Watch his Lordship's pen!"

(Scott) "Yes. We were discussing about the product that was being offered by the company called Ceridian, which was called at the time TeleMoney."

(Hylton) "What is TeleMoney?"

(Scott) "TeleMoney is a product that offers cash advances to people who have credit cards. It is a product which would enable the customer—"

(Justice Panton) "I am hoping that before I leave the scene you can talk as fast as you want and I will be just putting it in and reading it at the same time."

(Scott) "My apologies, sir."

(Justice Panton) "You don't have to apologize. I am just telling you what I am hoping. Five years, ten years. The lawyers won't have to tell you to slow down."

(. . .)

(Hylton) "Now you can go back, Mr. Scott, to page 161 of the Bundle."

(Scott) "Yes."

(Hylton) "There is a handwritten note at the bottom of that document?"

(Scott) "Yes."

(Hylton) "Who wrote that?"

(Scott) "I did."

(Hylton) "Can you tell me what it says?"

(Scott) *"Dalton. Please note urgently and take appropriate action."*

(Hylton) "And then you signed?"

(Scott) "I had also signed the front part but I added afterwards 'and take appropriate action' and I signed again."

(Hylton) "What was your reaction, if any, to the statement in that memorandum to the effect that Mrs. Knight was unable to locate the Merchant Agreement, and was advised by Mr. Beckford in Operations that the account was opened by Mr. Yap?"

(Scott) "At the time my reaction would have been that Mr. Yap as General Manager of Technology and Operations may have been testing, may have been doing tests. I have no idea as to why he would necessarily open these accounts. Further, based on what I saw here, I thought it was necessary that he take corrective action to protect the bank."

Back in the benches I leaned forward and shoved a bewildered face near Chris's. "I don't believe it!" I hissed as quietly as I could. "He's using *TeleMoney* as an excuse?" But Chris could not look up. His hand was already flying across a note pad with the words "cross-examination" on the top.

Hylton took his witness through several more pieces of correspondence, including the July 2nd VISA letter that bore his handwritten note to me urging me to *take appropriate action.* When asked by his own Queen's Counsel why his notes fell short of instructing me to close the accounts, it was Mr. Scott's pathetic argument that as a colleague he had no authority to give me instructions. Clearly he had forgotten that it was on the basis of his department's written instructions, signed no less by his subordinates, that my department had promptly closed the accounts. Clearly neither he nor the plaintiff's legal team thought to ensure that Alarene would not punch holes in this statement the very next day.

Hylton then moved on to the matter of the contract with FTA and signature card for the Daily Settlement Account with the Suburban Bank in Bolingbrook, Illinois. While Scott admitted to signing both back in 1991, he attempted to convince the Court that he only did so obligingly, in both cases. He went at length to explain that he had assumed I would follow the procedure for executing Board Resolutions, a procedure he claimed supposedly existed within the bank at the time. He remained stuck on the theme of my talent for skillful persuasion for much of the time he sat on the witness stand.

When it was time for my Queen's Counsel, Dennis Morrison, to begin the cross-examination, I thought I detected Ewart shifting in his seat ever so slightly. Morrison took Scott back to early 1993 when the meetings with Todd and McGranahan were taking place. Slowly, Morrison lifted the lid off what smelled to be a simmering pot of miscommunication and lackadaisical approach to structure and detail on the part of the bank. The healthy dash of bucking egos made the brew even spicier. While Scott admitted to having had initial talks about telemarketing with them, he claimed that by March the discussions on that subject had ended:

> "The discussions in March, you say, were not in connection with telemarketing? You had discussions in connection with something else?"

"Yes."

"Which was?"

"TeleMoney."

"Were these discussions which you were having in connection with TeleMoney taking place with the authority of the Managing Director?"

"To have discussions, I don't need the authority of the Managing Director."

"Was he aware of that?"

"I don't know."

"Did you make him aware of that?

"I don't normally make the Managing Director aware of conversations that I have."

Then there was the WTS Marketing and Service Agreement document that I had passed on to him in March of 1993 through my secretary, after having received it from Richard McGranahan. He claimed to have not seen it until preparing for the trial. He did, however, admit to seeing and signing the Trade Secret Information document and Letter of Intent—but claimed that I had called him into my office where together Bill Todd and I once again supposedly convinced him to sign on the spot. It was Mr. Scott's contention on the stand that he had assumed he was signing a document that would allow the bank to engage in testing the technology that would enable it to enter into the TeleMoney or Quasi Cash business:

"In what circumstances did you affix your signature to this document?"

"Mr. Yap called me into a meeting with Bill Todd. When I went in, Mr. Todd—wherein he provided me with copies of the documentation (. . .) which included the Letter of Intent on the next page. After reading it, going through it, it described the features that we were discussing other than telemarketing, called TeleMoney. It was my understanding that in order for us to do the testing, we needed to sign to allow access to the technology. It is on that basis I signed to allow us to get access to that technology."

(…)

"Was your Managing Director, Mr. Wiggan, aware before you affixed your signature that you were going to do so?"

"No."

"Did you make him aware of this development subsequently?"

"I don't remember?"

"Might you have, do you think?"

"I really don't remember."

He clung to the same shaky memory line when it came to the question of whether or not he had met Mel Reaume in March of 1993, citing his job requirement to meet new people on a regular basis. Dennis let that go, but pressed a little harder on the point that he, Ewart Scott, was only first aware of the bank's involvement in the telemarketing business in May, when Alarene handed him the VISA memorandum:

"Now, you said in answer to my learned friend, that when you received this memorandum, you assumed that Dalton, Mr. Yap, was running some tests. What do you mean by that?"

"Technology Dalton is responsible for. (…) I was not privy to the details of what he was doing. But one thing is clear—on receiving this memorandum I thought that he should take whatever action necessary."

"But this memorandum from Mrs. Wong was in fact referring to *live* transactions, was it not? It speaks of ten transactions being disputed by cardholders?"

"Yes."

"What kind of 'testing' do you think might have been in progress that could have *that* result?"

"I have no idea. However it was my impression that whatever it was, he should take appropriate action."

"You said you assumed he was carrying out tests but you have no idea what tests?"

"With due respect, I am not an expert in technology. I have no idea."

The plaintiff's Queen's Counsel engaged in further re-examination once Morrison was finished questioning Scott. Mr. Hylton had, he told his Lordship, just two questions. The first, which for me seemed somewhat irrelevant, dealt with the current employment of those individuals associated with the trial. From Scott's answer, almost all had left the bank. The second question at the time also seemed puzzling, but it was Scott's suddenly fulsome answer that I found quite telling:

"In answer to another question, you said that the arrangement with the TeleMoney project was never implemented?"

"Yes."

"Why?"

"We got two of their machines and started testing it. We never got around to implementing it and it was subsequently cancelled. I hope the machines were returned."

I could only suppose at the time that the plaintiff's lawyers were trying to prove that TeleMoney had indeed been under serious consideration, to the point where Scott could claim it as the focus of the Letter of Intent, as far as he was concerned, but Ewart's answer proved two things. One, he was quite clear on the particulars of the tests being done for TeleMoney. Two, he could not therefore convincingly turn around and use ignorance on the same point as his defence for signing the Letter of Intent. Call it gut instinct, or maybe it was his slightly raised eye behind his spectacles, but somehow I felt that his Lordship agreed with me.

Maria Green and George Beckford followed in that order in the afternoon session. Each spoke freely and frankly on the issues that the Operations and Technology Division handled day to day such as chargebacks and the opening of accounts. Their testimony showed the Court that my division acted within reason, and according to whatever guidelines were in place, with me at its helm. I'd love to say that we all listened attentively as they took turns explaining methodically items that ranged from obvious to the technical to the plain boring. I watched his Lordship nervously for any signs of a stifled yawn as he continued to labour over his notes. Quite frankly, I couldn't have blamed him if he had succumbed to one.

The plaintiff's witnesses would answer without hesitation that yes, those accounts were in fact ordered opened under my instructions, a point I never disputed. Under examination by Norman Wright, George would acknowledge that while he could name me as the person who ordered the accounts opened, he could not say whether or not I had been following instructions by Marketing, nor was he privy to communication between the division heads. He confirmed that, to his knowledge, VISA International and MasterCard were indeed raising red flags, but also reported, in an equally direct manner, that it was his opinion that I took what he considered to be sufficient action, and investigated their concerns in a satisfactory time frame. When asked about the issue of the chargebacks, Beckford verified that the high percentage of chargebacks shown for the period in question was not a reflection of the percentage that would be settled in favour of the cardholder. Not surprisingly, his reply to questions posed by the plaintiff's Michael Hylton concerning the July 19 meeting with Worldwide Marketing accurately reflected my own impression of that pivotal meeting:

"Do you know who was present at that meeting?"

"I can recall Mr. Yap, Mrs. Alarene Knight now, was Wong then, George Lumsden, Maria Green and myself. I can remember those persons and Mr. Greenlese from Worldwide Marketing being present at the meeting."

"Do you recall any proposal being put forward at that meeting?"

"There was a proposal to open a merchant account in that name for WorldWide Marketing."

"Was there any indication in the course of that meeting as to what address would be used for Worldwide Marketing Company?"

"The address, yes. The address to be used was supposed to be an address in Jamaica, a local address."

"Prior to that meeting, were you involved in any discussions at which that issue was raised, that is to say, the account for Worldwide Marketing and a local address?"

"Yes."

"Could you tell us the circumstances, who said what to whom?"

"I had discussions with Mr. Yap regarding that issue. The issue stemmed from the fact that VISA International had asked us to cease processing transactions for those merchants on the basis that the transactions did not originate in our region, meaning that their regulations required that the transactions needed to have originated in the particular region where the processing is done."

"Did he say anything else?"

"That is the reason why the account was now being opened with a local address for the transactions to originate locally, hence we would be able to process it."

"So an account was later opened in the name of Worldwide Marketing?"

"Yes, an account was opened."

On cross-examination, Norman Wright would address the same issue with Beckford and take it a step further.

"You remember any instructions being given to check the question of a local address or local setting up of an office for this particular company?"

"Yes. I remember there was a discussion."

"And to be even more specific, you remember Mrs. Wong being asked to undertake this particular exercise which would have fallen to her responsibility as the marketing person, to look about that?"

"I don't specifically remember that."

"But as the marketing person that would have been her responsibility."

"Yes."

When it comes to giving testimony, i.e. offering evidence on a matter, credibility becomes the pulse on which the Court must put its finger. At the end of the first day of testimony, we felt it was clear who had been perceived as being sincere.

That weekend, I retreated into a self-made capsule that had room only for my lawyers and perhaps a little too much comfort food. We parted company only to retreat to our homes for some sleep, after hours of literally charting the testimony dished out thus far against the corresponding document numbers. My bubble, now smaller than ever, didn't even allow for the basic manners my poor mother had taught me. I blocked everyone out. My only objective was to hone our argument, and see the sun rise the following Monday so that we could push on and get the hell over with it. I refused to come up for air until we were through. And I, the reluctant star of the show and final witness, had yet to take the stand and face the music.

The trial resumed on Monday just minutes after ten. Alarene Knight was promptly sworn in shortly after that. Like her former colleagues, she was sharply dressed and made for a competent-looking fixture on the witness stand. Unlike her counterparts, however, she appeared quite at ease as she nudged into her seat, seemingly prepared to make the most of the task ahead.

It was a rather entertaining, almost animated, Alarene who smiled and occasionally giggled as she offered her testimony, at times even leaning in towards the lawyers and his Lordship. If I didn't know better, I'd have thought she was actually flirting. I can only speak for my lead counsel, Norman Wright who would cross-examine Mrs. Knight. He was none too amused.

The plaintiff's Queen's Counsel, Michael Hylton, was the first to question the witness. Alarene answered fulsomely his questions on a myriad of administrative issues, a lot of which naturally focused on the merchant agreements and approval process in general. As expected, like Ewart, she too claimed to have had no knowledge of how the merchants in question were acquired by the bank, and denied any involvement on her part. She did, however, concede that she had met some of the individuals involved back in January of 1993 at a meeting she'd been asked to attend by her then-boss, Ewart Scott:

> (Hylton) "Could you tell us what happened at the meeting, if anything?"

> (Knight) "The meeting was really for the bank to process off-shore credit card transactions, how we could process transactions offshore for these gentlemen."

> (His Lordship) "The meeting was to determine *how?*"

> (Knight) "Not *how*. To discuss the *possibility* of processing offshore credit card transactions."

I felt the scowl on my face grow as she went on about the dozens of frightful VISA International alert bulletins she had been receiving, none of which had been passed on to me. Corroborating Ewart's story, she cited the May 3 letter from Soublette as one of the first indicators that new merchants had been brought on board, which resulted in her memo to Ewart Scott—in which she pointed the finger at me. She became further animated when Hylton asked about the July 2 memo from VISA, describing how she had quickly scribbled 'Urgent' on the top left hand corner, and barged into a meeting in which Ewart was sitting to discuss the matter with him. It was her version of the pivotal July 19 meeting while still under Hylton's examination that had me seeing stars:

> (Hylton) "If you could look now at page 291, a memorandum from George Lumsden to Dalton Yap? The first paragraph refers to a meeting on July 19 and

to a proposal put forward by Worldwide Marketing. Do you know anything about that meeting?"

(Knight) "Yes. I was invited to sit in on that meeting."

(Hylton) "Who else was at that meeting?"

(Knight) "Mr. Scott, myself, Mr. Lumsden and two other gentlemen. I don't recall their names."

(...)

(Hylton) "What did they want?"

(Knight) "They wanted to open merchant accounts, which to me, if they wanted to process off-shore credit card transactions, however, they would have to domicile it here in Jamaica."

(Hylton) "What do you mean by domicile?"

(Knight) "In other words, as I said when I spoke of merchant accounts, have a local address coming out of Jamaica as per VISA/MasterCard regulations."

(His Lordship) "So it was going to be a pretense in terms of the address?"

(Knight) "As far as *I'm* concerned!"

(Hylton) "Was there any indication in that meeting as to what the nature of the business was, how the transactions would be entered into?"

(Knight) "I really can't remember.

(Hylton) "What was your reaction?"

(Knight) "Amazement!"

(Hylton) "You were amazed?"

(Knight) "Yes. Because VISA was calling, indicating that we were about to lose our licence and it seems to me, we were trying to get around the process for off-shore transactions."

(His Lordship) "To get around the system?"

(Knight) "The system by domiciling the transactions in Jamaica."

(His Lordship) "When the transactions were really offshore?"

(Knight) "Yes."

(...)

(Hylton) "Was a decision arrived at, at that meeting, as to whether the bank would go further to opening the new accounts?"

(Knight) "No. No decision like that was arrived at."

Alarene continued to dazzle on the witness stand after the lunch break. I clenched my teeth as I sat there speculating the effect her testimony would have on the final outcome, especially where the July 19 meeting was concerned.

When Norman stood up to begin cross-examining her, I could tell that he had had enough. The absence of the normally gentle Nelson Mandelaesque look in his eyes was the tip off. This time they pierced. He began with questions about the January meeting in 1993, and then the one in July. I don't know how my trial compares to others, but this one touched on a range of emotions. We even had flashes of humour that had the courtroom chuckling at times:

(...)

(Wright) "Mrs. Knight, you have told me that you have an excellent memory?"

(Knight) "I do."

(Wright) "Now, please remember what I ask you. And just answer the question and not ramble on. Can you answer the question? Could you say if either of the two gentlemen who were in the first meeting in January were in the meeting in July?"

(Knight) "No."

(Wright) "Fine! This is how you should do it, please. Could you look at page 291 of the second bundle, 1(B) please, Mrs. Knight? Could you please look at the letter, Mrs. Knight? In that letter, Mr. Lumsden recognizes the potential for new business. I am looking at the part that says: 'with reference to our meeting of July 19, the proposal put forward by Worldwide Marketing appears to be an attractive source of new business, and one which could utilize the capabilities of our credit card technology.' You have seen that?"

(Knight) "It is not addressed to me. I am just looking at it. It is not c.c.'d to me. This is the first time I'm seeing it."

(Wright) "You said you were at that meeting?"

(Knight) "Yes and I was very silent."

(Wright) "It is possible, Mrs. Knight, to have a telemarketing arrangement which is profitable, isn't it?"

(Knight) "Yes, because telemarketing is—"

(Wright) "Just answer the question. Please don't anticipate what I'm going to ask you next."

(His Lordship) "She is confusing you?"

(Wright) "No. She can't succeed in that, Mi. Lord."

(His Lordship) "She couldn't, Mr. Wright? Don't be too sure."

(Wright) "Maybe I should call her by her maiden name and we would have a Wright and a Wong?"

(Knight) "That is an assumption. My maiden name is not Wong."

(Wright) "You know, they say two Wrights don't make a Wong. I know you don't want to spend all day here, so let's try and get on."

He then turned to the subject of the pivotal meeting. His objective was to further drive home the fact that even the plaintiff's own witnesses were not in agreement on the bank's internal procedures, and could therefore hardly rap me on the knuckles for disobedience:

"(...) You told us that you were amazed at the proposal being discussed at the meeting. Did you express this? In fact, I think you said you were silent?"

"I spoke to Mr. Lumsden *after* the meeting."

"Your *evidence* is that you were silent at the meeting?"

"Yes. I was."

"My learned friend had asked you a question to which you had started to give a reply—I don't think I got all your answer about how an account is closed, and I understood you to have said it requires a memo from the Marketing section?"

"Yes."

"That is so? Where an account has to be closed, it requires a memo from the Marketing section? Such a memo would be sent to the Operations section?"

"Right."

"And they would act upon it?"

"Right."

Ewart was not in the courtroom at the time, but it didn't prevent me from picturing him sitting there, gulping that one down and getting a sudden brain freeze from it. I leaned forward to share the thought with Dunkley and found him adding yet another note on his yellow pad. He had caught a point I had missed: how telling it was that Alarene claimed to have expressed her concerns *after* the July 19 meeting to George Lumsden—the author of the resultant memo to me approving the new business, and the only JCB person at that meeting who did not testify. And didn't it also seem somewhat odd that she claimed not to have seen the resultant memo until it was shown to her in the courtroom?

It was in the afternoon session that Norman would go after the plaintiff on the allegation that I defied orders to close the accounts, further forcing the plaintiff to retreat into an increasingly tighter corner:

"(. . .) You wrote a memo to Mr. Scott on May 3 and you related what Mr. Soublette had said. (. . .) What action did you take?"

"I reported it to my superior, my General Manager, the same day I got the information from Mr. Soublette and I reported to him directly."

"He was General Manager of the bank?"

"No."

"You were in charge of Marketing?"

"Yes, but no."

"No? I just asked you if you were in charge of Marketing. Apart from the report to your General Manager, Mr. Scott, you took no further action?"

"Well, Mr. Scott—I left it in the hands of—"

"Apart from that letter, you took no further action."

"Not exactly."

"And in fact, the first time you did that which the Marketing Department was required to do, namely do a memo, is the step you took on July 6 (. . .), when by letter to Lesley Ann Hew of Operations, you directed that these accounts be closed immediately? Am I correct?"

"Yes."

Whether intentionally or not, Alarene delivered one to my solar plexus when Norman raised the issue of her management of the department before it was split in 1991. She not only claimed that the US$140,000 worth of MasterCard paper came about *after* FTA had been brought on board—a complete contradiction to Wiggan's version on the same matter—she then insisted that the only reason the operational side was handed over to me was because the portfolio had grown so much. It was because of that, Alarene said, that Wiggan decided to split the department in two, and at no time did I or anyone ever bail her out of any situation. I stifled a look of disbelief. Even Chris couldn't help but turn my way to share his amused look.

The bank's legal counsel, Camille Facey took the stand at half after three. She was the last witness to be called to testify for the plaintiff. Her examination-in-chief and cross-examination lasted only twenty-five minutes in all. She stonily admitted that her department had indeed examined and approved the FTA contract in 1991—the same offensive contract which allowed

FTA to make limited, but nonetheless unilateral withdrawals from the Daily Settlement Account. She then took her time to carefully explain the procedure by which the bank would open an account with another bank. As I listened, I marvelled at the fact that the process, which she was so eloquently describing in beautiful detail for the Court, never made it into something called an internal procedures manual.

Adjournment was taken at five minutes to four that afternoon. After a few utterances from the clerk of the court, each side gathered documents, knocked heads together and conversed while making their way to the door. I squeezed my eyes open and shut a few times to get some more moisture in them as my family waited for me in the hallway.

Within minutes we were crossing over to the parking garage, slowing our pace down just enough to drink in some of the afternoon sunshine, now softer in its final hours. After a full day indoors, the friendly weather felt comforting to the skin. No one commented on the downtown rush hour traffic. By now all manner of vehicles were crawling in a mostly northern direction, under full view of the hills in the background. Dunkley, Norman, Dennis and I walked just ahead of everyone to exchange opinions on the day's events. We paused where our common path ended. Dunkley held back as the other two bid their goodbyes and made for their vehicles.

"Okay, Yap. So far, so good. We're not sporting any black eyes yet. No sign of any smoking gun either. Tomorrow we give our opening submissions. You take the stand day after that. Let me handle the late-night work. All you have to do between now and Wednesday is try to relax."

I think even Chris knew how ridiculous that sounded.

WEDNESDAY, SEPTEMBER 25. Day five of the trial, and the first of my three days on the witness stand.

The news media had been kind enough to make the announcement for my curious public. By now I was becoming familiar with the routine—go through security check, register with the clerk, start walking to your designated courtroom. Around you, the echoes of voices and shoe soles shuffling through the tiled corridors compete with your thoughts as you dodge the cloaked attorneys sweeping past you in twos or threes, their cloaks fluttering behind them at the tails if they're moving quickly. Some walked in suits and carried their robes in blue cloth bags, which were usually slung over their shoulders. In the sea of blue bags, I noticed a handful of red ones hurrying by.

Chris explained that the red bag was a badge of rank, so to speak. It was a silk's way of saying that here was a junior who has done or does exceptional work. This was a junior counsel with whom they were well pleased. It was also an indication that the junior could be on his or her way to silk.

I began to view our courtroom with the sentiments of a patient in a doctor's office. You know the place, you know you need to be there in order for things to get better, but you're cursing the reason that brought you here in the first place. I was a repeat patient. My eyes had learned where to find its particular signs of wear and tear, like the church-style wooden benches that had lost their lustre and squeaked when you moved forward or backward. Or the stagnant dust that covered the long fluorescent light bulbs. I had already stopped struggling with the dull ambient lighting, which also felt tired, as if the bulbs had lost their enthusiasm for serving the public. Through the crack in the door's jamb, the busy sound of others shuffling around in the hallway trying to get to their own courtrooms was now a familiar sound in my ear. A bit harder to ignore was the occasional muffled melee out on the street, between what usually seemed to be an irritated truck driver blaring his deep horn, and a clearly smaller, but no less indignant vehicle.

I had decided on a moderate and greaseless breakfast of just toast and coffee that morning, after carefully weighing two options. Eat less for better intestinal control, but run the risk of running out of steam, or eat heavy for strength, but run the risk of becoming ill from nerves and a full stomach. These things one has to think about when about to face a stressful moment. The last thing you want while under the x-ray lamp is to be slammed with a cold-sweat stomach gripe.

This time my family could not brave watching me in court. They didn't have to explain. I understood. My mother, still in Mandeville with the children, called me no less than three times, crying into the phone about luck and good fortune. Each time I thanked her patiently and begged her not to worry. Each time I tried to distract her with requests to kiss the children for Pauline and me.

The evening before, my legal team and I had replayed the shaky evidence the plaintiff had pulled out of their magic box. Over another home-cooked meal we examined our individual notes and growing list of contradictions and holes in the plaintiff's argument. I was almost disappointed. The hulking monster that had been taunting me for the last three years was little more than a man on stilts. It now seemed apparent that the plaintiff was taking a different approach—trying hard to make the case fit the evidence, but in the end they were left with a bunch of square pegs and round holes.

That night, I lay in my bed replaying the bank's case in my head. Outside, a white owl screeched after its prey. Maybe it already had it caught in its claws. A victorious kill. And then I turned my thoughts to our opening submission.

We had all felt good about Dennis Morrison's performance. While there was no jury for which to display persuasive theatrics, I felt that my Queen's Counsel, even in his decidedly more conservative manner, had delivered our argument spot on. He had nicely set the tempo for my upcoming testimony. You know instinctively when someone believes in what he has said when there is no searching for words, when the cadence of his speech falls flawlessly in line, and his eyes rest comfortably, no—unabashedly—on his captive audience.

The Court calls Mr. Dalton Yap to the stand!

For the few seconds that I stood there before being sworn in, I was swallowed up by a feeling that the centre of the universe had suddenly shifted to me on the stand. In a small way it had. Today the press had their eyes on me. Like Wiggan, I chose to remain on my feet instead of taking a seat on the wooden stool. I would, when my feet began to prickle, eventually lean on it, but I stood the entire time.

Norman handled my examination-in-chief, and gently pushed off with the obligatory and sundry questions confirming my date of birth, address and other personal facts. I used them as practice to find the right pace so that his Lordship could follow, and so that I could steady my tremble.

At first, the experience of giving testimony under oath was what I had imagined it to be. Dunkley and Norman had more than prepared me. In a way the preparation sessions were more for peace of mind. I already knew the case better than the other side did because I had lived it. One by one I returned Norman's questions with a frankness I could not have manufactured. Steadily, we went through the allegations and presented, for all the eager ears, my understanding of what had happened.

Like Ewart Scott, I confirmed that it was not the bank's style to automatically issue job descriptions. I watched everyone listen to Norman, as he painstakingly went through each one of my performance evaluations, and even had me confirm that I had, in fact, turned down an offer by the Group Chairman for a leap up the ladder. Once we delved into the heart of the matter, the questions became even more specific, each drawing from me a rush of energy. At some point, as my lawyer continued to nudge at me for answers in the requisite polite manner, I could feel the bile building inside me. I grew increasingly irritable as mental fatigue slowly took over.

By the second day I was a wheel spinning in mud, unable to get where I wanted to go. All I could think of now was bursting out of that stand and screaming about lies and betrayal. Norman would get me close to my wish when he took me back to what was perhaps the most crucial issue— the signing of the contracts that opened the doors for the telemarketers:

"Now, you told us the circumstances in which you say you signed or were given instructions by Mr. Ewart Scott. He came into your office and he showed you a letter and he said certain things, 'run with it', and so on. Now, Mr. Scott in his evidence on this point says as follows: *He called me into a meeting into his office. When I went in, Mr. Bill Todd—wherein he provided me with copies of the documentation.* (...) Now, part of his evidence, where he said you actually called him into your office, you have any comments on that?"

"That is *not* true that I called him into my office."

(...)

"And part of your evidence is that when Mr. Scott gave you the letter, it had a signature on it as we saw on page 121?"

"Yes. He had already signed it and said, 'Look, go with the system, sign it.'"

"Did he advise at the time from what source he had got that letter or how it had come to him?"

"I mean, Bill Todd was there. It could have come from Bill Todd."

"Did he tell you?"

"No. I didn't ask him."

"He just came in with the letter signed."

"Yes."

"Can you think of any reason why Mr. Scott would have given a different version in this incident from the one you give? Saying you called him into the meeting?"

(...)

"I mean, the man fired me at the end of the day. I think he is trying to shift blame. (...)"

And in that one sentence I had summed up what our three years of defence-building was trying to say: Yes, someone definitely screwed up royally, but it was not Dalton Yap.

No decent courtroom scene is worth much without something for the reporters to munch on. I unexpectedly gave them their treat in the final minutes of my examination, after two days of careful but continuous questioning. With his eye now firmly on the finish line, Norman began to pummel me with the drive of a man on his last reserve of adrenaline. He came at me with the list of allegations, one after the other after the other. I stood there shaking, exhausted and angry, with only my unchecked emotional responses to hurl back through the air. *That's not true! No! I deny that! No! That's false! Not true, sir!* The end finally came when he brought out my dismissal letter, and handed it to me. I swallowed the burning knot stuck in my dry throat:

"You mentioned this morning, Mr. Yap that you had been fired by Mr. Scott? He was the one who signed the letter?"

"He was the one, yes."

(...)

"And you said he probably was just trying to shift blame on you?"

"Yes."

"And the letter repeats a number of these allegations about negligence, non-compliance and so on. (...) Have you always denied the contents of this letter?"

"*Yes.* I *begged* him to allow me to talk to Mr. Wiggan or Mr. Danny Williams who was then Chairman of the Board, but *nobody* wanted to listen to me. Nobody in the bank."

"You wanted the Board to do what?"

"To explain the allegations. I was given a resignation and asked to leave the bank. After five years, after I had given what I thought was good service to the bank—I mean, you cannot treat people like that! You cannot get up and kick a man out of the door after five years of service! I did work in the bank! Long hours I spent there and moving up and down !"

"Mr. Yap—"

"And I have to pay outstanding charges to live in Mandeville, you know! Okay?"

"Mr. Yap—"

The court records will show, literally, that at this point the witness, Dalton Yap, speaking loudly, begins to cry. I may as well have broken down in the streets. A few days later, the news media reported the emotional moment that brought the curtain down on my examination-in-chief.

My final day on the stand came on October 16, after our application for a continuance was approved. Under cross-examination, Mr. Hylton raised the issue of the businesses I was personally affiliated with—attempting, I can only suppose, to shine a suspicious light on the 1991 start-up dates. Yet he did not even delve into my bank accounts or the source of the funds.

In a way I was not surprised. We had made it clear from the start that the paper trail on my accounts was as transparent as could be. On re-direct by Norman, I would have the opportunity to confirm that I had indeed disclosed all my personal matters to the bank, and nothing more was made of the subject.

As expected, Hylton touched on most of the issues, taking time to chew more slowly on the meatier ones. He tried to discount my version of how the Daily Settlement account came to be opened. He suggested that I had a greater role in the preparation of the contract with FTA, and tried to show that I should have been more aware of the eyebrow-raisers in the bank's accounting reports. I admitted to being blank as to how the LMP account was still open in July, but stood firm on my reasons for opening the Worldwide Marketing account.

He would not end before insinuating that I was, all along, trying to contain information within the Operations Division for self-serving reasons, which explains why I, among other things, was not happy about VISA's direct correspondence with my colleague.

BOTH SIDES GAVE their closing statements the following day. As it was the eve of a three-day weekend, the atmosphere was a lot like sitting in a classroom the day before a holiday. You're holding your breath while your teacher is still at the front of the classroom trying to squeeze in the last lesson. Finally the blessed school bell shrills out announcing your immediate release and temporary freedom.

Each side took more than an hour to deliver its final words of persuasion to what I thought to be by now an exhausted Justice Panton. He was not the only one eager for the end. Shoulders that had started out taut and square, were now rounding at the edges. Dennis Morrison delivered our closing submission. The plaintiff had the privilege of the last word. At the end of Hylton's oration, somewhere between his Lordship's final words and the clerk's bellowing, Dunkley turned to me with a look of accomplishment all over his face. For the very first time, I could see him allowing the fatigue to seep into his eyes.

"Well, Mr. Yap. The fight is over. Now we wait." By then my mind had begun to shut down, and all I could do was nod at my lawyer and friend. He and his team had delivered a brilliant performance.

As I steadied myself on my feet, I paused to look at his Lordship as he stepped down from his dais and disappeared into the privacy of his chambers. He had a lot of work to do now.

Dunkley caught my stare. "Dalton?"

I gave him a weary sigh. "I'm just wondering—"

"Yes?"

"I'm wondering if he got it all."

TEN

Just days after my trial had ended in 1996, a friend who had been following my ordeal closely all along, asked me what great lesson I had learned from all of this. I hesitated as I reminisced on my father's motto that if you worked hard enough and walked the path of a truly honest man, you wouldn't have to worry about people banging on your door at midnight. And for the first thirty-two years of my blessed life, the man who had raised his family in a spirit of trust and human decency had been right, and I had walked around with the stride of a truly free man.

Now my father's words had the sad ring of a sentimental fairy tale story in a child's bookcase. So I turned to my friend and told him what I now knew for certain. When it comes to your job, I said to him, assume that no one has your back but you. Establish a paper trail. Do it like your life depends on it. People *will* make mistakes, and people *will* be sloppy. It's an insidious habit. And you can easily get caught in their sticky mess.

Now almost a year later, we were finally being summoned back into court to learn my fate. Justice Panton was ready to hand down the panel's judgment. I can only credit my sanity during the agonizing wait to the distractions that surfaced in between. Once the trial was out of my skin, I secretly began to entertain visions of a real life. A productive life. In

214

anticipation of the Mareva and my legal woes being lifted with the Court's ruling, I kept an eye out for my next opportunity as a businessman. I could feel that old enthusiasm returning. Soon, I was able to establish my own small plastics factory. The lucky break came, thanks to a friend who offered me some abandoned equipment of his that had been sitting dormant under a tarpaulin in the corner of his warehouse. "Dalton, take the machines and at least get started," he had said. "Get back into life again." And so I did.

Pauline and I welcomed our third child on January 9, 1997. Our family was immediately thrown into a new world with a much-needed and joyful distraction. I understood from the moment I first held Jason that I was being given a fresh chance at fatherhood. Failure was not an option. The Government of Jamaican was thinking along the same lines. By early 1997 it had introduced the Financial Sector Adjustment Company (FINSAC), a resolution trust company set up to stem the tide of the country's sinking local financial institutions. In an unexpected twist, FINSAC appointed the plaintiff's able assistant counsel, Patrick McDonald, as its Corporate Operations Executive. Hilary Reid would eventually step in to fill his vacant spot. Dunkley restrained a smile on hearing the announcement. A change of hands, he explained, was not exactly good news for the other side.

Meanwhile, I'd continue to harass Dunkley, whose daughter was also born that year, about the frustrating delay on the part of the courts. Was I to take this as a sobering sign? Was this normal? Could there be a problem we're unaware of? Barely pausing after my trial to turn his undivided attention to his other clients, my lawyer patiently took my calls. He also reminded me tirelessly, and usually in quick bullet-point style, that the bank had not proved its case in the end. Hopeful but still cautious, I moved forward.

By the time August rolled around, I began to resemble the island, which had itself been grappling with a nasty drought for most of the summer. We were both visibly drained from the long and debilitating absence of some good news from above. I kept glancing skyward watching for the first signs of promising clouds, and an end to the oppressive heat and general depression. But more was yet to come.

On a muggy Monday, September 22, Justice Panton took the bench before the somber reunion of *Jamaica Citizens Bank v Yap,* my family and a few reporters. It was to a hushed courtroom that he finally shared his understanding of what had transpired at the bank. I sucked back quiet short breaths as he began to sift through the plaintiff's and defence's claims, carefully connecting the dots of what he deemed to be the salient pieces of evidence. His Lordship also made reference to my performance evaluations, acknowledging in his words that I "shone" as an employee, according to the plaintiff's annual assessment. I shot a grateful look at Norman, who was also holding his breath.

Justice Panton finished going through the claims. Then he noted to the courtroom that, in addition to considering the evidence and counsel's submissions, he also gave weight to the demeanour of each witnesses as they gave their testimony, and to the fact that the witnesses were all still active players in the bank. I suppressed a hopeful lurch in my stomach on hearing that. We had indeed been blessed with a pragmatic judge. And then he began reading his findings, which went along these lines:

FTA

The Agreement with FTA and the opening of the account:

His Lordship felt that the plaintiff was no doubt experiencing difficulty, if not embarrassment, where the US$140,000 of unprocessed MasterCard paper was concerned. He found that the defendant, having been asked to find a processor, did just that. Clearly, however, FTA Card Services would not have provided this service without a formal contract. He further found that the defendant not only passed on this contract to his Managing Director, Mr. Wiggan, who in turn sent it to the Legal Department for vetting, but that Mr. Wiggan signed it upon having it returned to him by the latter. Justice Panton said he found it unlikely that the bank's top officer could have signed such an important document without full knowledge of its contents. On this matter, his Lordship declared himself to be "at a loss" as to how the defendant could therefore be the root cause of the agreement and the subsequent opening of the account, when the defendant was merely carrying out the instructions of his employer.

The Resolution:

While he found that the bank's Board did not, in fact, pass the resolution allowing for the opening of the account, he further found that the plaintiff's interests were nevertheless "well protected." With regard to Neville Parkinson and Ewart Scott's role in the opening of the said overseas account, he found it unlikely that this could have happened without Parkinson's "concurrence and approval" as the officer in charge of the plaintiff's finances. Referring to Mr. Parkinson as a "key player" whom the plaintiff chose not to call as a witness, his Lordship fully accepted the defendant's testimony that Mr. Parkinson persuaded him to "sidestep the Board," and accepted that the defendant was acting on the assurance of a senior officer that there would be no harm in doing this.

Mr. Palmer, the plaintiff's officers and the account:

Mr. Justice Panton found "unsustainable" the allegation that the defendant allowed Mr. Palmer to commit fraudulent withdrawals, while doing nothing to prevent this, including alerting the bank. Calling the confusion amongst the plaintiff's officers over job responsibilities an "undesirable state of affairs", his Lordship ruled that, in the absence of a job description that held the defendant responsible for the monitoring of the account, he had to find the general manager of finance responsible in this case. He further found that Mr. Palmer had indeed been sending statements on a regular basis to the plaintiff, which seemed to elicit neither comment nor action by Mr. Parkinson. In the matter of Ken Palmer's fraudulent activities, Justice Panton felt that some of the bank's senior officers had perhaps "fallen asleep on their watch". However, the defendant, he said, was not one of them. In his summary concerning the FTA matter, his Lordship cleared the defendant of all charges of negligence and breach of contract, and instead pointed a finger at the combination of the contract into which the plaintiff knowingly entered "under legal advice," Mr. Palmer's fraudulent actions, and the "laxity" of those in charge of the bank's finances.

Telemarketing

Justice Panton's first focus in the telemarketing matter was the executive meeting in which the plaintiff claimed to have decided against venturing into telemarketing. Raising the issue that Ewart Scott and Lloyd Wiggan could not agree when it had taken place, Justice Panton then commented on the absence of the minutes amid the "flood" of documents submitted to the Court. Despite all this, Mr. Justice Panton found that telemarketing was likely discussed in an executive meeting in early 1993, but could not conclude that a decision had in fact been taken to "stay clear" of it, based on the events that followed. Calling Scott's signature on those subsequent Agreements "damning," especially when it appeared alongside three of the telemarketing companies that were part of the trial's focus, Justice Panton labelled as "unacceptable" Scott's explanation of "testing" as his reason for signing the documents. His Lordship levelled harsh criticism at my former colleague, calling his explanation a "feint", as he clearly knew more than he was leading the Court to believe.

He held a similar dim view of my former boss. Finding it "too remarkable to accept" that the Managing Director only first realized following a vacation in July that the bank had engaged in telemarketing, he saw as "telling" Wiggan's lack of shock or uproar at what was supposedly a blatant breach of company policy. It was his "cool attitude toward the manner," said his Lordship, which led him to believe that the Managing Director had been well aware of the plaintiff's involvement in telemarketing. To Mr. Justice Panton, it appeared that the plaintiff sought to lay blame once the project began to generate losses. He further expressed his surprise that only scribbled notes took the place of an emergency meeting to address what was claimed to be an urgent situation—a clear indication that no policy had been breached, at least up to this point in July.

Where the defendant's behaviour was concerned, Justice Panton accepted the well-documented opinion that I was a "model employee" and "excellent worker," one often called upon by the plaintiff to assist in matters outside of my division.

The opening of the accounts:

His Lordship agreed with the unchallenged fact that the defendant had given orders to open the accounts. However, he further found that the defendant had "inherited" a situation in which contact with the offending telemarketers, direct or otherwise, had already been established by other officers of the bank. This, he said, was seemingly supported by Ewart Scott, who went on to sign certain documents indicating his intention to pursue the new line of business. Also accepting the undisputed evidence that the Marketing Department was responsible for background checks, Justice Panton noted that the same department did not investigate said merchants once their involvement with the bank became known.

The closing of the accounts:

Puzzled by the same theme of inaction, his Lordship posed the question as to why the Marketing Department did not give written instructions for the accounts to be closed following the May 3 memorandum, this being the time that Ewart Scott claimed to have first learned of their existence. His Lordship then offered the reply that no such instructions were given then, as there was no policy in place prohibiting their existence. He further found it "unreasonable" that the plaintiff would try to exonerate the members of the Marketing Department, from which a letter instructing the closure of said accounts was finally issued in July. As for the complaint that the defendant delayed in responding to VISA's complaints, his Lordship accepted Mr. George Beckford's testimony that in this area the defendant acted appropriately.

HIS LORDSHIP'S RULING was now almost over, but I was not home-free.

In the matter of the re-opening of the LMP Marketing account after July 6, Justice Panton found that I was both responsible and aware of the implications of doing so, even though there was no loss as a result suffered by the plaintiff. He further found that the opening of the Worldwide Marketing account in July constituted a breach of the plaintiff's "now-known policy" not to accept telemarketing merchants, making me therefore liable for that merchant's losses to the plaintiff amounting to US$106,226.04 plus interest at 12.5 percent retroactive to June 13, 1994. The words whistled in my ears like a thousand flying arrows.

I said nothing.

THE DOOR SLAMMED behind me causing Dunkley to raise his eyes. "Follow me to my office," he had said in court. "We'll talk there."

Dunkley studied me carefully as I slowly eased into a chair in front of his desk with the deliberate motions of a man aware of his every joint and muscle. I loosened my tie just as slowly. "Well, Mr. Yap! Congratulations!" he said. "You've won." There was hesitation in his tone as he tried to read the controlled look on my face. I said nothing. Chris leaned back in his chair and compressed his lips. "Okay. You're disappointed."

I shot out of my chair and threw my hands out at him. "What the hell do you think?"

"Okay, Dalton. I know it's not the complete exoneration you wanted, but as lawsuits go it's a damn good judge—"

"Damn good judgment?" I cried in disbelief, my head turning to face him. "Damn good judgment you say? What about my good name, Dunkley? It's still got mud all over it!"

"I know," Chris said quietly. "Yes, I know." Then he sighed heavily and threw his head back, his gaze now at the ceiling. I could almost hear all the expectations he'd been harbouring for the last four years spew out on his breath. "My God. We were so close. We were right—we were right there!"

"What the hell happened?" I asked, trying not to shake. "It's like Justice Panton completely forgot about the July 19 meeting *and* the memo that came from Lumsden afterward."

"Can't explain it," Chris said passing a hand over his face. He looked exhausted. "That surprised me too. I thought we'd made a strong case around both. Shit. I don't know, Yap. Maybe he just simply forgot that one point with all the other details flying at him. I mean, there was a lot to take in."

"And exactly how did the plaintiff prove that it had established policy after July 6 to cease the telemarketing business?"

221

"They didn't."

"Well, Panton thinks they did! What was it he said? The now-known policy?"

"I know, Dalton, I know. I get your frustration," he said. "But look, we did manage to whittle the suit from US$2 million to almost nothing. All they got in the end was 5 percent. In the legal world, that's a victory. I don't know of too many lawyers who would disagree with that."

"Damn it, man," I said. This time my eyes flashed. "You know this is not just about the money! Look, Chris. I am grateful. No, I'm raw with gratitude for what you all did in court for me. But understand that I *have* to purge my life of this disgrace in absolute terms or else I'll be forever explaining myself to my children! I don't want—"

I stopped to shift my pace to a slower canter and cleared my throat. "Listen to me and put yourself in my shoes. I'm looking into the future to thirty, forty years down the road when my grandchildren are in school, doing research for a project. I don't want for them to buck up this case and see their grandfather's name all over the newspapers like some common criminal. That *cannot* happen, Mr. Dunkley. You understand what I'm saying? If I die tomorrow, I need to know that I'm going to my final resting place with my integrity unchallenged. I am *not* leaving this world until I'm completely exonerated." I continued venting for the next few minutes while Chris tried, but only very gently, to make me see the results from an lawyer's point of view. I stopped only when he finally gave up.

"Okay, Dalton," Chris said, pulling his desk calendar in front of him. "Okay. You win. All I'm going to ask at this point is that you think about it some more. We have six weeks to decide. Appeal or let it go. I'm asking you to just think it over for a bit. And please, Yap, keep in mind that we can now return to the matter of the Mareva injunction, and seek an order for an inquiry to be held in respect of damages. There's a good chance that you can still collect something for that."

I didn't hear him. "I can't believe you're not fully behind me on this, Chris," I said, my tone heavy with resentment. In our four years of battle, this was the closest he'd ever come to sitting on the fence.

He held up a hand to correct me. "Dalton, that's not the issue here. As my client and as my friend, I'm going to let you make the final decision. I won't tell you what to do. And I will go full guns in whichever direction you choose. You have my word. All I ask is that you keep in mind the fact that the plaintiff is a big, powerful, rich bank with some major face to save. But, as your lawyer, I am obligated to advise you that if the plaintiff really wants to, it can drag this nasty mess out until your hairline becomes acquainted with the back of your neck. Are you hearing me?"

I combed my fingers through my hair as I headed for the door. "I hear you. Consider me advised."

Outside the air was unusually still. In the distance, I could see the clouds gathering.

THE RAINS CAME the next day.

The dry earth soaked up each fat raindrop like a stray animal lapping up its first puddle of water. In the interior, low-lying clouds frosted hills and mountain peaks, causing them to disappear temporarily. Forecasters warned of possible flooding in low-lying areas. It was enough to make the news. So was the ruling on my case.

The news media reported my blow, with the numerical terms waving smugly from the headlines. Each time my father would fling the papers down amid a barrage of choice Chinese and Jamaican curse words, leaving my mother to search our eyes pleadingly for a translation of the article. In the matter of my innocence, my parents and family were in full agreement.

"Son, do *not* admit to what you did not do," my father pleaded with me one night as I sat at the kitchen table, my head in my hands as I questioned and regretted my harsh reaction in Dunkley's office. "You fight them all the way to the end. They push you, you push back."

I had by then already met with Norman Wright and Dennis Morrison. Both gave variations on Dunkley's warning. *You can leave it be, Dalton, and consider yourself almost vindicated, which for many is as good as it gets. Or you can appeal it and reopen the whole ugly thing. Do you really want that?* In fairness, neither ever told me what to do. They merely suggested which path they would take were they in my shoes. Deep inside, I knew they wanted the pain of my ordeal to end for my sake.

For the first few nights I was the only one awake while my family slept. The rain was my companion as it continued to pelt the wood shingle roof. I tried to get the feel for the new shoes I was in—declared mostly innocent and just a little bit guilty. I decided I didn't like it much.

CHRIS PUNCHED AT the up arrow on the television remote control button once again. It was his third time going through all the cable channels. Nothing.

In the darkness, with only the glow from the television illuminating the room, he let his mind roam over the trial and Justice Panton's ruling. Chris knew instinctively that the Court had taken to his client's spirit. He could feel it. From the words chosen, and even the tone with which the ruling was given, it was clear that it had seen his client as a man of probity. A decent man who was just doing his job. That's what made it difficult for Chris to come to terms with the final outcome.

Intellectually, Chris appreciated that his Lordship had delivered a somewhat Solomonic ruling. A little bit of pie for everyone served up with a side order of comfort in the knowledge that Dalton could better digest a hit of US$100,000 as opposed to US $2 million. Emotionally, it was no different than turning into the final lap of a punishing marathon, only to face defeat in the final minute. Just as you're close enough to see the finish line, you suddenly buck your toe and go crashing to the ground as your competitor steals past you to freaking victory.

What to do now? Chris struggled to clear his thoughts. The feeling was not a familiar one. Usually his gut instinct would be loud for him to hear it without effort, but this time there were questions. Lots of them. He had given his client his word that he would let the man make the final decision, and was ready to commit to that. He had to.

Dalton Yap had gone above and beyond the expectations of a paying client—practically spoiling his legal team with his willingness and ability to keep pace—to research, pore over documents and stick toothpicks in his eyelids to stay up until dawn to help build his own damn case. After missing the first Mareva appeal, the man was there for every court appearance, whether for mere mentioning or the actual trial. The Court liked him. His staff liked him. The peanut vendor liked him. He had become the kind of client that made a lawyer want to march into court and rip justice out of the concrete walls.

This time, however, they were standing at the edge of the highest precipice they had faced so far. For the moment they were relatively safe. Following the ruling, the defence had applied for, and had been granted, a six-week stay of execution on the payment of the money as a prelude to walking into the Court of Appeal, but they still had the option to stay put and accept Justice Panton's decision.

For weeks, Chris kept his distance from his client, hoping to give him room to think. He even prayed on it a little. If things went terribly wrong, he thought, Dalton could stand to lose it all. Not just his money, but his sanity. Chris knew he couldn't write a cheque like that on someone else's account. Neither was he comfortable with simply allowing the client to be the architect of his own destruction. He just wasn't that kind of lawyer.

Chris telephoned me literally the day before the six weeks were up. "What are we doing, Dalton?" he asked carefully. By the second line of skin-scorching expletives, Chris understood what my answer was.

That evening, he sat alone at a friend's kitchen table with a fresh notepad, a blue ink pen and a cold can of grape soda. And there, the young lawyer poured out of his heart the notes to my grounds of appeal without consulting a single person, or lifting his head to check the time. By nine o'clock the next morning, he had typed and filed them. We were heading back to court.

LIFE IS, INDEED, stranger than fiction.

By early January 1998 we were back to actively juggling two cases—the lawsuit and the Mareva. We were already standing in line for the first, preparing for round two in the appellate court, but with the plaintiff's failure to prove much of its case, we were now before the Honourable Justice Harrison with an application for an inquiry as to damages. It was now time to collect on the Mareva's built-in recourse.

Once again we were tossed out on our asses. In April, Justice Harrison denied us the order of an inquiry for damages, stating that the plaintiff's failure to prove fraud did not mean that its argument was without merit, or that there was no reason for the injunction given the circumstances. It was not the birthday present I was hoping for. Dunkley immediately filed an appeal.

Meanwhile, my former employer was about to be taken down, and swiftly. The homegrown star had started to show signs of fatigue from treading in a widening sea of competition. Soon it was being deemed financial-industry flotsam and, by the end of 1998, was FINSAC's next rescue attempt, along with four other so-called failing local banks. The resultant institution was to be aptly named "Union Bank Holding Company Ltd". The new bank needed a new chairman. This time, FINSAC came knocking on our door for our Mr. Dennis Morrison. Incredibly, I had lost my lead counsel to the enemy.

Chris leapt up immediately to build a Chinese Great wall for information around our now former Queen's Counsel. He delayed his own shock at the crippling blow for a time when he'd have the luxury to do so. Now he was about to be thrown into an even stickier paperwork hell by the plaintiff, which was now demanding the name be changed to Union Bank for the purpose of the lawsuit.

I, on the other hand, exhibited no such emotional control. "I don't *bomboclaat* believe this!" I screamed into receiver when Chris called me with the sick news. Much to our relief, Morrison would graciously offer to stay out of the case and let the new executive take over. Dunkley seized the opportunity to tell the other side that we felt sure about winning the appeal, but that his client was just a man, and one who was growing tired. *Did the new Union Bank want to call it a day and save itself another few years of legal fees?* he offered through Michael Hylton. To his credit, Hylton did meet with his client and put the question to them. They returned a resounding "no." Their decision would make for another watershed moment in the case.

It was, in fact, the answer Dunkley had expected. With legal bills creeping up to the ceiling, he knew that the bank could not have been happy with the final outcome. Not when they were originally chasing US$2 million. In a way, it was also the answer my lawyer had been secretly hoping for. It would give him one last chance to make things right for his client.

Once again, the young lawyer hit the pavement in search of silk. This time, with my own legal bills soaring beyond reach, I had to rethink the size of my legal team, and bid Norman a reluctant goodbye.

HILARY PHILLIPS, Q.C. was a seasoned lawyer with elegantly greying hair, a firm handshake and warm eyes that looked straight into your core. She was also legal royalty. Her late father was Sir Rowland Phillips, the former and highly-respected chief justice in the 1960s.

Her selection by Dunkley, however, went beyond her experience and solid reputation. Phillips was known for jumping straight into the deep end, where she'd swim nose high in documents and gather evidence until she was satisfied she knew a case better than her own life story. She would do just that when Chris finally pitched my case to her. After carefully studying the material, she called to say she concurred with him, but wanted to meet with me first before committing.

"She agrees, Yap," Chris called to tell me hurriedly that evening between mouthfuls of his dinner. After months of careful searching, I could hear him beaming through the phone. "She thinks we've got a good claim on the appeal." We had at last found another believer. We agreed to meet at her office later that week. Now both sides had a Hilary. Hilary Reid for the bank, and Hilary Phillips for us.

I knew from the moment I met Queen's Counsel Phillips that I was the luckiest accused man to ever to be dragged into a legal war. She was a lot like Dunkley; spirited and spiritual. I felt an instant comfort at the sight of a simple gold cross pendant around her neck. While I had never actually taken a serious bite out of religion, I acknowledged now that maybe I needed a little taste of it. Perhaps that was the missing ingredient in my ordeal.

We had arranged to meet Friday afternoon to talk casually in her firm's library, a stand-alone building across from the parking lot. It was a converted garage that now resembled a cozy cottage, beckoning with huge bay windows and pristine white paint. Inside, it was just as inviting. The deep room pulled you in with its warm hardwood flooring and dark wood trimming on crisp white walls. To the right, floor-to-ceiling shelves groaned with thick law books and cardboard boxes filled with files. A bright red fire extinguisher sat perched on the wall to one side of the door, not far from the library sign-out book that lay open with a pen in its crease. Nestled alongside the sunny windows between two huge green plants was an old mahogany table that could seat ten. Above, recessed pot lighting provided soft but focused illumination. The room smelled of aged, used books. It was the scent and feel of competence. Slowly, my shoulders began to ease.

It all seemed to fit. A quick background check amongst my friends on Miss Phillips had produced positive feedback. "Seasoned lawyer," one friend said. "Absolute integrity," said another. I decided that if Hilary Phillips would have me as her client, I was going to be happy to hire her as my Queen's Counsel.

I was not the only one sizing up the new guy. Hilary had not known me before and had not worked with Dunkley before. She made her own assessment of the pair in front of her, and the journey she was contemplating taking with them:

'When I first met Dalton, he was initially very intense, quiet, contained, and yet sincere. Even emotional. And you certainly didn't have to ask if he and Christopher Dunkley had been through a lot together. You could see it. They were equally passionate about the case having been on the ground from the first awful news. But what impressed me most was that Dalton was very familiar with his own case. He answered my questions forthrightly. At the end of it, I was satisfied that the information in the records about his ability, his focus and his determination to do well were entirely *inconsistent* with the allegations made against him. So I felt that if we went through the records carefully, and Chris had already sent me the whole of it along with the notes of evidence, we could pursue it. I was satisfied there was an argument.

Once that was officially decided, we got ready to do matters my way. That meant a completely thorough application. I was determined that we would remove the blot from this young man's record, get rid of the hopeless charges, and make the bank pay—even though the truth was that money could hardly compensate for the obvious damage to his reputation, to his family and to his spirit."

ONCE HILARY OFFICIALLY joined our team we applied for and were granted a new court date in order to give her more time. The Court would give us audience in November 1999. I remember groaning at the thought of stringing my life along for almost another entire year. Dunkley laughed. "Show some appreciation, man. At least they're squeezing you in before the new millennium." The delay in fact gave my lawyer a much-needed breather. In addition to the bulging pile on his plate, he was relocating his firm to an office in New Kingston.

From this point onwards an extraordinary synergy boosted the three of us into high gear. With Hilary at the helm, we prepared for the upcoming trial with the precision-like ease of a new age factory line. This time around I was at practically every meeting they had. They talked while I took notes, poured refills of water, picked up take-out dinners, and tried to punch holes in their arguments. If there was something for us to incorporate in submissions, or file in court by a certain date, I was on the other end of the telephone with their secretaries two days before the deadline with a friendly reminder. Those would be followed by post-deadline calls. Another set of computer-generated cross-reference charts helped us chisel out even stronger main and alternate lines of argument, with the relevant document identification, page numbers and paragraphs. And this time, a little technological ingenuity called the Internet helped us to swap information faster than we could say "Mareva Injunction."

Hilary was genuinely impressed with the work we'd done before her involvement. She was particularly happy with Norman Wright's move to include my performance evaluations in the first instance trial.

Bundle four, in fact, had dealt entirely with my work record. Every annual and semi-annual statement highlighting my ability and exemplary conduct was there, signed by the very men who, in the end, had turned on me. It was at this point that the irony hit me. It was Wiggan who had introduced performance evaluations at the bank.

Hilary explained the significance of Norman Wright's decision in one of our meetings. "Not only did Norman ensure that your work record became a matter of *public* record, Dalton, he had the judge scratching his head over the inconsistency of an employer accusing a man with such a consistent background. So much so, that Justice Panton obviously felt impelled to include some very positive statements about you in his judgment. Thanks to him, we're now able to march into the Court of Appeal with those same statements and say look, Mi Lordships, the plaintiff is accusing Dalton Yap of behaviour

231

that completely contradicts his five years of outstanding service. So let the plaintiff show the Court what drove him to make such an incredible switch."

In the same conversation I'd ask her about the issue of motive, and the likelihood of the plaintiff trying to fabricate a case around one. She was ready with her answer. "The fact is you don't necessarily have to have motive to do wrong. You could blunder by simply being incompetent. That is precisely why the real issue in *this* matter is your past conduct, and what it is likely to be."

If I was the happiest about Hilary's passion for my case, and clearly I had to be, Dunkley was right behind me. He needed that ally to make his work shine.

With the determination of a freshman student, the lead counsel began the uphill process of memorizing the exact location of every important document in the bundles and the weight of each one to our argument. Poised and ready to back her up if she missed a number or document title, Dunkley and I spent equal time studying the new charts and engaging in role play.

This time our argument focused on challenging the findings of Justice Panton in the matter of LMP Marketing and Worldwide Marketing. We needed to show once and for all that the bank had *not* established a policy after July 6 to discontinue accepting telemarketing merchants. We needed to prove that Marketing had indeed *approved* of the opening of the Worldwide account. We knew in our hearts the argument was simple enough. The evidence supported it, but the Court had missed it before. This time we were going to pummel them with the facts until they begged us to stop.

After a few months and several dozen takeout dinner practice sessions, the three of us were practically talking in our own code, riddled with chart pages and document numbers. There was no question that by then the latecomer knew the case better than the plaintiff did. We were feeling incredibly sharp, and absolutely prepared.

NOVEMBER 1999 CAME quickly. Once again the island settled down into more agreeable temperatures as summer relaxed its restless grip. Once again I returned to my closet to select the appropriate suits. Conservative all the way. Nothing flashy.

Meanwhile, in damp Mandeville, my 75 year-old father continued to nurse a stubborn cold. He'd come down with it after being drenched in an afternoon downpour while tending his garden. Mom was spending more time in Kingston helping Theresa, who was struggling with a draining divorce. She checked on him daily by telephone, urging him to make homemade Chinese soups. But a week later his voice had lost its boom. Pat eventually put her foot down and made an appointment for him with a doctor in Kingston.

My father called me the morning she arranged to have a driver bring him in from Mandeville. I was already in Kingston wrapping up my last week of meetings with Chris and Hilary before the trial. I didn't hide my worry when I asked him how he was really feeling. "Oh, you know my big daughter," he said dismissively. "She born to fret over all of us." I relaxed at his attempt to poke fun at Pat, and told him we'd see each other later on.

I REMEMBER THE exact moment and place my father and I literally passed each other that Thursday afternoon. With the bumper car frenzy of Kingston already an hour and a half behind me, burgeoning May Pen was already a speck in my rear view mirror. Home was now a mere forty minutes away.

233

I pulled down the sun visor while I continued to put more distance between me and the capital city. The glow from the sinking sun was unusually impressive that afternoon—an almost tempestuous ball of orange retiring in the west with great fanfare. I remember thinking about the cheering audience it was sure to have at Rick's Café in Negril. Those tourists were going to be in for a treat.

I first saw my father's car approaching in the distance as I came upon the flat, easy stretch of Four Paths before the lone gas station. I still remember the seconds that followed.

At first I can just make out Dad's small frame in the passenger seat. Immediately I smile, ready to take my left hand off the steering wheel so I can exchange a hello wave. We're drawing closer and closer. I'm getting ready to turn my head to follow him for as long as I can. Several seconds later, we're close enough to see each other's face and I begin to wave. It is when we are at our closest point that I suddenly notice that he looks cold, uncomfortable, even though he's wearing one of his heavier sweaters. While I'm trying to decipher this, my father locks eyes with me. He barely manages to wave back. There is no smile from him, and now mine has disappeared into a troubled frown.

The date was November 11. That was the last time I would ever see my father alive.

WE HAD NOT seen Dad's heart attack coming; nor his passing. My family huddled shoulder to shoulder. The finality of it was more than any one of us could bear alone. In the centre, our broken hearted mother struggled through her tears to say goodbye to the only companion she had ever known.

Chris and Hilary flew to my side with words of sympathy and suggestions of delaying the trial until I was emotionally ready, but I did not allow it to fade into the background. That's not what my father would have wanted, I told them. That was not what his legacy was about. We would proceed.

We buried my father the following Sunday. After wiping our tears, my family and I returned to our arena in downtown Kingston, less one.

Between November and December, my legal team delivered one sound argument after another on my behalf before the panel of Messrs. Justice Ian Forte, then President of the Court of Appeal, Justice Donald Bingham and Justice Clarence Walker. The seamless flow between my lead and assistant counsel was almost riveting. No matter the direction Hilary blazed while on her feet, Dunkley followed in her wake. From the bench, he fed her a steady stream of well-timed hand-written notes offering points she could incorporate into her argument. Or notes on the exact location of a particular document, just in case she had a brief, but rare, memory lapse.

I couldn't help but put my nerves on hold to admire their work. On Day One the Judges were casting suspicious glances at our trusty chart. By Day Three they were asking us to refer back to it. The esteemed panel was faced with pure genius. The team of Phillips and Dunkley was absolute legal magic, and an absolute privilege to watch.

Still devastated by my father's passing, I had fully expected to walk into my trial numb, but that didn't happen. Perhaps Hilary was right. Maybe God really was carrying me when I could no longer carry myself. The part of me that decided to accept that also wanted to believe something else—that my father was sitting there too, cheering me on.

And this time, with no heart to fail him, he was roaring like a tiger.

Eleven

A fter the trial was over, I had asked Hilary about the quick prayer she had said in her office with us before heading for court on our first day. "Lord, let justice be done," were the words my lead counsel had whispered, with head humbly lowered. "My father taught me to say that instead of please let me win," she explained. "Remember, Dalton. We are, first and foremost, officers of the Court."

I was out of breath by the time the millennium celebrations took over. With my father now gone and the Court of Appeal's judgment pending, I opted for a more subdued greeting of the New Year. I watched the second hand of the clock with my family and a handful of close friends. At the stroke of midnight I imagined him toasting the milestone century with a little brandy swirling in the warmth of his hand. It was then that I realized that I was now the head of the family.

ONCE AGAIN I slipped into my emotional cocoon while waiting impatiently for word from the Courts.

This time, however, I was able to maintain longer periods of calm. My new plastics factory was finally taking shape and made for a safe place to channel my energies—especially in the mornings when I missed my coffee companion the most. Around me, my family, long familiar with the intense look in my eyes, took up their usual positions in the distance and held their breaths. Now a little older, my first two kids were beginning to understand that their daddy was waiting on some very important news. Certainly my daughter did. While I managed to function, my mind flickered on the Court of Appeal's decision at least several dozen times a day. Quite frankly, I could hardly focus on little else.

In late March, the news media jolted us with the announcement that FINSAC had plans to sell Union Bank to the Royal Bank of Trinidad and Tobago. Still involved in the lengthy due diligence stage, the deal was expected to take some time before it was completed.

"Nnoo—no it won't affect us, Yap," Chris decided after taking yet another panicked call from me. "Not for now anyway." But behind his composed tone I could hear his mind racing through the wire. "First things first," he continued. "We wait for the appellate court's ruling. In the meantime, give me a little time. I need to check into something," and then he hung up.

In April I blew out forty candles on my chocolate birthday cake as my friends and family cheered on. Inside, I felt like eighty.

FREEDOM CAME ON Thursday, June 15, 2000.

Seated at the back of the courtroom with my equally nervous family, I wrestled with the poor acoustics to hear Justice Clarence Walker read his panel's judgment, and the words I'd been waiting to hear for some seven wretched years. I don't recall how I actually managed to remain in my seat. I wanted nothing more than to be standing right under their podium as the panel of three finally addressed the issues at the heart of our appeal.

In the matter of the existence of the "now known policy" subsequent to July 6, the panel found that Justice Panton's findings were not sustained by the evidence, which meant therefore that there was no such policy for me to contravene to begin with. They also agreed that the lower court did not give due effect to the July 19 meeting, nor to the subsequent memorandum indicating approval from the Marketing Department, both of which were crucial to the opening of the Worldwide Marketing account. In the matter of the re-opening of the LMP account, the panel found that there was no direct evidence to prove my involvement, a point Mr. Michael Hylton had eventually conceded in the trial.

Calling Hilary Phillips's argument "compelling," the panel made specific reference to my excellent performance evaluations and reputation of being a model employee, and stated that, given my history, it would have therefore been "highly improbable" that I would have acted as charged.

In the end I was cleared of all allegations. Every last stinking one.

Hilary best describes what followed next:

"When the judgment came down, we weren't too sure that Dalton had heard it all because he'd been sitting at the back of the courtroom. But when we turned to walk toward him and his family, we found them in a tight circle holding hands quietly, heads touching—as if praying. It was one of those very tender moments that make you pause on the spot. It was very special. Very special and very private.

Dunkley touched my shoulder as he made his way outside to feed the hungry reporters with a statement about our plans for legal action against the bank. I held back and waited for Dalton. To be honest, I almost felt a little shy just watching. Then, after a few moments, the man around whom this nasty ordeal had been swirling for seven years, lifted his head and saw me. That's when he broke away from his family and walked up to me. With the biggest smile on a face I had ever seen, he gave me a thousand squeezes in one huge hug. I could almost feel him releasing all the energy and years of pent up sadness and frustration while he kept whispering 'thank you' over and over again. And then his eyes welled up as he started to talk about his father. If only he could have hung in there long enough to see him clear the family's name, he was saying. Throughout our time together I had always been frank with Dalton, never sugarcoating anything, never offering platitudes, if even to make him feel better. I wasn't about to change that now. And so I told this brave young man what I believed in my heart. I said 'He knows, Dalton. Your father knows.' "

FOR THE FIRST time since 1993, I was thrilled to see my name in the news media. The public announcement of my vindication and plans for legal action against the bank tasted as sweet as the first juicy mango of the season. I sank my hungry teeth into it and let the syrupy juices run down my chin. My family and I had by now collapsed in pure, shameless joy.

As for my legal team, when I'd finally exhausted all the possible combinations of words in the English language to express my gratitude, I showered them with some from the two Chinese dialects I knew. But there was more work to be done. The trial now over, the Mareva issue was about to step into the spotlight and with the allegations against me now completely wiped out, we were going for aggravated damages. Nothing less. The door behind which my retribution sat was now glowing through the cracks. I could hardly wait to open it.

Incredibly, six weeks later I found myself applying the brakes to the festivities. The bank was still not out for the count. This time they wanted to take the matter to the Privy Council. Dunkley was dumbfounded. "They cannot be serious," he said shaking his head in disbelief. "We just tore them a gaping new one. Crater-sized! And still they're flailing their arms at us?"

This time I laughed and I told Dunkley he should take it as a compliment. "Maybe they can't handle the fact that a slingshot took down the lot of them. It's killing them."

In August, the bank announced that it was officially applying to the Court of Appeal for leave to take the case to the Privy Council. Just two short months later, the Government named Queen's Counsel Michael Hylton as the country's next Solicitor General. The media confirmed that Hylton would take up office effective January 1, 2001. This time it was the other side that had lost its lead man.

Dunkley and I scratched our heads over the strange turnstile effect the case seemed to have developed. "Well, I guess the esteemed Mr. Hylton gets to keep his zero losses record after all," I said to Chris, but my lawyer wouldn't comment. He only nodded with a wry smile.

It was Queen's Counsel Dennis Goffe who took the baton from Hylton. By then the departing lead counsel had already prepared and filed the appeal to the Privy Council. Dunkley said he was sure the case would languish. "They've got none of the original lawyers left," he reasoned. "Goffe can't possibly want to take this to the Privy Council. They're not going up there, Dalton. They're not."

For a while the matter did seem to show signs of fading as 2001 rolled in. At least the silence convinced us of that. Even when on February 19, the Court of Appeal granted Union Bank final leave to appeal to the Commonwealth's highest court, Chris reacted with little more than a peripheral glance. He assured me he was keeping an eye on them. I decided to keep my eye on him.

Christmas for me came in October of that year. On the nineteenth, the Court of Appeal gave us the thumbs up for the

Supreme Court to assess damages. Justice Henderson Downer handed down the ruling on behalf of the panel that included himself, Justice Clarence Walker and Justice Algernon Smith. Describing Ewart Scott's action against me as "deceitful" and his performance in court as "a feint," the panel advised that I seek exemplary damages from the bank. Chris noted that I seemed to be cosmically linked to the month of October. "Shit really happens to you around then, huh, Yap." He advised that we'd have to put our pursuit of the undertakings on hold until after the Privy Council, as the bank could put a stop to it until after the Council's ruling. "That's if they really go there," he said.

By now it was official. This would be the first Mareva case in Jamaica's history involving an assessment of damages. My unwanted attention had won me a dubious spot in the country's legal annals.

It was now public knowledge that I stood to claim millions from the bank. This time, technology brought me cheers from supportive Jamaicans across the globe—strangers who jumped on the Internet to share their happiness at my victory, and disgust for the ugly hand dealt to me:

Make sure you get every cent you are due!

Lesser men may have jumped off a bridge!

Days later the bank, only weeks away from its official name-changing ceremony and now temporarily straddling the name RBTT/Union Bank of Jamaica Ltd., issued a circular to its staff announcing that Dalton Yap's fight was with FINSAC and not the bank.

The announcement got a smug rise out of Dunkley. Oh, I don't think so! I believe was his response. As they were the ones who had started the name-change issue, my attorney was openly happy to turn it on them. "Just playing the same little game," he said.

It was then that he revealed the results of his sleuthing. After the March 2000 announcement of the pending sale to

RBTT, he had quietly begun to check on matters with the Registrar of Companies. At first I didn't make the connection and threw my hands up. "The Registrar? What for?"

"Call it a hunch," he said. "Old habits die hard. I figured if they could be sloppy before, we could count on them to be sloppy again." And he was right. Sure enough, the requisite paperwork at the Registrar's office was incomplete. Chris went straight to the new bank's legal counsel with our proposal. Change the name on the lawsuit to RBTT, he said, or we'd sound the alarm and reduce their grand opening to a small thud. "Let them cogitate on that one!" he said.

I had to hand it to my lawyer. He did his job well.

ON A SUNNY but comfortable November 28, government officials, the bank's top brass and members of the press attended a corporate flag-raising ceremony at the New Kingston branch of RBTT Group. They gathered on the wide, shaded sidewalk to witness Union Bank officially change its name to the Royal Bank of Trinidad and Tobago. After several decades of proud service to its customers, Citizens Bank was about to fade away once and for all.

I arrived when everyone was already in place. Wearing casual slacks and a short-sleeve shirt, I made no attempt to conceal my presence, nor the camera in my hand. Instead, I mingled easily with the crowd, smiling and handing out my hellos like party favours at a soca fete. Then, as the RBTT Group Chairman began hoisting the new corporate banner, I started snapping pictures of the colourful fabric meandering its way up the bare pole. The military band struck up a lively score at the precise moment it reached the top.

Through my camera's lenses I could see the frown lines on the foreheads of some of my former colleagues. Several had remained—including one in particular who, according to a sympathetic friend conveniently lodged in the middle of the crowd—immediately became inconsolably distracted, and couldn't stop asking why the hell I was there.

He wasn't the only one. Those who had spotted me had their heads bent together in whispered conferences, while keeping their eyes firmly my camera. Missing, of course, was my old boss, who had left the bank in 1996 just days before the trial had ended. The word on the street was that he was now in the United States searching for gainful employment.

The idea to crash the party had been Dunkley's.

When I had asked him why, he explained that we needed the pictures as backup proof of the name change, just in case there was more resistance. "But beyond that," he said with an indignant frown, "They're just really irritating me now. I want to see them squirm."

THE YOUNG LAWYER WAS tired. Outside, Elise collected his messages.

Alone inside his office, Dunkley switched on the radio in time to catch the end of an old Christmas carol, one of his favourites.

Dunkley stared at his overwhelmed desk. He swore he could hear it groaning under the weight of his working files. For a few seconds he gazed at the framed pictures of his wife and children. His kids were no longer babies in diapers. Had he missed too much family time? Erica had long bought into his defence of Dalton and let him do his job without complaint. He'd have to make it up to them when it was all over. Maybe they'd take a nice family vacation.

He moved his eyes over to the calendar, and then to the telephone.

This was the itch he did not want to start scratching. The bank's legal team had not said a single word to him since firing their first warning shot about appealing to the Privy Council. Dunkley opted to maintain the silence. Once more, the two sides were engaged in a chicken version of your-move-first, but this time the field had grown quiet. Eerily quiet.

Dunkley still believed the other side might be bluffing, but if not, his second big hope was that someone over there would look at the case as it now stood and be more realistic. He had to admit though, their persistence was now bordering on the impressive.

Again he was forced to weigh action against impact. An early telephone call seeking confirmation of their intentions might actually prompt them to reach for their passports and possibly infuse some real momentum into the case. Just the right amount of interlude might sway them to accept the fact that the show had ended, and head for the nearest exit. All this he explained to me each and every time I called to ask him what the hell he was waiting for, and why couldn't he just pick up the damn phone and make the call, but he didn't cave in. "Just hold on, Dalton. Just a bit longer. You have to trust me on this."

Chris understood that I was in a panic about another mad dash to the deadline. I was not, I kept reminding him, a last-minute man. I did not enjoy working with my hair on fire like he did, but my lawyer held firm.

Meanwhile, Chris was wondering deep down if the case hadn't evolved to become something else. Was it now a silly sandbox fight between two firms, with one refusing to take its beating with a spoonful of grace? Or was it a case of some energetic lawyer wanting to be the one who cleared the hurdle that others had stumbled over? Had the case gone on for so long that it was just hard to let it go? There was no question that the Yap case had caught the curiosity of just about every judge, lawyer, and even law student in the country.

Or was it something else? Could it be that an ambitious FINSAC had not listened to counsel's advice to yield? And if that was so, what was Patrick McDonald really thinking about all of this? He knew the case well enough. Did he honestly think they could win?

Whatever the reason, Dunkley decided to wait it out. He would admit only later on that he had by then developed somewhat of a mental block where this case was concerned:

"I admit that I was drained. Maybe even a little afraid I had finally run out of tricks. Truthfully, I was secretly hoping it would just go away once and for all. It had been almost ten years. More than half my career."

ONE HOT AND breezy afternoon in the last week of March 2002, Chris picked up the receiver and called Myers, Fletcher & Gordon. Two minutes later he was slamming the phone down and cursing at the walls. We were on for the Privy Council, and the court date was less than two weeks away.

My lawyer took a deep breath, and slowly dialled my number.

I WANTED BLOOD. "You thrill-seeking bomboclaat! What the hell are you trying to do to me? I told you to call them, Dunkley! I told you! Why the hell did you leave it hanging for so damn long?"

Chris had called me, fully prepared to receive my wrath in silence. You can't fight an angry man, he would always say. You just have to let him talk. You have to hear him out. So he dutifully took the unyielding earful without a complaint or whimper. However, by the end of the conversation, he had brought me down to a manageable simmer. I was at least breathing through my nostrils without spewing droplets of

245

water. I had had my moments with my lawyer before, but this time the edge was dangerously close.

"Look here, Christopher Dunkley," I gasped into the receiver. "Don't frig with me now. We cannot fumble. Not now! You hear me? It's been too long a fight! Too long! You hear me?"

"Yap." His voice was steady, bordering on blasé. "Time for you to look at my track record now. Have I dropped the ball yet? No? Exactly. So you have my word—it'll all be fine. I'll simply ask for a short adjournment, and in the meantime Hilary and I will get cracking. Now, go talk to your family and deal with your travel documents. And pick out a couple of your heavier suits. London can be cool in April."

Chris told me in the same conversation that he got the feeling the bank's lawyers themselves were surprised that they were actually proceeding. "Call it instinct," he said, "but if I didn't know better, I'd say they really don't want this either."

The truth was that Chris was not quite as relaxed as he appeared to be. The wobbling stack of files on his desk alone was indication that he now had to do some creative scrambling if he was going to even board the plane much less prepare a statement of case. Elise's eyes grew wide when he gave his already stressed out and now newlywed secretary the unhappy news. Her working days were about to merge into nights once more. She was not happy. A quick call to Hilary confirmed that she too was overloaded.

Chris was working up a nice shade of purple. The other lawyers' cool and flippant reply that their tickets were indeed booked and confirmed, and that an adjournment was neither here nor there to them, was just about the worst thing Dunkley could hear. Especially when he was still convinced that they actually needed the postponement more than we did. "They've lost their minds over there!" he ranted. "McDonald and Hylton are gone, and this thing is getting ahead of the new guys.

But instead of admitting to it and coming to a levelheaded agreement with us, they keep pushing. *Un*believable!"

Thinking that he could just call and request a postponement, as was often done in Jamaica, Chris promptly rang up the Privy Council office in London. It was an unaffected Mr. Williamson who replied with a firm but ever so polite "Oh, Mr. Dunkley, yes. So terribly sorry. We'd love it if you could join us, of course, but if you absolutely can't—"

There would be no short adjournment. I peppered Dunkley for that one too.

Once more, both he and Hilary immediately cleared their schedules and turned their attention to the matter of my defence. I was not to worry, Hilary kept saying. We were the respondents and it wasn't our appeal. And besides, our performance at the local appellate court was, in many ways, a practice run for the Privy Council. For her this would be a second appearance at the Privy Council, but first time as lead counsel. I dissected and clung to her every word.

The cocktail combination of Hilary's serene confidence and Dunkley's incensed enthusiasm had me walking around in an odd state of eager-fear. I was eager because deep down I knew we had a fireproof argument. I was also in a hyped state for my legal team. This was a moment over which most lawyers in the Commonwealth either bit their nails to the quick or dreamt of during their law school days. I had to admit I was anxious to see them kick legal ass over there.

I was also filled with fear. For me, the Privy Council was my absolute final stop. As much as I tried to block it out, the 1994 Mareva appeal shock kept floating in my head. I decided I needed to ensure that Chris and Hilary could do their jobs without distraction. I didn't even want them to have to go find their own icy mints over there. So I called Pat. "I was wondering, since you already know the way around London, would you—?" My sister didn't wait for me to finish the question. She agreed to join us as our travelling assistant.

That Friday night, Dunkley sat and drafted the entire respondent's statement of case in one sitting—fifty-two paragraphs. After ten years of working on the same slab of material, he knew the feel of its every angle and texture. I'd be grateful that he was one of those crazies who produced some of their most succulent work while sweating in a pressure cooker.

The next day, Saturday afternoon, Dunkley tracked down his lead counsel at a Pulse fashion show rehearsal at one of the larger hotels in the city. While the models worked the catwalk to the intricate blueprint instructions of their choreographer, music pumping through the huge speakers, the two took pen to his work. With just a handful of adjustments, they honed the statement into a most perfect silver bullet. Days later, we fired it off to London by email. All we had to do now was pack.

Dunkley called me a few days later with a loud "Hey, Yap! You're really going to like this one!" and almost immediately started howling into the receiver. I could tell this was about to become another one of his many 'I told you so' moments. As his smugness had only meant good things for me in the past, I started grinning as he shared his fresh discovery. It seemed as if the plaintiff, now known as the appellant, had prepared its statement of case after ours had been submitted. Perhaps Dunkley had been right all along. Either the other side had planned to fly to London on autopilot, or they never really meant to go at all.

Had we really called their bluff?

ELISE HEAVED A frustrated sigh.

As she locked her eyes on the small but growing pile of unsigned letters in her boss's in-tray, she sighed and wondered how she was ever going to make it disappear, and then allowed herself a private chuckle. Now engaged in a battle for her boss's attention with a most alluring opponent, Elise felt as if she was watching her own child gleefully counting down the days to his birthday party.

In the ten years she'd been working for Christopher Dunkley, she'd never seen him jump around quite like this, but then again, she had never seen her boss head for the Privy Council. Even the other secretaries had to hide their smiles from him.

Ever since her Mr. Dunkley had announced that he and Ms. Phillips were heading to London for the final leg of the Yap saga, it felt like the entire office had practically moved there. Now it was all about getting on that airplane to cross the great Atlantic. Where her boss had been a grammar fusspot before, he was now a one-man militia—either screening Elise's correspondence to the Council's agent or drafting the letters himself.

"You know I'm not playing with the other side," he'd lecture through the open door of his office. "You know that when I sort anybody out, I have to look good. Right, Miss Elise? So pay close attention to my letters, now, ma'am. We can't be roughing up the nice people while making typos and grammatical errors. Not at this firm, we can't." Elise Crawford knew she'd have to wait for the trial's end before her boss could even touch ground again.

I took Dunkley's near lightheadedness as a good sign. All indications showed in fact that we had every reason to puff our chests out. We had shrugged off an almost decade-long attempt by the bank to bury me. We had made it through two successful appeals and had managed to turn the defendant into the Royal Bank of Trinidad and Tobago. So while other cases were fighting institutions that no longer existed, we had locked in a brand new bank. One way or another, we were going to get me my damn apology money.

Our Privy Council hearing was set for the morning of April 11, at 10:15 a.m. sharp. I believe I finally allowed myself to soak in the thoughts of a happy ending the day Chris called to confirm our flight and accommodation plans. While I was impressed with his thought to detail, I was not in the least bit surprised. Christopher Dunkley may well have been the kind of control freak that high school kids like to mock inside a classroom, but run into life-altering trouble, and you could only hope to have him on your side.

It was all perfectly orchestrated. He and Hilary would leave Kingston on Sunday night, one day ahead of Pat and me. Chris would travel economy while Hilary, who struggled with a bad back, would go club class. They'd arrive in London Monday morning and use that day to shake off the jet lag before opening up their briefcases for one final round of preparation work. Pat and I would also fly economy and join them on Tuesday. We would all stay at the Sussex Gardens Hotel by the theatre district. On Wednesday we'd all pay a quick reconnaissance visit to the Privy Council. Showtime was Thursday. And on Thursday evening after it was all over, we'd all go see The Lion King. He'd already booked the tickets.

"The Lion King?" I repeated into the phone. "This is the fight of my life and you're talking about seeing a musical? Are you serious?"

"Oh yes," Chris laughed. "Quite. Miss Phillips says she intends on having a grand time from start to encore finish."

TWELVE

L ONDON COULDN'T have greeted us with a softer blue sky or more perfect spring temperature. Standing on the sidewalk outside the arrivals terminal, I pulled in a deep, grateful breath. After the eight-hour flight, the air felt refreshing in my lungs. My legs were also welcoming of the chance to finally stretch.

I was surprised. The last thing I had expected to feel about being in London for my trial was good, and yet I hadn't felt that energized in a long time.

My sister took over from the moment we landed at Heathrow. Once we got settled in our cab, she rubbed her hands with a grin as we rolled out of the airport and headed for the centre of the city. "We're here!" she sang. "*Big Ben* country!"

Pat had been in a charged mood ever since we hugged and kissed our families goodbye and checked in at the British Airways check-in counter Monday night. Not only had she managed to wrangle us an upgrade to first class, she had secured seats in the symbolic first row. It was typical Pat Yap. "Look—if you don't ask, you don't get," she said with a sniff. I started laughing, eyes rolling.

Meanwhile, awaiting us on the plane was a small shocker. Sitting in a row close to our newly assigned seats were none other than Dennis Goffe and the other Hilary, Hilary Reid.

251

While I stood there momentarily stuck between laughing and cringing, my sister's brain had already shot way past the stickiness of the situation. She shrieked under her breath. "Dalton! They're in row four! It's a sign!"

"What?" I murmured through my smile after offering the opposing counsel an awkward but nevertheless pleasant greeting. Dennis Goffe had likewise returned a very cordial response—almost sociable. No one mentioned the obvious and unpleasant purpose of our trip.

"Have you forgotten your Cantonese, boy?" she hissed. "Four rhymes with death! *Sie!* Yes, man—we're going to win!"

Pat and I maintained our jovial mood well into the flight. Across the aisle in row four, the atmosphere didn't seem to float much above solemn. You didn't have to ask which party was going to have its reading light on for most of the flight. Eventually we began to feel some sympathy and toned down the jokes. "Lambs to the slaughter," she had sighed as she settled down under a blanket, muttering something about what's going to hit them next.

"Bloody hell!" Our young cabbie waved an irritated hand at a red mini that had just cut into his lane ahead of us. Once again the engine geared down. Ever since we had gotten closer to the city limits, the ride had taken on a more noticeable stop-and-go motion normally associated with traffic in a bustling city. For the moment Pat and I had slipped into happy tourist mode and didn't think to complain. We left that to our harassed driver.

Instead, we allowed our eyes to roam and take in the always appreciated change of scenery from our island in the sun. Around us, Londoners and tourists strode along clearly demarcated sidewalks, which often took them past modest private gardens tucked away behind old stonewalls, or understated but elegant wrought-iron fences. Some pedestrians—either the experienced or the pessimistic—

toted umbrellas or light trench coats today. For the moment no rain seemed to threaten from above. Pat sighed and smiled, as if looking at a longtime friend. "Crossroads of the world. Always such a smart-looking city."

The Sussex Gardens Hotel was your typical charming London hotel, and sat just minutes from central Oxford Street. Already at work, Chris and Hilary were in the makeshift office they'd set up in Hilary's room. Pat and I were to room with Hilary and Chris respectively. We greeted each other with hugs, and gave them an exaggerated tale of our flight across the Atlantic with a decidedly unsettled enemy. Chris laughed and commented on their decision to travel first class only to face defeat. Then he chided us for not ordering champagne with our dinner. "C'mon, guys. It would have been the perfect follow up to crashing the flag-raising ceremony," he laughed. "Imagine their faces!"

For the remainder of the day Chris and Hilary continued their two-man mock trial session, while Pat and I allowed our bodies to adjust to London time. On Wednesday morning Chris, Hilary and I filed into a cab after a light continental breakfast. Pat went her separate way that morning to gather some essentials for us, including hairpins for Hilary's wig. As we pulled away, we each glanced at our watches.

It was Hilary's idea to case the joint in advance. Although not her first visit to the Privy Council—she had first gone as assistant counsel to the Honourable Mr. Carl Rattray—she felt we'd be more at ease on the day of the trial if we reduced the number of potential surprises, like the travel time we'd need from the hotel during the morning rush hour. She also wanted to get a look at some of the law lords. That was Hilary; leave nothing to chance.

"I want to get my ear attuned to their voices, get a feel for the tenor of their questions, see how they treat counsel, detect who is the dominant personality on the council, that sort of thing," she said. "In the days of old, some of the law lords had tended to be rather aggressive. Some even had the potential to be offensive or just downright rude, especially if the Queen's Counsel was unfamiliar with their record or had the audacity to present a matter without merit. And then some lords could be quite courteous. I just think it's best to find out."

LESS THAN THIRTY minutes later we were standing on pristine Downing Street. The building that housed the Privy Council was a modest, almost unassuming structure. Quite frankly, it took me by surprise. This, after all, was supposed to be the scene of the final battle. Chris caught my frown and grinned at my puzzled expression. "What? Not exactly what you pictured?"

Dressed casually, yet with the significance of the Privy Council in mind, we walked into the reception area and went through the necessary security check. Soon after Hilary was introducing herself to one of the councillors. His appraising gaze had what seemed to be a distinct 'and-who-might-you-be' question.

Perhaps he didn't believe that Hilary was really Queen's Counsel from Jamaica. Perhaps he was just a little taken aback by our odd looking trio standing there with great aplomb but in less formal attire. We were, by our ethnic collection, not an easily forgettable group. Hilary, with her Egyptian extractions, was the shade of coffee with cream. Chris sported a light brown complexion. I was clearly Asian and the tallest of the three.

At the end of the foyer were two rooms. One was called the "robing room" in which lawyers put on their robes, wigs and bands. The second was a final preparation room, where one gathered one's notes and, no doubt, final thoughts. In the latter stood two doors on either side with signs affixed: "Appellants" and "Respondents." Each took you into the actual area and to your correct seats in front of the panel—without forcing you to cross in front of the law lords.

That day we entered the visitor's gallery to watch the proceedings and surfaced to the left of the law lords' view. What we walked into was a hushed room, beautifully adorned with elegant woodwork, tiled floor and grand windows. It was the kind of room that made you stop and do a slow full circle. It was a huge area with an incredibly high ceiling. The law lords were sitting at a horseshoe table on the same level as everyone else, and not on an elevated podium.

Immediately behind them were shelves of books, making the courtroom seem more like a massive judge's chamber. I was surprised that their Lordships were wearing only suits and none of the usual robes and wigs. Hilary reminded me that in England they reserved such apparel for the House of Lords, their highest court. "In here, they're really sitting in council, not court," she said. Despite the cavernous feel of the place, the acoustics were amazingly superb. We could hear every word, every syllable uttered by both the presenting counsels and their Lordships, who were also outfitted with microphones.

We watched and listened in silence for almost an hour. I decided that the law lords fell on the courteous side. No monsters on this panel. Finally I leaned over and asked Hilary if she was nervous. She answered in the negative. After thirty years in the profession, the courtroom may as well have been her living room, she assured me. That said, she admitted she still looked for that slight buzz when going in for the fight, that dash of tension—and she had it with this case, she assured me. "I have faith in this case, Dalton," she told me, without blinking or even using a hand gesture. You couldn't help but believe her. Hilary was ready for tomorrow.

Once back at the hotel, Pat secured us dinner and dessert so that we could work straight through the evening. She arranged our wake-up calls for the following morning. Finally, at nine we closed our files for the last time.

THE MORNING OF the trial we said Hilary's little prayer in her room as a group. It put us where we needed to be that day—in a spirit of true calm and confidence. None of us had to reach for antacids. By the time the cab dropped us off near Downing Street, we were practically finishing each other's sentences. It was approximately quarter after nine. One hour to spare.

Inside the Privy Council chamber, this time in the appropriate attire, we were alone with the opposing counsel across the aisle. Both sides were busy arranging their bundles in front of them. Pat and I were seated in the visitor's gallery to the side. I raised an eyebrow at the obvious lack of freshness on the faces of the opposing team. "They look like they just flew in, man," I whispered to Chris. He and Hilary had just walked over to us from the respondents' side to exchange some final words of encouragement.

Chris nodded in agreement. "Either too much last-minute scrambling," he suggested with a touch of humour in his tone, "or they've been taking in some city tours." Hilary said she wasn't so sure. She respected her opponent; she knew him to be a fellow professional who believed in thorough preparation. They had run neck-and-neck over the years on several matters before this one, and so she wasn't about to underestimate him. "But faith in the case," she added with a wag of the finger, "is an entirely separate issue," and then she and Chris made their way over to greet them.

My eyes roved around and eventually settled on the elegant curved table and row of chairs that faced us, waiting to be filled by the Privy Council lords. Behind that was the room from which they would soon emerge. I imagined them in there as we waited. At the appointed time, the clerk appeared. "Clear the room, please!" he bellowed. We all immediately stood up and exited through the doors through which we had entered. We remained out of sight as their Lordships took their seats.

Moments later we were again being summoned to return to the huge chamber. We duly bowed to the panel of five and waited for their nods before taking our seats. Pat gave me a supportive touch on the back. I sucked in a deep breath. Three law lords from yesterday's panel had returned today. We were all sure we detected a look of recognition in their restrained second glances.

After the calling of the case, Hilary and Dennis took turns announcing their respective representation. Seated before us were the esteemed panel of Lord Steyn, Lord Hutton, Lord Millett, Lord Rodger of Earlsferry and Sir Denis Henry. They were a surprisingly young panel. My Queen's Counsel would eventually add "attractive" to that description, and bestowed one in particular with "movie-star looks." Within minutes the trial was underway—the final leg of my painful ten-year journey.

We knew we were going to win within minutes of hearing Mr. Goffe present his case. He had started out on fairly solid footing, reading his statement of case. It seemed clear enough, but the shakiness began the moment questions concerning the allegations came flying at him from the panel. Requests by the law lords for the Queen's Counsel to direct them to a certain page or document were met with pauses, which were usually followed by incorrect pagination. Visibly frustrated, their Lordships continued bouncing the appellant team in search of answers. Queen Counsel Goffe's assistant ran her hands back and forth through the bundles in attempt to offer help, but it would not be enough.

From the uneasy grimaces on their faces, I could tell that Chris and Hilary took no pleasure in watching the scene unfold, even though Goffe and Reid's shaky performance served our purpose. My team had actually wanted their fellow Jamaicans to put on a good show in London, even though they still wanted to defeat them. Inside, Hilary was anxious for her esteemed colleague, but it was too late. From where I sat, the disconnection between this new opposing team and the decade-old matter was all too obvious.

When it was finally time for Hilary to rise to her feet, a wave of electricity flashed through my body.

It didn't take her long to warm up. Within minutes she was fielding questions from the panel like a batsman on a roll, speaking quickly but eloquently. The contrast between her and her opponent was quickly established. She met every one of their Lordships' requests to be directed to certain documents with the grace and flow of a seasoned orchestral conductor. When Lord Millet asked for an analysis of a particular point, she immediately returned with her answer—backed by the page numbers and paragraphs of the cross-examination that spoke to it. When Lord Rodger asked if she'd be arguing differently if the evidence did in fact show Mr. Yap's actions to be negligent, her immediate and frank reply was met with subtle but noticeably satisfied nods.

After a while, only three of the five law lords were asking questions at all—Lords Millet, Steyn and Rodger. Having cleared the questions, Hilary then began to tell a narrative that flowed like the perfect soliloquy. She spoke with unnerving ease—as if speaking of herself. She was, in my mind, the epitome of lawyer perfection at that moment. Queen's Counsel Hilary Phillips blew them away. A modest woman by nature, even Hilary had to admit that she knew she was having a good day. She could feel it in her bones.

By the time they stopped for the lunch break, we knew we had them. Even so, we were not willing to relax. Not just yet. The bulk of our case had yet to be presented.

Pat dashed out to grab us some lunch while we huddled in conference over Chris's notes. Chris wasted no time telling us that while he felt we were home-free, he was not completely satisfied. There were certain points he still wanted to raise and drive home, he repeated to Hilary. For safety's sake he wanted us to cross that certain threshold. He wanted us to get to that safe place.

I immediately understood what he was saying. By now, even the other side was congratulating us. We returned pleased smiles and equally gracious comments, but inside Chris and I were nursing old nerves over this unhappy déjà vu. We'd been here before—a step away from victory, receiving handshakes from the other side one minute, only to be slapped with a surprise defeat the next.

Chris and Hilary sat hunched over the list of items he wanted her to go through in the afternoon session. I sat next to them in silence listening, not wanting to break their concentration. Before long, Pat sailed in with a bag of assorted sandwiches with fancy names, but we merely picked at them. Quite frankly, I don't think we would have noticed if she had returned with a hot gourmet meal served on china. Still thinking one step ahead and with only minutes to spare before the break ended, Dunkley ran around collecting the names of those present—the judicial secretary and council agents—in the event we were stopped midway through our response, only to suffer disastrous results.

At the end of the hour the clerk summoned us back inside. Once again we filed in, determined to make our final push. Just as Hilary was preparing to stand, their Lordships indicated that they did not need to hear anything further from her. Hilary immediately settled back in her seat with a respectful and prompt nod, while Dunkley moved as if to bolt out of his. From the side I could see him leaning forward, his arms braced on the table. Hilary said nothing but discretely touched his arm as if to hold him down. I pressed my lips shut and bit down. After almost ten years of litigation, our final act had boiled down to just two hours, and we had not yet finished saying our piece. Had we done enough?

The last thing we heard their Lordships say before dismissing us was that they would duly advise Her Majesty in council. And with that, our day at the Privy Council was over.

THAT NIGHT WE sat close to the centre of the theatre, which was filled to capacity. On stage, the famed musical thrilled its audience. Hilary threw her enthusiastic cheers at the stage, ablaze with lights and costumes that had come from the depths of the most wondrous of imaginations. She'd been aching to see the famous musical for years. She leaned over, keeping her eyes focused on the stage. "Positively *fantastic* show, isn't it?" There was no response and so she turned her head.

Hilary said she wasn't sure which made her smile more— the magical spectacle on stage before her, or the amusing scene that lay beside her. As the rest of the theatre erupted in successive waves of deafening applause, Chris, Pat and I slumped motionless in our seats. With heads reclined and eyes sealed shut, we were like children who had succumbed to slumber at the end of a truly exhausting adventure.

KINGSTON. TUESDAY, MAY 28, 2002

I was trapped in morning rush-hour traffic like a mosquito on sticky flypaper. Dunkley called on my mobile, insisting he needed to see me about something. Since I was in town that day, he suggested, with one too many uncharacteristic *ahms,* it would be better if we met in the privacy of his office to talk it over. Before I could ask—the beads of sweat already beginning to form on my brow—he was hurried off the phone blaming another urgent call he had on hold. Forty-five minutes later I burst into his reception area. I charged past Elise and into his office, cursing him and at least two generations of his ancestors. Dunkley just sat behind his desk and let me go on for a good few minutes before quietly holding up a plain brown envelope.

"What's this?" I shook as I snatched it from him.

My lawyer merely bit his lips, turned his head to the side and let his eyes drop to the floor ever so slowly.

My mouth went dry as I carefully pulled out the contents. "Dunkley?" It was the Privy Council's judgment. I tried to read it but my hands were shaking too badly. I gave up trying and shook it at him. "Dunkley I can't read this thing! Tell me, man! What does it say?"

"You're completely cleared."

I stopped shaking. Around me everything seemed to fall silent. "You mean it's really over?"

"Over."

I don't have any speech impediments, but that day I stammered out in words what I did not want to gush out in tears. It would have been too much. Elise couldn't stifle her huge grin as she watched from just outside the doorway. Her small frame almost went off balance when I buried her with a grateful hug. "I'm so happy for you, Mr. Yap," she said. "So very happy."

One good turn deserves another. We decided to extend the prank to Hilary, who immediately responded to Chris's worried tone when he called to say he was heading to her office right away. Her face went ashen when she raced to her reception area and saw the two of us standing there, eyes cast to the ground. "Hilary," Chris said with a deadpan voice. "I ah, I think you need to see this," and he slowly handed her the same plain envelope.

261

It was pure carnival after that. Our communal jubilation practically tore through the walls of her office. Not only had the Privy Council dismissed the bank's appeal and called for it to pay my costs, it spoke of Hilary's exceptional performance:

> *Their Lordships, having similarly had the advantage of the well-marshalled and well-presented submissions of Miss Phillips, are satisfied that the Court of Appeal reached the correct conclusion, and that this is one of those exceptional cases where the appellate court was entitled, indeed bound, to interfere with the decision of the trial judge on a matter of fact.*

Dunkley was not to be left out. For his outstanding work he would be presented with a red bag.

Two days later, the media announced my final victory. Dalton Yap was once again a man of honour.

A YEAR WOULD pass before I finally settled with the bank for an undisclosed sum.

The number-crunching process included one final move by Dunkley, who quietly reversed roles and slapped a Mareva injunction on the bank when it attempted to offer us Government bonds as payment. As expected, they scurried off to court to try and have it overturned, but we were victorious there too.

I was alone the day I went in to collect the settlement cheque from the bank's lawyer at their New Kingston head office. Waiting for me in her office was a young professional in a sharp suit. She was new to the bank and looked at me curiously as she placed the envelope into my hand.

Inside I was smiling at the almost dry, unceremonious end to what had been a nightmare start to my decade-long journey—in a sharp looking corporate office very similar to this one. I wondered what this young lady had heard. I imagined what she might be thinking as she brought to a close the debacle started by her predecessors.

I remember thanking her. I also remember adding, for what it was worth, that employers in general should think better of their employees and treat them as real people. The statement came more in the tone of a personal wish than lecture. It was not my intention to drag her into a fight that was not of her making. I didn't stay long. She smiled politely as I wished her a good day and walked out the door.

It didn't occur to me, until I had stepped out into the sunshine and felt the warmth on my face, that it was a Friday afternoon.

Epilogue

T he test that brought me to my knees also brought me more knowledge than one man could ever dream of gaining in life.

It armed me with the unshakable certainty that my family will remain intact no matter the obstacle, and confirmed that in my birth family lies an irreplaceable support system. Many before me have fallen to a similar fate with disastrous results because they did not have this kind of cushion that broke my fall.

I now know who my friends are. I will be forever grateful to Charles, Bobby, Richard and Wayne Chen of Mandeville for their unflagging support. They stayed by my side while most others fled. True friends are better than money in the pocket. I have indeed been blessed with the strongest of bonds, both old and new.

Dunkley remains a busy lawyer, but is now a changed one. By his own admission, the seasoned professional now treads even more cautiously where conflict is concerned. He has seen how if you allow someone with enough resources the right opportunity, they can destroy your life on a whim. He now practises law with the assumption that somewhere, hiding in the shadows, is the presupposition that one is guilty until proven innocent.

Fortunately, today the increased transparency in Jamaica's legal system has left less room for trial by ambush. Actions now demand more justification.

Nevertheless, Dunkley remains vigilant on behalf of those who seek his help. Hilary has since become a Court of Appeal judge. To this day, Hilary, Dunkley and I remain locked in a spiritual fellowship, and can still launch into parts of our saga with a mere mention of a word or name. Every now and then we'll reflect on our day at the Privy Council—which has since been relocated to the Supreme Court Building in London's Parliament Square.

Norman Wright is now Queen's Counsel, while C. Dennis Morrison, like Hilary, became a Court of Appeal judge. Both Norman and Dennis remain respected friends to whom I will be forever grateful. Justice Seymour Panton, who delivered the first judgment at the lower court in my matter, is now President of the Court of Appeal, which makes him Hilary and Dennis's boss. Thomas Powell is clearly a pseudonym, but the real Powell remains a close friend who has yet to ask for the full story. He has it now. Every now and then I'll hear from some of my other friends and colleagues from my old division, most of whom, I am pleased to say, are making much of their careers and personal lives.

Were it not for the talent, faith and strength of my legal team, my small band of friends and devoted family, I would not be where I am today. They were my sea of stars.

In my post-corporate life, I have become the successful entrepreneur my late father had always wanted me to be. I enjoy my busy routine, which I constantly adjust with a healthy dose of balance. I also stepped back into the Chinese-Jamaican community, and joined the long-established Chinese Benevolent Association (Jamaica) in 2002, at the encouragement of one of its elders and former presidents. Its membership elected me president in 2003, a hectic but rewarding office I proudly held for three years.

In the telling of my story, I tried to remain true to the feelings and emotions that had claimed me at the time, including the unflattering ones. I was, after all, an angry, confused and depressed man. Today, the image of Jamaica Citizens Bank stands in my mind like a lone building in a ghost town. With the exception of a couple of former managers who did not testify against me, I never did hear from any of my former management team colleagues—most of whom have long since moved on. I sincerely wish for them whatever success or benefit their particular capabilities and expertise can bring them. I can say this because I understand and believe that people are much more than their mistakes. This is a truth I have always acknowledged.

As for me, Dunkley says the old naïve Dalton died in 1993. In a way he's right. I've been cured of the fear of confrontation, and no longer hesitate to state my position if I need to. The experience has not left me bitter—life is too short—just wiser. I can still laugh until tears come to my eyes. I continue to treat people with the same respect and consideration that I expect in return. I honour my commitments as I always have, and truly believe that our initial intention is to do right by one another. However, now I look more closely into the soul of the person standing before me. I listen more carefully and ask more questions, both for their sake and mine. It's not a bad way to be. As a business owner, I look beyond the titles of individuals and beyond the complaint being levied at them by others. I try to observe their characters, their personal lives, their families, and the hurdles they've endured to make it thus far in life. I offer them this courtesy as a human being—because once upon a time, I stood facing those whose refusal to see me almost led to my ruin.

Finally, a word on the reason I decided to tell the story of my legal ordeal. Experience is a good teacher. I want the well-intentioned individual going to his or her job every day to learn my lesson—that the universe is not necessarily going to be fair just because you've done right by your employer. Trickery will lurk in places least expected when self-preservation rears its ugly head. Give your employer your best effort always and exhibit trust, but do so with a spoonful of street smarts. Take the necessary steps to stitch together that safety net for the fall that may or may not come. Be your own best protector in a world driven by the need to win and survive. Always be prepared. Above all else, be consistent in your conduct.

Since 1993, I have met several individuals who have fallen to a similar fate. With none of the wherewithal needed to right the wrong, most have had to walk away quietly with mangled pride and the hope that they can start over elsewhere. To them I lift my hat for they do not walk an easy road. I was one of the lucky ones.

Sources

It is no exaggeration that I kept almost every official document, slip of paper, sympathy card and research notebook that this decade-long battle generated. It is from all these documents, my own memory and that of my legal team, family members, colleagues and close friends that this memoir was written. The official records and sources on which I relied include:

Record of Appeal

In the Court of Appeal
Supreme Court Civil Appeal No. 121 of 1997
On Appeal from the Supreme Court of Judicature of Jamaica
(Suit no. C.L. J-320 of 1993)
Between Dalton Yap (Appellant) and Jamaica Citizens Bank
Limited (Respondent)

Volume 1

1. Notice and Grounds of Appeal dated November 3, 1997
2. Writ of Summons and Endorsement dated October 8, 1993
3. Reply dated April 12, 1994
4. Further amended statement of claim dated September 17, 1996
5. Final judgment dated September 22, 1997
6. Written judgment dated September 22, 1997

Volume 2

Items 1 – 77 – documents related to the case.

Volume 2A

Items 78 – 144 – documents related to the case.

Volume 4

Notes of evidence

Volume 4A

Notes of evidence

Bundle of Documents

#4 – Having to do with Mr. Yap's performance evaluations etc.

Judgments

1. From the Supreme Court – Justice Panton (first instance)
2. From the Privy Council

The Gleaner (Jamaica) – misc. articles

The Jamaica Observer – misc. articles

ABOUT THE AUTHORS

DALTON YAP was born in Hong Kong in 1960, and grew up with his younger siblings in a small village near Tai Po in the New Territories. At age twelve, he and his family made Jamaica their new home, first settling in Papine, St. Andrew and then in Mandeville, Manchester where he spent most of his early adult life.

At the time of the lawsuit, he was General Manager of Technology and Operations at Jamaica Citizens Bank. During the trial's ten-year period, Yap ventured into the manufacturing, restaurant and food retail sectors, and became a successful entrepreneur in his own right. He now lives in Toronto with his wife Pauline and their three children.

ALEX LEE was born in Portugal in 1966. She grew up first in Kingston, Jamaica and then Toronto, Canada. As a professional writer, much of her work has been for corporate clients. She has also authored and co-authored several mini-memoirs, with *A Matter of Conduct* being her first full-length collaboration. She is now based in Miami, Florida, USA.

CPSIA information can be obtained at www.ICGtesting.com
Printed in the USA
LVOW041943120912

298504LV00001B/1/P